6|18

D0041018

I LOVE CAPITALISM!

I LOVE CAPITALISM!

AN AMERICAN STORY

Ken Langone

PORTFOLIO/PENGUIN

Portfolio/Penguin
An imprint of Penguin Random House LLC
375 Hudson Street
New York, New York 10014

Photo credits:
© Ann Billingsley: Pages 1 (bottom), 3 (top right), 4 (top), 5 (top),
6 (middle), 8 (top), 14 (middle), 15 (bottom)
Lisa Berg: Pages 3 (top left), 6 (top)
John Calabrese Photography: Pages 8 (bottom), 16 (bottom)

Most Portfolio books are available at a discount when purchased in quantity for sales
promotions or corporate use. Special editions, which include personalized covers, ex-
cerpts, and corporate imprints, can be created when purchased in large quantities. For
more information, please call (212) 572-2232 or e-mail specialmarkets@penguinrandom
house.com. Your local bookstore can also assist with discounted bulk purchases using
the Penguin Random House corporate Business-to-Business program. For assistance in
locating a participating retailer, e-mail B2B@penguinrandomhouse.com.

Library of Congress Cataloging-in-Publication Data
Names: Langone, Kenneth G., author.
Title: I love capitalism! : an American story / Ken Langone.
Description: New York : Portfolio, 2018. | Includes index.
Identifiers: LCCN 2017056583| ISBN 9780735216242 (hardback) |
ISBN 9780735216259 (epub)
Subjects: LCSH: Langone, Kenneth G. | Businessmen—United States—Biography.
Entrepreneurship—United States. | New business enterprises—United States. |
Home Depot (Firm) | BISAC: BIOGRAPHY & AUTOBIOGRAPHY / Business.
| BUSINESS & ECONOMICS / Leadership. | BUSINESS & ECONOMICS /
Entrepreneurship.
Classification: LCC HC102.5.L36 L36 2018 | DDC 381/.45683092 [B]—dc23
LC record available at https://lccn.loc.gov/2017056583

Printed in the United States of America
3   5   7   9   10   8   6   4

Designed by Daniel Lagin

To my wife and sons with my everlasting love and gratitude

ACKNOWLEDGMENTS

I have enjoyed writing this book because it gave me reason to reflect on all the wonderful memories of my life. I've been blessed to have so many caring people help me as I traveled life's roads. Their encouragement, support, and interest in me have been big factors in my life.

First and foremost is the importance of my faith as part of my life's journey. Whenever I was in tight spots or facing difficult circumstances with little or no chance for a good outcome, my faith kept me going. I know I am more sensitive to the plight and needs of others because of my faith—my spiritual beliefs dictate no less than that. I would be a shadow of myself without my faith in God.

The luckiest day of my life was that Monday evening in early June 1954 when I first set eyes on the love of my life, Elaine. Counting a two-year courtship, we have been together for sixty-three years—WOW. When things went well Elaine cheered me on and when things weren't so good she was there to encourage me to stay the course and to let me know she would always be there for me—win, lose, or draw. She has been my life partner, my soul mate, and my best friend—my love for her grows with each passing day. One of the great blessings God bestowed on me was bringing Elaine into my life. Most of what I write about probably never would have happened had Elaine not been with me. I am forever hers.

My parents, John and Angie Langone, were the very best parents a child could have. They gave my late brother Michael and me the one thing that matters most to a child—unconditional love, and lots of it! My brother died much too young but not before he taught me my prayers and helped me do all my Cub Scout projects. My lasting memory of him is as my protector—I wish Our Lord had given us more time with him. Mom and Dad worked hard so that we could have a better life. They taught values by living them and they stressed the importance of hard work and education. While they struggled financially they made personal sacrifices to make certain we had plenty to eat, a warm and comfortable home, and happy things to look forward to. Every day that goes by I miss them more and more.

Elaine and I are blessed to have had Our Lord send us three fine men, Kenny, Bruce, and Stephen. I know I am a better person because they are my sons—their love and respect for me is a source of great strength. They have always encouraged me in all my endeavors and have not allowed our accomplishments to diminish their humility or their caring for others. My one regret is that my career kept me away from home more than I would have liked, but thank God, Elaine made up the difference. Every time the boys and I are together, the first thing we do is kiss and hug, and we end every phone call with an expression of love for each other—it doesn't get any better than that! We are also blessed with loving and caring daughters-in-law, Jessica and Nhung, and two grandchildren, Manny and Sophia. I hope and pray the examples we set for them will lead them to happy and productive lives.

My parents-in-law, Marion and Dick Abbe, and my sister-in-law, Janet Rider, accepted me into their family as a son and brother rather than as an in-law. Their kindness, thoughtfulness, and generosity knew no limits and my father-in-law enjoyed a special place in my career, especially as he helped me get started on Wall Street. His wise counsel and insights saved me from many mistakes I might otherwise have made. No one could have had kinder or more loving in-laws than I did.

Reflecting on the early years of my life, I remember the love and support of all my extended family—my grandparents, my aunts and uncles, my cousins. I remember the family gatherings every Sunday at 1:00 p.m. at Grandma and Grandpa Laucella's in Port Washington; the aroma of the gravy (not sauce!), the meat balls and sausages, the braciole, the fresh bread from Frappaolo's bakery down the street; the table that, no matter how many were there, always had room for one more. And after lunch, each of the grandchildren performing in the family rendition of "Ted Mack's Amateur Hour." Most of all I remember the love, respect, and affection we held for each other. How kind God was to send me to such a warm and loving family.

There are many people in my professional life that have been so important to what I've accomplished, none more so than my assistant and friend, Pam Goldman. There can't possibly be anyone more challenging to work with than me, and Pam pulls it off virtually flawlessly—as she's done for twenty-five years! I have a bad habit of saying yes to too many things and Pam always makes sure things work out. She can keep more balls in the air than anyone I know and she does it always with a smile and good cheer. I am grateful to her beyond what any words can describe. And then there is my friend and driver, Alvaro Gallego. Alvaro has been with me for twenty-six years, and no matter what the demands of my crazy schedule are, he's always there. Alvaro is one of the best examples of what a hardworking, dedicated person can accomplish if he applies himself and takes advantage of everything our great nation offers. *Alvaro es mi amigo!*

Although in the beginning I had great trepidation about writing this book, the experience turned out to be special in every way possible. My collaborator, Jim Kaplan, was a kind and thoughtful partner. Every suggestion he made—every one!—improved the book. His commitment to clarity and meaning always brought my thoughts to the points I wanted to make or the story I wanted to tell. In addition to that, he is a superb writer who has an incredible command of the king's English. We started on a purely professional basis and we ended enjoying each other, having fun, and becoming good friends.

The entire group we worked with at Penguin Random House made sure we kept the trains running on time, and my team— Adrian Zackheim, Merry Sun, Will Weisser, Tara Gilbride, Margot Stamas, Katherine Valentino, Lisa D'Agostino, and Kate Griggs— have been sensitive to my purpose in writing this book but firm when it came to issues they knew more about than I did. I could not have had a better agent than Bob Barnett. He was thoughtful, thorough, and realistic and he made certain there was always a meeting of the minds. I am grateful to the entire team for this most positive publishing experience.

As you will read in the book, Yankee Stadium wouldn't be able to hold all of the people who helped me in my career. It's likely that I've forgotten some of them, not because they didn't make the cut but rather because my memory is not perfect. In advance, I apologize to them for this oversight. I thank each person or group on this list for playing a role in my life and my career. Along the way they guided me, helped me, advised me, or supported me. For that I am most grateful. The mistakes I've made have all been of my own doing.

Lenny Altman

Adam Arnott

Bindy Banker

John Bartolotti

Carol Bartz

David Batchelder

Gerry Bell

Art Benvenuto

Bill Berkley

Joe Billera

Frank Blake

Arthur Blank

Jonathan Blum

Jules Bogen

Frank Borman

Eric Bosshard

Larry Bossidy

Ari Bousbib

Ed Braniff

John Bravman

Greg Brenneman

Gordon Brewer

Ron Brill

Elliot Broidy

Dick Brown

Bobby Buckley

Walter Buckley

Arthur Calcagnini

Donald Calcagnini

Dave Calhoun

Geoff Canada

Tony Carbonetti

Al Carey

Terry Cassidy

Paul Chiapparone

John Clendenin

Armando Codina

Gary Cohn

Bud Cone

George Conway

Lee Cooperman

Brian Cornwell

Dave Cote

Tom Coughlin

Bill Cowie

Archie Cox

Berry Cox

Ed Cox

Mac Crawford

Greg Creed

Jack Cullen

Doug Curling

George Daly

Will Danoff

Fred DeMatteis

Mel Dickenson

Jamie Dimon

Cardinal Timothy Dolan

Bob Donato

Fiona Druckenmiller

Stan Druckenmiller

Steve Dula

Jimmy Dunne

Marvin Ellison

Michael Erlbaum

Gary Erlbaum

Steven Erlbaum

Bob Fagenson

Pat Farrah

Tom Fazio

Mike Fedyshyn

Larry Fink

Bill Flaherty

Arminio Fraga

Luis Fraga

Alan Frazier

Paolo Fresco

Dale Frey

Bill Gayden

Peter Georgescu

Suzy Goldberger

Pam Goldman

Joe Grano

Bob Graper

Dick Grasso

Hank Greenberg

Ron Greenberg

Bill Greve

Bob Grossman

David Gruenstein

Gil Haakh

Davis Hamlin

John Hamre

Bill Harris

Ira Harris

Jon Harris

Mitch Hart

Russell Headley

Ed Herlihy

Ray Hermann

Bonnie Hill

Steve Holzman

Stan Hubbard

Labe Jackson

Tom F. Kane

Tom W. Kane

Mel Karmazin

Alex Karp

Henry Kaufman

Steve Kaye

Cristina Kepner

Art Kinney

Joel Klein

Dave Komansky

Robert Kraft

Dick Kromlich

Jimmy Lee

Steve Levin

Randy Levine

Marty Lipton

Joe Littenberg

Walter Loeb

Art Long

Joe Lonsdale

Dan Lufkin

John Mack

Shorty Mahanna

Ed Malone

Charles Mangum

Bernie Marcus

Tom Marquez

Jim Marshall

Jim McCarthy

Joe McFarland

Allen Mebane

Craig Menear

Mort Meyerson

Roberto Mignone

Ted Mirvis

Bob Moser

John Mountain

Angelo Mozilo

Bishop Bill Murphy

Tom Murphy

John Myers

Gary Naftalis

Blair Nance

Bob Nanovic

Tom Neff

Nader Niani

David Novak

Michael Ovitz

David Parker

Michael Pascucci

Larry Pedowitz

Frank Pellegrino

Ross Perot

Andy Pearson

Dean Poll

John Printon

Scott Probasco

Chris Quick

Msgr. Robert Ritchie

Gerry Roche

John Rosenwald

Nathaniel de Rothschild

Eddie Rowan

Lew Rudin

Jack Rudin

Bill Rudin

John Runnette

Msgr. Francis Ryan

Herb Sarkisian

Julian Saul

Lew Schott

Zach Schreiber

Alan Schwartz

Stan Shapiro

David Shapiro

Larry Silverstein

Geoff Skidmore

Bob Smith

Derek Smith

Duncan Smith

Gary Sojka

Michael Solomon

Joe Spector

Frank Spencer

Rob Speyer

Jerry Speyer

Paul Standel

Bob Stansky

Michael Stansky

Al Steinhaus

Gene Step

Brendan Sullivan

Bill Summers

Sidney Taurel

Andy Taussig

Tom Teague

Carol Tome

Paul Tudor Jones

Dan Tully

John Turner

Jeff Unger

Larry Victor

Peter Vlachos

Dorothea Wahrburg

Fitz Walling

Tom Walter

Andy Warlick

Gus Watanabe

John Weinberg

Msgr. Jack Weist

Jack Welch

Tony Welters

Hudson Whitenight

David Wiederecht

Frank Wilkens

Webb Williams

Faye Wilson

Ernie Wuliger

David Zaslav

Gerson Zweifach

All the associates of the wonderful companies and organizations I've been fortunate to be a part of:

Autofinance Group

Bucknell University

Choicepoint

Electronic Data Systems

The Home Depot

Invemed

IVAC

Micelle Technologies

NYU Langone Health doctors, nurses, staff, and board of trustees

NYU Stern School of Business

Ohio Mattress Company

Parkdale America

Patlex Corporation

Salem Leasing Corp.

Unifi

United States Satellite Broadcasting

Wachtell, Lipton, Rosen and Katz

Yum! Brands

The world belongs to risk takers.

—Ken Langone

A kid once said to me, "Money doesn't buy everything."
I said, "Well, kid, I was poor, and I can tell you right now,
poverty doesn't do a very good job either."

CONTENTS

I LOVE CAPITALISM!

1.

I OWE BUCKNELL $300

This book is my love song to capitalism. *Capitalism works.* Let me say it again: It works! And—I'm living proof—it can work for anybody and everybody. Blacks and whites and browns and everyone in between. Absolutely anybody is entitled to dream big, and absolutely everybody *should* dream big. I did. Show me where the silver spoon was in my mouth. I've got to argue profoundly and passionately: I'm the American Dream

---

I grew up in Roslyn Heights, Long Island, during World War II and just after. There was never much money. My father was an excellent plumber, though not a financially successful one; we lived from paycheck to paycheck. Because he couldn't make enough to provide for the family, my mother had to go to work: she got a job at the school cafeteria, and the little bit she brought in helped make ends meet. But I didn't realize that I was poor, and I had a wonderful childhood.

Just over the hill from Roslyn was a vast tract of hills where sand and gravel were mined. The area was called Cow Bay, and

1

Cow Bay sand was much sought after for all kinds of construction in New York City: roads, sidewalks, building infrastructure—anyplace concrete was used. Both my grandfathers came over from Italy when they were young, and both of them worked in the sand pits. It was dangerous work; there were avalanches all the time. My father's father, who had a good business head, also had a store in the pits—the company store, where he sold the miners and families vegetables and canned goods and you-name-it. And he bought real estate; owning property was the name of the game for immigrants, the road to riches. My grandfather bought a lot of properties that eventually became very valuable, but then in 1932 he was killed by a car; nobody ever found out who hit him. After he died, his sons fought over who was going to pay the tax bills on the properties, and none of them did, so the real estate was sold to cover tax liens.

My father's father died three years before I was born, and my father's mother had died in 1919, in the flu epidemic, so I never met her either. My mother's parents, I knew. My maternal grandparents were working people. My grandmother stayed home. My grandfather had left school when he was six years old and never went again. When he died in 1952, at seventy-two, he couldn't read or write, English or Italian.

My grandfather was a peasant. He was a lovely man, and from the time he was six years old until the day he died, he had a shovel in his hand. His right hand was totally deformed; the thumb had lost the ability to bend from sixty years of holding a shovel. His only entertainment was the opera on Saturday afternoons. He would work all week at the sand pits, then work odd jobs on Saturday morning. When he came home, my grandmother would have the bath ready for him, and he'd clean himself up. He always wore a vest, suit pants, and high-top black shoes, the kind with the hooks and eyelets. When the shoes got too old, they became his work shoes.

He would take his bath, get dressed, and eat lunch. He was a vegetarian; his favorite meal was fried peppers and potatoes and a piece of bread and a little bit of homemade wine. Saturday afternoon he'd eat his lunch, then he'd go under the arbor—he never owned a house; he always rented—and listen to the Metropolitan Opera, sponsored by Texaco, on the radio station WJZ. Last year, I was invited to the Metropolitan Opera's performance of *La bohème,* and I had dinner beforehand with the chairwoman of the Met, Ann Ziff. All through the meal and the performance I was thinking to myself, "Holy smokes, if my grandpa could see me now."

There was a man who lived in Beacon Hill, a nice neighborhood, his name was Mr. Davis. He was some sort of official for the State of New York, in the Transportation Department. My grandfather used to work on weekends at Mr. Davis's house; he would cut the lawn, do pruning and stuff. And Mr. Davis got him a job working on the roads. In those days, in the wintertime, they didn't have mechanical sanders; they had two guys in the back of a truck throwing sand over the side onto the snowy roads. That was one of my grandfather's jobs. It was steady work. And he had better benefits, such as they were; they weren't much, but at least it was better than the sand pits, and it wasn't as dangerous, though there was always a chance (especially at night) that one guy might hit the other with his shovel by accident.

My grandfather was working at Mr. Davis's house on a Saturday in August of 1952 when he reached for a branch to cut it and he had a stroke. He died four days later. Clearly, he had AFib—atrial fibrillation. But they didn't have Coumadin then; they didn't have beta-blockers. I have AFib, and I take a blood thinner. History. Genetics.

My parents, Angelina Teresa and John Francis Langone—Angie and John—were also very simple people. Neither of them ever got close to graduating from high school. My mother dropped out in the seventh grade. My father didn't want to work in the sand pits, so he went to trade school and learned to be a plumber. But for four years during the Depression, 1930 to 1934 (this was before I was born), my father didn't work at all, not only because of economic conditions, but also because of his health: he had colitis, and he was also manic-depressive. For four years, my parents effectively relied on the help of lots of relatives and friends.

By the time I was born, in September 1935, my father was working again, but my parents were still struggling financially. During World War II, my father worked in the Jakobson shipyard in Oyster Bay, putting plumbing in ships to be used in the war effort; my mother volunteered at the elementary school across the street from our house, Roslyn Heights Elementary School, helping to feed what were then called undernourished children. The government sent surplus food to feed these poor kids. After she'd done this for a few years, they opened a cafeteria in the school, for all the kids, and they asked my mom if she'd like a job.

Every morning she would make me breakfast and fix my lunch ahead of time—always the same thing, my favorite, American cheese on white bread—and then walk to work in the cafeteria. My mother was an incredibly sensitive person. She would identify kids who she knew were having a tough time, whether they had mental problems or learning problems, whatever it was, and make a special effort to be good to them.

I never wanted to eat in the cafeteria, because my mom worked there, so I would come home every day for lunch. Sometimes I brought a friend home with me: Arthur Kimball, a black kid. His nickname was Bubba. When my mother knew Bubba was going to come home with me, she would make him a sandwich too.

Our address was 58 St. Marks Place, Roslyn Heights. My parents bought the house in 1944 for $4,000; I can remember my father getting the mortgage. The payment was something like $28 a month. It was a small house, on a fifty-by-hundred-foot plot of land, backed up against the hill that led down to the railroad tracks. The house had an unfinished basement, with a coal furnace; on the first floor, there was a dining room, a living room, and a kitchen, with a little pantry. In the pantry was an icebox. The man who used to bring the ice came every three or four days. He had a piece of canvas on his shoulder, and he had ice tongs, and he had a chunk of ice sitting on the canvas. The icebox was wooden, and it had two compartments, one for the food on the bottom and one on top for the ice.

Upstairs there were three bedrooms. My brother, Mike—he was five years older—and I stayed in one, my parents stayed in another, and from time to time my parents would rent out the third bedroom, say if there was a new schoolteacher who needed a place to stay before getting settled.

My father found work as often as he could. He was a union plumber—Local 457, the Plumbers Union—so if he was on a job and the job wound up, he'd be out of work until he found another.

Dad was very meticulous and neat. Whenever a job ended, he'd go home and tell my mother, and she'd wash his coveralls. They had an old-fashioned washing machine, the kind with the agitator that went back and forth and a hand-cranked wringer on top. The next morning, his coveralls would be nice and folded, and he'd take his metal lunch pail with the thermos in it and go out in his car and look for union work. He'd drive all over, from job to job to job, and just ask. If he found a job at eleven o'clock in the morning, he'd say, "Can I start now?" And usually the foreman would say, "Sure. You want to start now? Start now."

Local 457 used to meet in Glen Cove, two towns over. The guys in the union hall liked my dad, but one day the union delegate came to the house and said, "You know, Johnny, it's not fair.

We've got guys down at the hall who are sitting there for days on end, and you're always getting a job." My father said, "Look, I've got two children; I need to pay my bills. When I lose a job, I can't sit at the union hall playing pinochle waiting for a boss to call in for a plumber. I get in my car and I go look for work." That's what the union plumbers did; they'd sit there waiting for work and playing pinochle all day, then go home.

"I'm in the union," my father told the delegate. "I pay my dues. The only difference is, I don't wait for somebody to call me. I go find them. I'm just going to keep doing what I'm doing." The union officials didn't like it; that was one measure of control they wanted to have over the members.

My dad worked as a self-employed plumber for a couple of years, 1948 to 1950. But he had a bad problem. He wouldn't send people bills. He'd send someone a bill three years after the work was done. He'd finished the work long ago, and the person would get the bill and say, "Hey . . ."

It wasn't out of any charitable impulse; he was just a bad businessman. He'd use his credit to the extent he could at the supply house, and it was only when he reached the point where he had no more credit that he'd start sending people bills. I remember my brother used to type them out for him, on a little Smith Corona portable typewriter, on these forms he'd had printed up. My father used to sit next to my brother and say, "Okay, two fittings, a half inch by three-quarters inch, fourteen feet of copper tubing . . ." And my brother used to send the bills.

My dad had good initiative but poor follow-through. I was different. I began working at age eleven. I was always on the lookout for opportunities, and I loved making money. I started out delivering newspapers. Then one Christmas I took some of my paper-delivery money and went to a greenhouse where they were selling Christmas wreaths for seventy-five cents each and bought a couple dozen. I had a broomstick with me—just the stick, without the broom head—and two kids I'd hired for a half buck each. We slid all the wreaths onto the broomstick, each kid took one end, and we went door to door. I charged a buck-fifty apiece for the wreaths and netted a nice profit.

My mother said to me one night, "You know, you're going to be very successful." I said, "How is that, Mom?" She said, "Because money skips generations. Your father's father was very successful. Your father and his brothers did the best they could, but not much came of it. Now it's your turn."

My dad had a panel truck: he'd bought it from a company called John Wagner & Sons Tea & Spice and had it spray painted forest green. He called it a route truck; it had no passenger seat. Every Sunday the four of us, then the three of us—Mike joined the army right out of high school—would get in my father's truck and go to my grandmother's for lunch, in Port Washington. My father drove, my mother sat next to him on a milk box, and I used to sit in the back where his tools were, where the guy that delivered the tea used to keep the tea.

In Roslyn Heights, there was a section called Roslyn Estates where the rich people lived. If you took the shortcut through Roslyn Estates, you'd come out at an intersection, Port Washington Boulevard and Northern Boulevard, and then you'd make a right on Port Washington Boulevard to get to Grandma's. And every time we drove through Roslyn Estates on a Sunday, my mother would say to me, "Would you like to live here one day?" I'd say yes. And she'd say, "Well, then you've got to work hard and get an education." And I listened. I knew damn well I didn't want to be poor. I wanted to be rich.

I had an after-school job in a butcher shop in Roslyn, and after work every night, from six to seven, I'd go work in a little store that made rotisserie chickens, cleaning up the grease from the rotisserie spits. The guy who owned the butcher shop didn't know I was helping the chicken guy, because he thought they were competitors. When I was fifteen, in 1950, a supermarket called M&H opened down the street and across the tracks from the butcher, and I moonlighted there too, helping them set up the store, putting the canned goods on the shelves at the same time I was working for the butcher shop. I caddied at the golf course. I started my own landscaping business, cutting lawns. When I got to be bigger and stronger, at sixteen, I got a summer job as a day laborer in road construction. I was a hardworking little bastard. Shit, man, as long as I'd get that money in my pocket, I was okay.

I was always on the lookout for opportunities. Next to the butcher shop I worked in was Altman Liquors, run by one of the few Jewish families in Roslyn Heights. One day, Lenny Altman—he was a terrific baseball player—said, "How would you like to work for me two nights a week?" The garbage was picked up Wednesday and Friday, and Lenny had all these empty cardboard boxes out back that the liquor came in. So on Tuesday and Thursday nights, I would take the boxes and walk them a couple hundred yards to the base of a big electrical tower that carried the electricity from the powerhouse in Glenwood Landing up into the communities. Right at the foot of this tower, that's where I used to leave the boxes, and the garbage truck would pick them up the next morning.

I don't remember how I found out, but I learned that the garbage guys used to take the boxes and break them up and sell them to a paper scrap dealer for money. This was just after World War II. So I went to Lenny. He paid me a buck a week, fifty cents a night. I said to him, "Look, I'd like to do what these guys do, sell the boxes for scrap." I said, "You don't have to pay me anymore, Lenny. Whatever I make from the boxes will be my salary." He said okay.

Four years later I'm out of high school, and I get a call from Lenny. Now I'm not working in the butcher shop anymore; I'm working for Bohack, part of a chain of supermarkets. I go over to see Lenny, and he hands me an envelope. He says, "I hear you're going to go to college." I say, "Yeah, I hope so." He says, "I've been holding this." And he hands me an envelope stuffed with dollar bills. Every single week, he'd been putting the dollar he would have paid me in the envelope, and now he gave it all to me. He said, "Here, I hope this helps you in college."

———

When I say I had the most wonderful childhood in the world, I mean every word. My parents gave me the one thing that a kid needs more than everything else: unconditional love. They were smart people, but they were ignorant when it came to formal learning, so they didn't press me academically. They just wanted me to go to school, and they had one dream—that I would go to college. My brother never went. He was not a student. But the problem was that even though I was a bright kid, I wasn't a good student either.

I was never academically curious in high school. I didn't apply myself at *all*. I did the absolute minimum. I was too busy having fun and working at all my various jobs: the butcher shop, Bohack, caddying at the country club, selling Christmas wreaths. Oh, I was a pistol. I remember I convinced the guy who owned the dry cleaner in town that I could put in a lawn at his house, and I made him order humus and soil and peat moss, and then I got involved with a girl and I never went, and the guy had mounds of this shit sitting in front of his house. I was just a kid!

Math came easy to me—I was always good with numbers—but that was it. College was my parents' dream for me, not mine. In my senior year, 1953, I didn't have a dream; I just had hormones. That year there was a girl I was crazy about who wouldn't give me the time of day: the logical next step, my seventeen-year-old brain told me, was to join the marines. Maybe I'd get sent to Korea, I thought. I could become a war hero and show *her*.

The problem was that I was young for my grade; I wouldn't turn eighteen until the September after I graduated, so I would need my parents' permission to enlist, and my father was furious at me for not wanting to go to college, and my mother wouldn't give her permission either. She said, "No. I have one son in the service already. When you're eighteen, you can do what you want. I'll at least have a clear conscience, that I didn't let you go before." Then Eisenhower screwed me up by ending the Korean War that summer.

I had some friends in Port Washington who had gone to Bucknell, three guys a year or two older than I, and that spring they invited me up for a house-party weekend. I got there Friday night and had a hell of a good time. The next morning while my friends went to class—Bucknell had classes on Saturday morning, but there were going to be more parties Saturday afternoon and night and Sunday morning—they said, "That building over there is where the registrar is—the guy that admits kids to Bucknell. Go see him."

It was their idea, not mine. House parties were great; I wasn't thinking about actually going to college. "Just go see him," they said. "Keep you busy."

So I went over. "Why not?" I thought. So I walked in and met this guy, the registrar. His name was George Faint. I must not have looked too enthusiastic. (I was also hungover.) He said, "What are you here for?" I said, "My friends thought I should come and talk to you." I told him I was about to graduate from high school. "Well, what are you doing next?" he asked.

"I'm going to go into the marines," I said.

"Let's talk a little bit," he said.

We talked a little bit. If anything, I was brutally honest. I told him I didn't like school. I didn't like studying. He started asking me some questions, and I guess he could see that I had a brain. So I left, and then the next week I got a letter from him, telling me that if I wanted to go to Bucknell, he'd like to offer me a spot. At the bottom of the letter he wrote, "In college, you'll have to work much harder than you did in high school." Apparently, he had called up my school, and I guess somebody at the school said, "Look, the kid is bright, but he's sort of listless."

Anyway, this was when I told my mother, "Mom, I think I'm going to go to college."

I guess I had mixed feelings about it. And bear in mind that Bucknell cost $2,500 a year; it was going to be a real struggle for my parents to send me. My father was still so angry at me for having wanted to join the marines, and now for being kind of half-hearted about going to college, that he didn't go to my high-school graduation.

Graduation night, a Monday night in June 1953. I walk up in my cap and gown, and the principal of my high school, Mr. Ross, hands me my diploma. And then—this was the tradition—my friends and I, along with most of the other kids in our class, all went out to Montauk Point to celebrate.

The next day I come home at eleven o'clock in the morning and walk in the living room, and my mother's sitting there bawling. My first thought was "Who died?" She said, "Nobody died." "What are you crying for?" I asked her. She says, "You're going to flunk college; you're going to flunk out of college." I said, "What are you talking about?"

"Mr. Ross told me last night that you're going to flunk out of college," she told me.

My mother, in addition to being in charge of the elementary-school cafeteria, cooked there. And from time to time, she made spaghetti, Italian-style, and it was so good—as good as you'd get at a good Italian restaurant—that whenever the teachers from the other schools knew it was on the menu, they'd all go up there to eat lunch. My mother knew all the teachers, including Mr. Ross, the principal of the high school. And on my graduation night, Mr. Ross went up to my mother and said, "You know, Angie, you and your husband work so hard for what you have; I have to tell you, you're wasting your money sending this boy to college, because he's not college material."

And this was why my mother was sitting in the living room bawling.

I said, "Mom, I'm not going to flunk out of college. I promise you."

Now let me tell you how close I came to breaking my promise.

My dad did some extra work at night and on the weekends, I kicked in from my various salaries, and we managed to scrape together the tuition for Bucknell. Then September came and off I went, on my own for the first time in my life. For a while, I had the time of my life. It was liberating; it was fun. My God, it was fun. Parties every weekend, nobody telling you when to go to bed, nobody telling you when to get up in the morning!

But there was another piece to it, an uncomfortable piece. I would drink beer and laugh with my new friends, but when the parties were over, I felt alone, more left out than anytime before in my life. Bucknell was full of Waspy kids with money, the sons of doctors and lawyers and business executives, and here I was, an Italian American kid from wrong-side-of-the-tracks Long Island, the son of a plumber and a cafeteria worker. I can remember being uneasy telling people what my mother and father did. Ashamed. Inferior. I desperately wanted to be one of the crowd, but which crowd?

All the fraternities used to rush during the first semester, and I made it a point to visit all of them—and to take full advantage of their hospitality. There was a Jewish fraternity called Sigma Alpha Mu; they called it Sammy. To this day, I have a lot of good friends who were in that house. Anyway, at the beginning of rush week, the guys at Sammy offered me a pledge pin. "What's this?" I asked. "I thought you had to be a Jew."

"You're not?" they said.

I shook my head.

Well, they grabbed that pin out of my hands so fast you couldn't believe it. But thank God for Jewish guilt; they had the best food on campus, and plenty of it. That's something I think both Italians and Jews have an affinity for: we both like to eat, and we like to eat well. Anyway, steak night was Thursday night every week, and they'd always invite me. They had these thin T-bone steaks, platters of them. My mouth waters at the memory.

Ultimately, I joined Sigma Chi, because I had friends there. Now it didn't matter where I was from or what my parents did: I was a Sig. I had found my crowd, and I blended right in. And the fun continued.

Bucknell had a policy in those days, and it was a good one: halfway through first semester of your freshman year, you got your grades, and so did your family. Today the parents can't even get the grades; it's against the law for the school to give them. I don't get it. I know what I did with my sons. If I couldn't see their grades, they could pay for their own education. When the bill comes, I told them, you sign the check. I'm done.

Anyway, I had a course in economics—Economics 101. The textbook was Paul Samuelson's book. It met Tuesdays and Thursdays, in sections, then every Saturday all the classes met together in the auditorium with the professor. Every once in a while, on Saturday, this guy—Russell Headley was his name—would give us a blue exam book and a generic question and say, "Tell me about this." A couple weeks before Thanksgiving, he gave us one about the theory of supply and demand, which is a basic point in economics. The Saturday before break, at the end of the class, Headley said, "Before we break, is there a Mr. Langone in the room?" I raised my hand. And thought, "Oh shit." A couple hundred kids in the room, and he calls my name. *Oh no.*

"I want to see you after class," Headley said.

Class ends. I walk into his office. He was *the* professor. Intimidating guy. He takes my blue book, and he throws it on the desk. "That is the worst English I have ever read in my entire life," he says.

He lets that sit for a minute while I squirm in my chair. Then he looks at me and says, "I had to struggle to figure out what you were saying, but it's clear to me that you really understand economics."

That was interesting. *I* had had to struggle to figure out what I was saying. I didn't know if anybody else would actually understand what I meant.

"Tell me something, Mr. Langone," Headley said. "Has anybody ever told you you're stupid?"

"Yeah," I said. "A lot of people."

"Teachers?"

"In high school, sure."

"That's a shame," he said, "but the worst part is that you believe them." He looked at me. Then he said, "How are you doing in your other courses here?"

"About as good as I'm doing in yours," I said.

"Well, I guess you're going to be out of here in January," he said. He looked at me. "Do you want that to happen?" he asked.

"No," I said.

"What are you going to do about it?"

"I don't know what to do about it," I said.

"Well, tell me about your other classes," he said.

So I did. And Headley said, "If I make an effort to talk to your other professors, will you do your part?"

"What do you want me to do?"

"Work your ass off."

And here's what Russell Headley did for me: he went to all my other professors and said, "Look, I think this kid is a diamond in the rough, and I think we ought to make the effort to try and pull him out of his nosedive." Which, by the way, was totally self-inflicted. Nobody pushed me into a nosedive. I voluntarily dove in.

Headley did another important thing for me. When I entered Bucknell, I enrolled in a bachelor of science program; you didn't have to take a language or any liberal arts courses. Quite frankly, the BS program was easier than the BA, and that was what I wanted. I had very little intellectual confidence at that point in my life.

Professor Headley felt I could do more. He thought I would be better served intellectually if I took liberal arts. So I switched programs. I took philosophy, art history, even Spanish. I'd dropped out of Spanish in high school, in part because I didn't like the teacher but mostly because I couldn't seem to wrap my head around the conjugation of verbs. Suddenly I was understanding verb conjugations. I was really enjoying philosophy and literature and art history. My curiosity was blossoming. I'm forever in debt to Russell Headley, and Bucknell, for that.

———

And then, just like that, I almost blew the whole thing.

Every January, just before the semester ended, Sigma Chi had a weekend party called the Bowery Brawl. It was a theme party: you were supposed to dress like a bum, or worse. Guys competed to come up with the most original costumes.

I'd made a new friend in the fraternity, a fellow pledge named David Parker. A great guy; we're still close friends to this day. Anyway, one night in early January, David and I are in the fraternity house with some other pledges, getting pie-eyed on illegal beer—drinking age was twenty-one in Pennsylvania; we were just eighteen—and we're laughing about what our costumes are going to be. And suddenly David says, "I'm going to go as a shit."

"What do you mean you're going to go as a shit?" I ask.

"I'm going to dye a pair of long johns brown," he says, "I'm going to put on a brown stocking cap, and when people ask me what I am, I'm going to say I'm a shit."

Oh boy, did we laugh. It was the kind of thing that seems brilliant when you're eighteen years old and half-drunk.

It was a Friday night. After we'd had more than a few beers, a bunch of us piled into cars and went to a diner down the road called, if you can believe it, Dine-A-Mite. Lewisburg's Biggest Little Diner, it called itself. As we were all sitting around a table laughing about Parker's costume idea, I had an inspiration. "Hey, how about if I get a toilet seat for you to put around your neck?"

That did it. Everyone thought that was the greatest idea in the world. While they were all howling with laughter and banging on the table, I went into the men's room and—I'm not bragging about this!—started trying to pry the seat off the toilet. But it wouldn't come off. I pulled and pulled, and the damn thing wouldn't budge. Finally, I yanked the son of a bitch, and the whole toilet bowl came up off the floor. There was water all over the place; water was running out under the door of the men's room. And meanwhile, my pals were raising hell in the diner—a couple of them did damage—and Sadie, the owner, called the police, and the state cops came, and off we went.

They took about ten or twelve of us in, booked us, then released us on our own recognizance. And of course, the police notified Bucknell about what happened. Damage had been done to the diner, and Sadie was pressing charges. The dean of men, a guy named Mal Musser—ironically, he was a Sigma Chi alumnus—called us in, more or less got to the bottom of the story, and effectively encouraged David and me to take the hit for everybody else. Musser felt if there were fewer kids involved, the whole incident would be less prominent. Now, was it fair for David and me to take the fall when other kids were also guilty? Not really. But the unfairness of it didn't make my own behavior one bit less egregious. I had screwed up, big-time. And oh boy, was I scared.

"Look," Musser told Parker and me, "you kids go work it out with the justice of the peace, and we'll talk when you get back." That made me feel a little better. So David and I went to the justice of the peace—his name was Paul Showalter—and pleaded guilty to disorderly conduct.

"Okay, that's a misdemeanor," Showalter said. "You each have to pay $37.50, plus damages." That was a lot of money. We came up with it. We go back to the campus, and we walk into Mal Musser's office, and we tell him that we did it, and it was all over, and he said, "Fine." Then he says, "Go back to your rooms, pack your stuff, and get out of here."

"What do you mean, 'Get out of here'?" I said.

"You're out of Bucknell," Musser said.

I started to cry. My first thought was about my mother. "This would kill her," I thought. David was crying too. Musser's office was in Roberts Hall; David and I ran across the quad to the admissions office, which was in Carnegie Library. There was a guy in the admissions office by the name of Fitz Walling; Fitz was also a Sigma Chi alumnus, and he was the chapter adviser. David and I went in, both in tears, and I told him what we had done. "Come on with me," Walling said.

So the two of us follow him, and we go back across the quad

to Musser's office, and Fitz says to Musser's secretary, "I want to see him right now with these kids." Before she has a chance to answer, he stalks into Musser's office, with us behind him. "I know what they did, and what they did is wrong," Walling tells Musser. "But I also know that they were not the only ones doing it, and they took the fall for your purposes. So you can do whatever you want to them, but you're not throwing them out."

It was a hell of a speech. Musser nodded. "Okay," he said. Then he turned to us. "You can go home at the end of the semester," he said. "But after that and for the next year, you're going to spend all your vacations right here on campus, raking leaves and doing whatever else the Grounds Department wants you to do."

Great. I only had one problem: What was I going to tell my mother about not coming home over spring break—or Thanksgiving, for God's sake? I called her up. "Mom," I said, "you can't believe what's happened. I'm so excited about my studies."

"What do you mean?" she says.

"Mom, I really want to catch up," I said. "So next time I have time off, I'm going to stay up here to study. My professors will be here then. It'll help me get a jump on my classes."

I could hear her sigh with relief on the other end of the line. "I've been praying to Saint Anthony every night that you would get serious, and he's answering my prayers," my sweet mother said. She went to her grave, and my father went to his, never knowing what really happened.

Many years later, though, it came up in an interesting way. One of my closest friends, a man named Walter Buckley, used to run the Bethlehem Steel pension fund. When Bethlehem Steel went under, Walter and his associates started a money management firm, and I agreed to invest $500,000 in it. That was 25 percent of their initial capitalization. One day Walter calls me up. He's a very proper WASP—*very* proper. It's hard to believe we could be as close as we are. If you looked at him and looked at me, you'd think, "Holy shit, opposites really do attract."

Anyway, Walter has something to say to me, but I can tell he doesn't know how to get it out. Finally, he says, "We had to file papers with the attorney general of the State of Pennsylvania to get our license, and because you own 25 percent of the firm, we had to submit your information."

I knew right away where this was going. "And they told you I have a criminal record," I said.

"I'm sure it's a mistake," Walter said.

"No, no, it's not a mistake," I said. I told him the whole sordid tale. "I pleaded guilty to a misdemeanor, and I paid a $37.50 fine and damages," I said. Did I hear Walter laughing on the other end of the line?

In the end, they got their license. I wonder if it had an asterisk on it.

———

End of my freshman year, June 1954, I got home from college, and a friend of mine told me there was a party over in Manhasset. Manhasset was not Roslyn Heights. Manhasset was the right side of the tracks—nice houses, nice lawns, nice cars. I walked into this party, and I saw this girl. She was tall. Blond. She had on white Bermuda shorts and a blue shirt with a collar, short sleeved. She had ballerina slippers on. That's what they used to wear then.

I talked to her for five minutes, and it was nice. Then I was moving around the party, and all of a sudden she was gone. I said to the girl whose house we were in, "Hey, that gal who was here, she told me she was going to give me her phone number, and she left before she gave it to me." Maybe I was fibbing a little bit. But this girl gave me the tall girl's phone number.

That was a Monday night. The next morning I started my

summer job, working as a day laborer for a Long Island contractor called Lizza and Sons. They were building the section of the Long Island Expressway from the city line to Shelter Rock Road in Manhasset. It was a long-term job, and I was thrilled to have the work; I had to join the Laborers Union, Local 1298.

At lunch the next day, I went to a pay phone at a gas station on the corner and called the tall girl from the party. The call was a nickel, as I remember. Her mother answered the phone, and I asked for Elaine—that was the girl's name. She picked up and I said hi. "Who are you?" she asked.

I said, "I spoke with you last night at the party. Would you like to go on a date with me this Friday night?"

"I can't," she said.

"Why not?" I asked.

"I just don't want to."

What could I say to that? "Okay," I told her, and went back to work.

The next day I called her again. Same answer. Maybe she'd been told nice girls don't get picked up by boys, even if it's at a party. There were different standards then than there are now.

So on Thursday I called her again, and I said, "Look. You go out with me tomorrow night, and if you don't have a great time, you'll never see me or hear from me again."

"I've got to ask my mother," she said. She was sixteen. I was eighteen. She got back on the phone and said, "I can go out, but I have to be home by eleven thirty."

I said, "Eleven thirty? Conrad Janis doesn't play 'The Saints' until midnight." There was a place down in the East Village then called the Central Plaza, and there was a guy who played the trombone who later became a movie actor; his name was Conrad Janis. It was Dixieland jazz, which was the rage then, and the Central

Plaza was a beer hall. You'd get pitchers of beer for a buck and a quarter, and you'd see girls flopping over in their seats, passed out.

"I've got to be home by eleven thirty," she said.

All right. We went with a high-school friend of mine and his date; I borrowed my father's car and went to pick her up. She lived in a nice house, in a nice part of Manhasset: her father, Dick Abbe, worked on Wall Street. They belonged to a country club, the whole deal. I'll never forget the sight of Elaine when she came to the door: she had a dress on with a crinoline, this thing girls used to wear that made their dresses stick out. She looked beautiful. And we drove down to the East Village and listened to the music and drank beer and had a ball. We laughed like hell. We got there about nine, and we left at ten thirty so Elaine could get home on time. My friend was fine with it.

We drove back to Long Island, and I dropped my friend and his date off, then I took Elaine home. I walked her up to her front door and said, "I had a great time."

"So did I," she said.

"I'll give you a call," I said, then I turned around to leave. I remember they had a slate sidewalk that went from the front door to the driveway, which was on the side. I got in my car, and before I backed out of the driveway, with the window open I said to her, "I'm going to marry you."

She laughed and shook her head at me. Then she put her key in the door and went in. And you want to know the crazy thing? She never dated anybody else ever again, and neither did I.

———

The beginning of any relationship is physical attraction. But I also enjoyed the fact that this girl came across as carefree. I was a little wild myself. In fact, after we started seeing each other, Elaine met a gal friend of mine from Roslyn—not a relationship, just a friend—who said, "I understand you're dating Ken Langone."

"Yes," Elaine said.

"Hell, he's nuts," this gal said.

"I don't know about that," Elaine told her. "All I know is, every time I'm with him, all I do is laugh."

She was carefree and I was carefree. It was a great time to be young, ten years after World War II, and things were starting to happen in America—big cars, jet planes, Elvis Presley (though I was never into rock and roll).

She was from Manhasset, I was from Roslyn, but I never felt like an interloper around Elaine. We were nuts about each other; we enjoyed each other. We had a great time together. We'd go to movies, or we'd go to Jones Beach. Cheap, simple stuff. We had many of the same interests; she liked sports, and so did I. I had run cross-country in high school, but Elaine was a much better athlete than I was. She was a very good tennis player, a seven-handicap golfer. I remember going to watch her play in a high-school basketball game while I was in college, and she was *good*.

She had a lot of friends; she was very popular. But the main thing I liked about her was that she was a free spirit. She didn't judge me and I didn't judge her. We just enjoyed each other, and we still do.

———

Supply and demand goes through everything in life. Early on I caught the fact that if you have a special talent, or if you have something unique that provokes people to do something that you can make a profit on, that's a good thing. Every two weeks while I was at Bucknell, my dad used to send me a $16 check for spending money: eight bucks a week. A big stretch for him, and a tough budget for me. Man, I had to go out and kill to eat. But necessity is the mother of invention.

Late in my freshman year, I'd hit on an idea. I remembered that as soon as they'd get to Bucknell as freshmen, a lot of the rich kids (practically anybody who wasn't me was rich) were buying stationery with their names printed on it or the Bucknell seal on it. Some guys waited until they pledged a fraternity, then put the emblem of their fraternity on it. I thought, "How could I make some money selling stationery?"

The lightbulb went on. Freshman orientation! For orientation at Bucknell, you had to wear a beanie and a kind of sandwich board—two sheets of white cardboard, one on your chest and one on your back, connected by a couple of pieces of string over your shoulders—with your name and hometown printed on each side. It was a little humiliating: that was part of the point. The first couple days you're there, you haven't met anybody yet, and you're melancholy; you miss your high-school friends, they've all gone someplace else. I thought that would be my moment to strike.

L. G. Balfour was a company in Massachusetts that made college rings and caps and gowns, and they also had a stationery division. Before I started my sophomore year, I got them to send me samples, and I put the samples on a piece of cardboard; I got all set up a week before freshman orientation. As soon as the freshmen arrived, I'd go into their dorms with my sample board and say, "Look, you're going to be writing a lot to your friends." I'd remind them that a long-distance phone call was sixty-five cents for three minutes; that was a lot of money then. I'd say, "Let's see, you have how many friends? Ten? You're going to write them two, three times a week?"

They're nodding. I can see they're homesick and blue. "Okay," I'd tell them. "Here's what you'll need for your freshman year, but you get a price break if you order enough." I guess you might say I was exploitative.

I made damn sure I got their check or money order right away, and here's why. Within two weeks after they got to school, they'd forgotten their friends at home, they'd made new friends, they were going to rush a fraternity; writing letters was the last thing on their minds. I had guys tell me years later, "You son of a bitch, I still have boxes of that fucking stationery."

Suddenly supply and demand was more than a theory to me.

———

Sophomore year, when I began dating Elaine, I used to come home most weekends. A Bucknell guy from my neck of the woods had a car, and four of us would ride with him; we'd pay him two bucks apiece, each way, for gas. On Sunday nights, we'd drive back to school, and sometimes we'd stop at a store on Forty-second Street called Tie City and pick up some neckties. Everybody at Bucknell had to wear a tie and jacket at dinner and in the fraternity houses. Those were different times!

Back in those days, all the college kids used to wear what you call rep ties—the silk neckties with the diagonal stripes. Tie City sold cheap rep ties for a buck apiece: you knew they were cheap because of how easily they wrinkled. With Tie City neckties you learned never to untie the knot, because those damn wrinkles would never come out. You'd just loosen the thing and pull it over your head.

Anyway, I used to buy a box of a hundred ties, all different colors, bring them back to Bucknell on Sunday night, then on Monday hit the freshman dorms and sell them for a buck-fifty, buck-seventy-five apiece—I could make fifty to seventy-five bucks on a box. Further adventures in entrepreneurship.

There was more. I knew a guy in my fraternity by the name of

Matt Sleeper. And Matt Sleeper, who was a senior when I was a sophomore, was the R. J. Reynolds representative for Bucknell. R. J. Reynolds was the tobacco company that manufactured Camels and their new filtered cigarette, Winstons (Salem would come later). Reynolds paid Matt twenty-five bucks a month, plus all the cigarettes he wanted, to distribute its products on campus.

Every month Reynolds would send Sleeper a big cardboard box containing twenty cartons of cigarettes. Each wax-sealed carton held twenty-five cellophane-covered four-packs of Camels and Winstons. And all Matt had to do was go to the fraternity dining rooms and put one of these four-packs at each place. Or go to the dorms, knock on the doors, and hand the cigarettes out. He was giving them away, not selling them; R. J. Reynolds was just building business.

Matt was about to graduate, and I wanted that job. I said, "Matt, how do I get it?"

"You've got to pay me," he said. "Whoever I recommend gets the job."

I asked him how much. He said fifty-five bucks. Fifty-five bucks was real money in 1954. But I would make it back in the first two months.

First, though, I would have to pass muster with O. R. Zimmerman.

Zimmerman was R. J. Reynolds's executive for college accounts. He worked out of Harrisburg, covering dozens of college campuses, and he visited his reps frequently. And Zimmerman was coming to Bucknell to meet with me, and Matt Sleeper told me, "You've got to smoke."

"What do you mean?" I asked.

"Oh yeah," Matt says. "You've got to smoke. When the guy comes to the interview, we're going to have lunch, and he'll tell you about what the job entails and so forth, and then he'll decide, but you'll have my recommendation. After the meal, Zimmerman is going to offer you a cigarette. And if you tell him you don't smoke, he ain't gonna hire you."

Matt smoked, of course. But I didn't. So a friend of mine taught me how to inhale. He taught me on Winstons, which had the filter. I got so I could just manage.

So O. R. Zimmerman comes to Bucknell, and he and Matt and I go to lunch at the Bison, this place on campus where you'd go after class to have a Coke and french fries. We sit in a booth. We eat, we talk, and it's all going well, and then Zimmerman whips out a pack of Camels and offers me one. I light up and inhale. And all of a sudden the—pardon my French—fuckin' room starts to spin. I just barely got "Excuse me" out, ran to the bathroom, and was sicker than I'd ever been in my life. Cleaned up, washed my face, went back to the table. And, long story short, I got the job.

And never smoked another cigarette.

———

Elaine and I got married in September 1956, the beginning of my senior year at Bucknell, and we were poor as church mice. Elaine was making a big bet on me. Who knew if I'd ever amount to anything? She was going to go to nursing school, and then she married me, and she didn't go to nursing school. Before the wedding, my father said to me, "Your mother and I are going to give you the same as we've given you every year; as for the rest, you're on your own." He was really adamant that you shouldn't get married unless you could afford to support your wife; fathers didn't do that for sons. Italian macho mentality.

At that point in my life, all I knew was that I wanted to make money. And where did you make money? Wall Street. My wife's father worked on Wall Street, in institutional investing at Shearson, Hammill. But that was just a lot of words to me then. All I knew about Wall Street was that was where you bought and sold stocks and bonds.

In other words, I knew nothing. But I read *Fortune* religiously every month, in the library at Bucknell. I was intrigued by mergers; I was intrigued by companies growing and how they financed their growth. I don't know why I was so fascinated by Wall Street. I wasn't from an Ivy League school; I really had no family connections; Elaine's dad and I didn't sit around discussing municipal bonds. It was all just exciting to me, in a way I couldn't put my finger on yet.

Elaine and I had barely enough money to see us from September to January—enough for food, rent on a little apartment on Main Street, off campus, and one semester's tuition for me. What that meant was I had to figure out a way to do two semesters in one and graduate early.

So I went to see the dean of students, Dr. Coleman; I needed to get his permission to take the extra credits. He wasn't encouraging. "I just don't think you can do this much work at once," he told me. "Sorry." I told him that if he wouldn't let me take the extra classes, it probably made the most sense for me to drop out right away. Why spend the money on my second-to-last semester, then leave in January a semester short of graduating? I could go to New York now and get a job, I told him, and save the tuition money.

He shook his head. "Okay," he said. "I'll let you take the extra classes. But you're asking for trouble."

"Maybe I am," I said, "but I've got no choice."

Coleman had an assistant, Martha Henderson. She had a desk outside his office like a secretary would, but she was really more than an assistant. She was the closet dean. When I came out of his office, she said to me, "How did it go?"

I told her Coleman had okayed the extra classes. "Well, you're on your way," she said.

"Miss Henderson, the truth is I've got a problem," I said.

"What's the problem?"

I said, "The problem is I'm short three hundred bucks."

She asked me what I meant. I told her my calculations had been a bit off; with the cost of the extra courses I'd be taking, I would be $300 behind by January. I said I was expecting to work in the post office that Christmas, so I'd make some money there, but I'd still be in the red.

She smiled. "Maybe we can help you," she said.

And thanks to Martha Henderson—I'll never forget her name— Bucknell lent me the $300.

I'll tell you a remarkable thing about that gift Bucknell gave me; it was a loan, but I really considered it a gift: I paid it back long ago, but I still feel like I owe them three hundred bucks.

And guess what? I'm glad I feel that way. Elaine and I have been extremely generous with Bucknell. But no matter how much more you do for the other guy, when he was there for you at a critical point in your life, you can never truly pay him back. Because that was the key to the door that let me go beyond that point. If I hadn't had it, who knows what would have happened?

2.

TRAINS, PLANES, AND COMBAT BOOTS

graduated from Bucknell in February, and we moved in with my in-laws in Manhasset. The plan was to stay just till we could get on our feet a little bit. Elaine found a job as a receptionist in Manhattan; I started looking for work. I had the vague idea of beginning a career on Wall Street.

Elaine's parents were very kind about putting us up—they even gave us one of their cars, a 1951 Ford coupe, as a wedding present—but I didn't want to be a freeloader. I did all kinds of stuff for them while I job hunted: painted the exterior of their house, stripped and refinished a piece of furniture, and painted the basement floor. I was always handy.

In the meantime, while Elaine got a job as a receptionist in New York City, nothing was happening on Wall Street, and I was getting itchy. A guy I knew worked for a company called Retail Credit, so I went in to talk to the people there and they hired me on the spot. I figured I'd take the job on a temporary basis until I found something better. Here's what it was: say Allstate Insurance has somebody who wants to buy car insurance from them; Allstate sends an inquiry to Retail Credit Company to do some background on this guy. So you drive by where he lives, you see what the house looks like, you talk to the neighbors. Basically, you're being trained to find dirt. The whole thing pissed me off, right from the start.

The company had a program: you had to do four cases a day. They would give you the four inquiries, and you would map out all the addresses in a road atlas and organize your trip (you had to provide your own car) so you're not driving back and forth, then go out and start knocking on doors. Most of the guys doing this work were not college graduates.

"Hi," you'd say. "We're doing some background on your next-door neighbors, Mr. and Mrs. Bellagio"—or whatever the hell their name was—"and we want to be careful that we're accurate."

Often as not you'd get this: "I don't know them very well."

But I had to keep pushing. "Well, have you ever heard them yelling next door? Have you ever seen Mr. Bellagio drive a car recklessly? Do you have any idea whether they're drinkers or not?"

Sometimes you'd get the door slammed in your face. "I don't want to talk to you," they'd say. "Get out of here."

Then, at two or three in the afternoon, you were supposed to go back to the office and write up what you found out about each of these four cases. But what if you'd found out nothing? Or just heard some gossip from the neighbors that made you feel bad about humanity? So I made my mind up: I'm not playing this game. The trouble was that I needed the job. They were paying me about $75 a week: not much money, but Elaine and I needed every dime just to cover our expenses. Fortunately, my in-laws weren't charging us anything to live with them.

So I thought, "I know what I'm going to do. I'm going to take my four inquiry slips, I'm going to go home, I'm going to have a nice lunch, and I'm going to type fairy tales! 'Great guy, upstanding guy . . .'"

I also found out that if you could take on more than four cases, you'd make extra money. So I began to do five or six cases a day. And on each slip I'd write variations of "Nice people, well liked, never saw them do anything bad."

After about six weeks, I got called into the boss's office, in Garden City. He said, "We'd like to promote you."

"To what?" I asked.

"We'd like you to do personnel work," he said. "We also do background checks on people our clients are hiring."

"Sure," I said. Why not? These checks were more in-depth, so you only had to do two a day. So I went about my merry way again, and again I was up to the same tricks: no matter who it was, he was the best guy on the planet.

I felt no compunction about what I was doing, because I thought what the company was doing was wrong. They operated on this assumption: everybody's got dirt, go find it. I resented that. Writing fiction, I felt I was robbing from the rich and giving to the poor.

And once more I figured, why limit myself? Why do only two a day? Hell, I could crank out forty a week! So I'm sitting at home, watching *The Price Is Right* on television at 11:30 in the morning, dreaming up wonderful things to write about all these candidates.

One day, after about three weeks, my boss calls me in again. "I've got to see you," he says.

"Sure," I say. "What's up?"

"Look, I want to talk to you about one case you got here," he tells me. He looks at my report. "You say this guy is a Little League coach, well thought of in his community. He helps his neighbors clean their gutters out. He's very active, he's a bowler, blah-blah-blah."

He looks at me. "Listen, Ken, help me out," my boss says. "How does he do all this from a wheelchair?"

I didn't have a snappy answer for that one.

"Go clean your desk up and get out of here," he told me.

It was time to get serious about Wall Street. My father-in-law knew a lot of people that I could talk to. He sent me to a man by the name of Maurice Hart, a senior executive at a firm called New York Hanseatic, specialists in trading foreign bonds. I went to see Mr. Hart at 120 Broadway, down in the financial district, and told him why I was interested in Wall Street, why I was fascinated by corporate finance and mergers and acquisitions. He gave me some contacts at investment houses and told me to come back after I'd met with them.

So I went around to a number of these firms—Halsey, Stuart; Clark Dodge; Kidder, Peabody; F. S. Smithers; Goldman Sachs; White Weld—and didn't even get a nibble. I went back to Mr. Hart and told him I'd struck out everywhere I visited. And he looked at me and said, "Let me tell you the lay of the land. We have Jewish firms for Jewish kids, and we have WASP firms for WASP kids. The Irish, we make clerks and put them on the floor of the stock exchange, and Italian kids like you, we put in the back office." Hart said, "I have nothing here for you. I don't want to put you back there; you're better than that.

"Okay, I'm going to tell you something," he said. "Go find a job where you can learn something about the business. With an institutional investor—say a bank—in its trust department."

Not Wall Street, in other words, but a place where I could get a leg up and learn the ropes.

So I told my father-in-law, and he said, "I have a friend at the Equitable Life."

Like other big insurance companies, the Equitable Life didn't just do insurance: half of the organization was devoted to maximizing profits by investing the money that came in in the form of premiums. The Equitable's investment department did private placements, meaning they bought notes and bonds directly from issuing corporations, not in the public market. They dealt in three categories of industries: industrials (corporations), public utilities, and railroads.

The Equitable Life had a very robust railroad bonds department, and the man who ran it also doubled as the head of personnel for the whole investment department. This was the man my father-in-law knew. His name was Hudson Whitenight—Huddy, everyone called him—and he was a lovely guy.

So my father-in-law arranged for me to go meet Hudson Whitenight in April, right after I'd blown out of Retail Credit. Whitenight told me they were just starting a new program to hire trainees in the investment department, but they were only looking at people with MBAs. I said, "How about if I go nights to get an MBA?"

"Would you really want to do that?" he asked. "It'd be a lot on your plate."

"Sure I'd do it," I told him. I suppose I pray at the feet of hard work. And I really was excited about the securities industry. I was just thrilled by the notion of financing buildings and railroads and raising money to buy and sell businesses. I loved every part of it.

Whitenight said he wanted me to meet with a few people about entering their program, and I interviewed with them over a two-week period. I was rough as a cob. A poor kid from blue-collar Long Island, not eloquent. But Huddy came from Pennsylvania, and he was impressed that I'd gone to Bucknell, and I guess the people I'd met with saw past my shortcomings. On May 23, 1957—I remember it was a Thursday—Whitenight met with me and said, "I'm going to offer you a job if you agree to go get an MBA in your free time."

He said, "I want you to know why I recommended you. You have a good education, and your enthusiasm is remarkable. If you really love your work as much as I think you're going to, you're going to be a big success. We're going to hire you at $82.50 a week—$4,290 a year. You're going to have to get an MBA while working here, and we don't have a tuition-reimbursement program."

"Okay," I told him. I couldn't have been more excited.

He told me I'd be working in the industrials department, under a manager named Bill McCurdy. I started on the first Monday of June, in the AMF Building at 261 Madison Avenue, fifteenth floor. I walk into McCurdy's office, and he isn't smiling. "I'm going to tell you what it's like here," he says. "Accuracy is the most important thing in the world."

Not "How are you?" or "Glad to meet you," or "We have high hopes for you." No small talk, no pep talk. "You're going to be working for Mike Fedyshyn," McCurdy told me. "When I want something, I want it right away, and I want it right the first time." That was it.

"Okay," I thought. "Tough guy. That's all right." So I went to Fedyshyn, and he liked me. He had me running numbers, filling out sheets with summaries of sales and earnings of companies the Equitable Life had investments in. For example, if there was a line for sales over the last ten years, they'd want me to calculate the percentage increase in sales year over year. It was meaningless shit. But I was learning, and I was knee-deep in annual reports and proxy statements—all the stuff I loved. The truth is that I loved what I was doing from the day I went to work, which is one of the great joys in life, I've found.

In May, my mother-in-law had found Elaine and me a little one-bedroom apartment in Auburndale, Queens—128 bucks a month, two-year lease. We moved in in May. We had my big $82.50 a week plus Elaine's receptionist's salary. Christ, we struggled. But my in-laws and my parents were good to us. We had a lot of hand-me-down furniture. We bought a secondhand china closet, I cut the legs off at the bottom and painted it blue over the mahogany. I remember we had an aluminum outdoor chaise longue in our living room for a sofa. But what the hell, you could sit on it!

We didn't plan to be poor. We just were. A big night out was a beer and a pizza at Rutha's on Northern Boulevard. We'd go to the movies. We had a little dog named Pinky. It wasn't all fun, believe me. But we had fun.

I enrolled at NYU right away and started night classes that summer, in July 1957. Every evening after work I'd walk up to Grand Central and get the Lexington IRT down to Wall Street. The subway station was right on the corner of Wall and Trinity, where Trinity Church was. Then I'd walk through the cemetery to the business school, which at that time was in the old NYU building on Trinity Place. No air-conditioning and not much heat either: you sweated in the summer, and you froze your ass off in the wintertime. The class was big: they had classes all over downtown to handle the overflow, at places like the Bankers Club and the Lawyers Club.

Elaine got a new job, as a medical assistant for a surgeon in Manhasset, Dr. John Mountain. (Remember, she had wanted to be a nurse.) The doctor had office hours on Thursday night, when I was at school. After her afternoon work with Dr. Mountain, Elaine would break for a couple of hours and go have dinner with her parents, and her parents would send me a plate of food. Elaine would bring the plate back to our apartment and put it on top of a pot with water on simmer, to keep the plate and the food hot. I used to get back from school at eleven o'clock at night, and she'd be waiting for me; she'd sit down with me while I had my dinner.

After two weeks at the job, McCurdy calls me in one morning. "You take a square peg and try to put it in a round hole, and it doesn't fit," he tells me. "If you take a square peg and put it in a square hole, it fits."

"Excuse me, Mr. McCurdy," I said. "Are you telling me that I'm out of place here?"

"Well," McCurdy said, "I'm not exactly saying that, but you might want to think about where your talents are best suited."

I realized (and later found it was true) that he'd resented Whitenight telling him, "This guy is going to work for you"—period. No ifs, ands, or buts. Did he look down on me because I had a blue-collar background? Maybe. I have no way of knowing for sure.

"Okay," I told him. What else could I say?

A few weeks later, I got a call from Whitenight's office. Whitenight said to me, "We have a statistics department downstairs on the fourteenth floor. The investment statistician is Bernard Bergman. You're going to go to work for him for six months."

I went down to meet Mr. Bergman, and he couldn't have been nicer. Bernie Bergman and his assistant, Rita Morris, worked side by side in a little office next to mine; Bernie was keeping close tabs on the Equitable Life's railroad-car-leasing business. Railroads were an interesting sector. At that point, the late 1950s, the national highway system was coming into being, and the railroads were all going broke. One of the ways they could raise money for the equipment they needed was through an instrument called equipment trust certificates—ETCs. It worked like this: the Equitable Life would buy the ETCs as an investment, the railroads would say what cars they wanted, and, using the proceeds from the equipment trust certificates, the Equitable Life would go buy the rolling stock and lease it to the railroads. The Equitable Life owned them: the railroads had to make a monthly payment, the same way you do on an automobile if you lease the car.

The Equitable owned more than ten thousand railroad cars—flatcars, boxcars, gondolas, and tank cars—and each leased for so much a day, depending on the type of car. Bernie Bergman had a system for keeping track of them: there was a three-by-five card for every car, tracking the lease payments month by month. He had a different-color card for each type of car. The boxcars were blue, the flatcars were buff green, the gondolas were pink, and the tank cars were yellow; every car was numbered. Bernie loved his work: he told me that one of his favorite things was to go home to Staten Island on the weekend and sit by the hi-fi and listen to an LP record while he worked on his cards. My new job was to bring those damn cards up to date. It was a mammoth undertaking.

For the first four or five weeks, I sat in my little office with my mechanical pencil, methodically writing the lease charges on the appropriately colored and numbered cards. It took a while to dawn on me that—except in the rare instance that a car was wrecked, in which case you noted the fact on its card and stopped keeping track—the numbers never changed. Never changed!

So I'm sitting there thinking, "Why am I doing this this way? There's got to be a better way." We were on Thirty-ninth and Madison; there was an office-supply store across the street. So I go in this store and I say, "Do you have an adjustable rubber stamp for dollar amounts up to hundreds, including cents?"

"No," they told me, "but we can have one made."

I was very excited. If the January lease payment for flatcars was, say, $93.55, all I'd have to do was set my magic adjustable stamp for that amount and stamp every buff-green card in the January space! Genius!

That custom-made rubber stamp set me back six or seven bucks, a lot of money to pay out of my own pocket, but it felt totally worth it. After another three weeks, I put all ten thousand cards in a big box and lugged it into Bernie and Rita's office.

"What's that?" Bernie asked.

"Those are the cards," I told him proudly.

He said to me, "What do you mean? You're done?"

"Yeah, I'm finished."

"Let me see them," he said.

"Sure," I said. I take the cards out, and he starts shuffling through them. He's looking and he's looking and he's looking. He looks up, he looks down, then he looks up again.

"How did you get this done?" he asks.

I said, "I went over to Maxfield's Office Supply, and I bought the stamp and a stamp pad. Every month I multiply the per diem by the number of days, and that's it; I stamp in the correct figure on all the pink cards, all the yellow cards, all the blue cards, all the buff-green cards."

Bernie looks at me. "I don't want them this way," he says.

"What?" I say.

"I don't want them this way."

"How do you want them?"

"I want you to write them by hand," he tells me.

"But this is easier to read," I say. "And there are fewer chances for mistakes."

"It's not, and there aren't," Bernie says. "I want them done by hand."

What could I say? I wasn't going to argue with him; I didn't want to screw up my job. So I went back in my little office and started over. It took me five months to do all those cards by hand, and by the end the mechanical pencil had made a little groove in the side of my right forefinger that I still have to this day.

Did I learn a lesson? Yeah—stay employed!

———

One day—it was the late fall of 1957—Hudson Whitenight calls me into his office. "Have you given any thought to what you're going to do about your military obligation?" he asks. He was a big military guy, very patriotic, a colonel in the army reserves.

"Well, I'm married," I said.

"Yes," he said, "but you want to do your part for your country."

I told him I agreed, and I did agree. Back at Bucknell, before

I got married, my plan had been to join the navy. I wanted to go to U.S. Navy Officer Candidate School in Newport, Rhode Island, and become a line officer, serving on a ship, as opposed to a supply officer, working on a navy base. I had no interest in being a land-locked sailor. But by 1957, with America at peace, the navy didn't want married guys as line officers, so that did it for the navy.

I found out there was an army reserve unit on West Fourth Street in Greenwich Village, and I went down there. They told me that if I signed up, I'd have to go on active duty for six months; I'd have to start within a certain number of days. After the six months, I'd have an obligation to the reserves for five and a half years: I would have to go to a reserve meeting one night a week and to Camp Drum, up in Watertown, New York, for two weeks each summer. I signed up. I committed to beginning active duty in March 1958, meaning I would complete my full semester at NYU, then reenroll in school after I'd served my six months.

I told Whitenight what I'd done, and he was delighted. Of course the Equitable Life would give me a leave of absence while I served, he told me. I'm sure he felt the army would season me. Everybody in the office thought I was immature, and they were right. I was twenty-one years old, for God's sake; I was a misfit! Every one of the other trainees had an MBA. One had been in the navy for four years before he got his degree; he was twenty-seven. Another guy was twenty-six. Another, John Turner, was twenty-eight. John had worked for GE for three years, and then he went back to Wharton to get his MBA. He ended up being my office mate, and we became the best of friends. John used to needle me about the damn railroad cards. It was clear that the rest of them were getting bigger responsibilities than I was. And bigger salaries. In contrast to my $4,290 a year, the guys with the MBAs were making $6,000 or $6,500.

But, I figured, I was getting paid, I was going to NYU at night, and I was learning, at school and at work. I was ravenous about learning; I couldn't get enough. I used to go to the public library on Saturdays to do more reading.

After working for Bernie Bergman for six months, I went back to McCurdy. He didn't like me much better, but he was around less; he had terrible arthritis, which kept him out of the office a lot.

In 1957 and 1958, the airlines were starting to take delivery of the first jets, and they were all borrowing money to buy the aircraft. The Equitable Life's industrials department—McCurdy's area of responsibility, and mine, now that I was back—was heavily involved. I had a chance to manage some of the work on the American Airlines financing, the TWA financing, the Eastern Air Lines financing. It was exciting—all the more so because, to start with, I knew next to nothing about what I was doing.

Each manager was assigned a lawyer in the legal department for investments. McCurdy was assigned an attorney by the name of Joe Spector, and Joe and I began to work together. He was much older than I was—he was about thirty-seven, it seemed ancient—and I was very honest with him about what I didn't know, which was almost everything. He said, "Look, don't worry about a thing. When you don't understand something, you call me."

I did, and Joe was as good as his word. He was a great guy, and he really took me under his wing. It also turned out—it was more striking in the late 1950s than it would be now—that he was gay. He invited Elaine and me to dinner in his apartment down in the Village one night, and there was his roommate, a guy named Pat, who cooked this great Italian meal. It was clear they were together. I remember—it's funny what you remember—that Pat had painted a picture of a nude woman with a big pubic bush and put it in the hallway of this apartment and that when Joe's mother, a nice Jewish lady from upstate New York, came in and saw this, she went and found a vase to put in front of the bush!

Anyway, Joe helped me enormously. And there's one very important point I want to make right at the beginning of this book: the thing I can't say and never will say is that I'm self-made. I'm not. To say that would be an injustice to all those people who brought me to the party. I'm grateful to every one of them, and Joe Spector was one of them. He's passed on, and I miss him. He was a good man.

Anyway, now I was working on all these financings, I was really excited, and I was doing well. I was also really intrigued by the subjects I was taking in business school: corporate finance, relevantly enough; securities analysis. Most of the people who taught in the business school worked on Wall Street; they were called adjunct professors. The man who taught securities analysis was the head of research at Clark Dodge. Another guy was in the corporate-finance department at Goldman Sachs. I was starting to meet people; I was networking.

Every morning I'd pack my lunch in a brown bag and take the Q28 bus from Auburndale to Main Street, Flushing, then take the IRT 7 train from Main Street to Grand Central. I'd come up out of the subway and put my lunch in a locker; Grand Central had public lockers that you'd put a dime in. I'd take the key and walk from Forty-second down to Thirty-ninth and Madison and go to work.

When lunchtime came, the man who ran utilities, Bob Benson, used to go with his trainees to a luncheonette across the street called Crosby's. A couple of others would always tag along, but I would usually tell them I had something to do. I'd go up to Grand Central, into the waiting room, get my lunch out of the locker, sit down on a bench, and eat. I would've liked to eat lunch with the other guys, but Elaine and I were broke. We had to pay our $128 per month rent, we had to feed ourselves, we had to pay car insurance. Our budget just didn't allow me to go to a diner and spend three bucks for lunch.

In January, the semester was over, and I stopped school for the time being. On March 23, I went into the army.

I did my basic training at Fort Dix, smack in the belly of New Jersey, south of Trenton. You weren't allowed to go home for the first four weeks. I had a black sergeant named Ralph Jefferson. He didn't say much. Great trainer.

The first day, we all got in our brand-new uniforms: fatigue jackets, hats, the whole deal. Jefferson said, "Okay, form four lines of twelve." Then he had each of us move from left to right, one at a time, until you came to a guy who was taller than you, then you stopped and fell in. Eventually, there were four lines in height order, with the four tallest guys at the head of each line. Then Jefferson announced, "You four guys are the squad leaders." That was it: I was tall, so I became a squad leader.

The four weeks were finally up, and we all got our first weekend leave. By the way, you couldn't leave before noon on Saturday, and you had to be back by roll call Monday morning. I took the bus from Fort Dix to the Port Authority terminal, then got the subway out to Flushing, then took another bus to get home; that was a long three hours, let me tell you.

Elaine and I were very glad to see each other.

My next weekend leave comes up and I'm packing my little bag, whistling a merry tune, when Sergeant Jefferson walks up to me and says, "Hey, Sarge."

Well, that was strange, I thought. I'm not a sarge; I'm a private.

"Hey, Sarge, you're standing tall," Jefferson says. "You got a good weekend planned?"

"Yes, I do," I say.

"Well, you've got to change your plans."

"Why is that?"

"Because you're staying here for the weekend."

"What did I do?" I said.

He said, "Oh, you did nothing." He said, "But look six guys down."

I looked down six bunks and saw another guy packing *his* bag.

"When your squad fell in this morning," the sergeant said, "that kid looked like his shoes were polished with a Hershey's bar. Now, he's going home for the weekend and you're staying here. And you're going to shine all the shoes of all the members of your squad."

We'd been issued paratrooper boots that went halfway up your calf. "I want the soles and heels polished as well as the tops," Sergeant Jefferson said.

"But what did *I* do?" I asked.

"Well, you did nothing," he said. "But I'll tell you one thing. You're never going to have one of your guys fall in again looking the way this kid looked."

"Oh, come on," I said.

He shook his head. "Nope. That's it—enjoy your weekend here."

So I stayed that weekend. I had to call Elaine and tell her I wasn't coming home. I stayed that weekend and literally spit shined twenty-four pairs of paratrooper boots—tops, soles, and heels. To do it properly takes about an hour per pair. I had a big can of Esquire paste polish, I had an old T-shirt, and I had a bottle of water. You apply the polish, let it dry, wet the T-shirt with the water, and buff the boot, let it dry again; reapply a thin layer of polish and let it dry, spit shine it again . . .

All twenty-four pairs of boots. Tops, soles, and heels. One hour per pair. They were all gleaming like mirrors by the time everyone else came back from leave. And I learned the importance of shining shoes. To this day (though I admit I don't shine my own shoes anymore), you'll never catch me with anything less than a high gloss.

When I got out of basic training, I was transferred to Fort Jay on Governors Island, the headquarters of the First U.S. Army. After I was there about a month, I was transferred to Fort Slocum, on an island off New Rochelle. From there, I got transferred to Fort Totten, which was in Bayside, Queens—my best weekend-leave commute of all.

I did okay in the army. I took orders and I didn't bitch. I went with the flow. I knew when I was going to get out, and I got out. And in September 1958, I went back to the Equitable Life and NYU.

"I've got some good news for you," Whitenight told me when I returned to the office. "The Equitable Life has a new policy, and from now on we're going to pay your tuition at NYU."

This was terrific. It also meant I could take more courses and finish that much sooner. I went back to school with the wind in my sails and did very well. I had a great relationship with my thesis adviser, Jules Bogen, who was really a luminary in the financial world; he did a lot of business writing and edited an important text called *Financial Handbook*. Many years later, when I was doing pretty well, I made a donation to NYU to have the faculty lounge named the Abbe-Bogen Faculty Lounge, after two men who helped me enormously when I was starting out, my father-in-law and Dr. Bogen.

One day Bogen called me into his office and said, "You know your subjects pretty well. Have you ever thought about teaching?"

That made me blink. I told him I hadn't, and it was the truth.

The truth was that I was standing there thinking, "Holy shit, only seven years ago I was on the edge of getting thrown out of college, and here I am being asked to think about becoming a college teacher."

"Well, you ought to think about it," Bogen said. "But you shouldn't give up your work. Would you be interested in teaching at night?"

"Very interested," I said.

"Good," he said, "I'm going to set you up with a friend of mine up at Washington Square."

Bogen sent me to a man named Hobart Carr, the head of the banking and finance department at the NYU School of Commerce, Accounts, and Finance. Carr was looking for an instructor to teach undergraduates corporate finance and securities analysis, two subjects I'd learned something about in the last couple of years. And so I started teaching in September 1960, the same month I finished my course work and my thesis, and in October I got my MBA.

The title of my thesis was a mouthful: "Anti-dilution Covenants of Convertible Securities." At the Equitable Life, something that became a trend was that if you lent money to a company, you had the right to convert the debt, if you chose, into the issuer's stock. So as your loan helped the company grow, you got a ride on the stock. It was an extra way of generating additional gains from of an investment, and it became all the rage at the time. But it was new, and the kinks had to be worked out. For instance, if I have a convertible bond, and the company goes off and issues a ton of new shares, my conversion might be diluted; I now own a smaller share of the company. So it became important to put covenants in the loan document to protect the value of your conversion rights.

I was feeling pretty good about life that fall. I'd gotten a couple of raises, and now I was up to $9,000 a year at the Equitable Life;

together with my income from teaching, I was making between $12,000 and $13,000 a year. I remember that when I graduated from Bucknell, my dream was to earn $10,000 a year. Elaine and I had moved from the Flushing apartment to a little rented cottage on a private estate in Brookville, just up the road from Roslyn Heights and in a nicer part of the world.

And we were expecting. For the first couple of years of our marriage, we'd had trouble conceiving, but in the spring of 1960 Elaine got pregnant, and our first child, Kenny junior, was born on December 21, 1960—one of the happiest and proudest days of my life. I was now a father.

At work, I'd been transferred from McCurdy to another manager in industrials, a man by the name of Ray Hermann, a career Equitable Life guy who'd started out as a clerk and worked his way up. He was a nice man. Like McCurdy, Hermann was doing financing for a bunch of companies, and he threw a lot of the work at me.

And the more Ray threw at me, the better I liked it. I worked late on Fridays, on Saturdays if I had to. I worked my ass off, and he respected me for it. I could feel my wings spreading. Ray treated me more like a son than a subordinate: he and his wife, Dot, lived in Floral Park, just a few miles away from us in Brookville; they used to take Elaine and me out to dinner sometimes at a little Italian restaurant near their house.

In August 1961, I went to army summer camp, at Camp Drum, upstate. And on August 13, Khrushchev closed the border between East and West Berlin and started building the Berlin Wall. It's a national crisis, a clear provocation by the Soviet Union, and President Kennedy activates 100,000 reserves. And lo and behold, I'm one of the 100,000.

"Get your affairs in order," we were told. "You're going to active duty September 15."

I'm doing well at the Equitable now; I'm really feeling my oats. Now, all of a sudden, my career is totally disrupted. I've got a wife and a nine-month-old son in a cottage out in Brookville. The Equitable Life has just built a new headquarters, at 1285 Avenue of the Americas, and we've all moved in. I worked in that building for one day.

And then, on September 15, 1961, off I went to Fort Bragg, North Carolina.

3.

BUILDING BLOCKS

'm at Fort Bragg, and I'm miserable. I'm a Spec/5 making a big $130 a month, which means I can't afford to go home, and my wife and baby are in Long Island. My career is interrupted. I've had to stop teaching. I'm feeling pretty damn sorry for myself.

One day I get a call that they want to see me at the personnel office. I go in and the lieutenant says to me, "We notice you haven't volunteered for Jump School." My brother was a paratrooper, in the Eighty-second Airborne Division; I wanted no part of it.

"Sir," I said, "I made my mother a promise."

He looked at me. "What do you mean?"

"My mother made me promise that I would never step out of a plane unless there were stairs to walk down."

The lieutenant got pissed off. "Funny guy," he said. "Beat it."

The next day I get a call to come back to the personnel office. "Oh shit," I thought. I walk in, but it's a different officer this time. He says, "I notice on your 201 file"—that's your personnel file—"that you taught at NYU."

"Yes," I said.

"What did you teach?"

"Corporate finance, securities analysis, business law."

"How would you like to teach for the army?" he asked.

"Where?" I asked.

"At North Carolina State."

Here's what it was about. We were no longer fighting in Korea then; we were not yet in Vietnam. But a small number of American troops were in Laos and Cambodia, with MAAGs—military-assistance advisory groups. These were highly specialized soldiers who trained the indigenous forces in communications, small arms, weapons, field medicine, the whole bit. It was a stressful assignment. After being overseas for six months, these soldiers would rotate back to Stateside bases for another half year before returning to Southeast Asia. And somebody figured out—not a bad idea—that while they were here for six months, why don't we offer them college-level courses, which they could take toward getting an undergraduate or master's degree.

North Carolina State was in Raleigh. I went up there and they said, "You'll teach two courses, one on Monday and Wednesday and one on Tuesday and Thursday, all at Fort Bragg. You're going to get paid $260 per month per course." That made an additional $520 on top of my $130 base pay. Suddenly I was slightly less impoverished.

"How do I prepare my classes while I'm soldiering?" I asked.

"We're also going to get you ED—Exempt from Duty—for two hours a day."

Well, this was beautiful. I knew the course material inside and out; I could just go back to the barracks and catch up on my sleep. So I ended up teaching at North Carolina State while I was in the army.

But I was still pissed off—about being seven hundred miles away from my wife and son, about my career and my NYU teaching being interrupted. When I walked into my first class at NC

State, I had a chip on my shoulder. "Okay," I told these soldiers, "I want to tell you something. You see that door you all just came through? Out there it's a different world; in here it's academic freedom." I said, "My name is Ken, and I am going to call each of you by your first name. I don't care what your rank is."

After the class, a huge guy, six five or so, a sergeant major, comes in and quietly says to me, "Professor . . ."

I interrupted him. "I'm not a professor; I'm an instructor."

He said, "Professor, you know, all day long I have to salute people and people salute me, and I refer to them by their rank and their last name. Don't ask us to be able to adjust just like that."

I said, "Do me a favor. You do what you want when you're not in this room, and I'll do what I want when I'm in this room."

That Saturday afternoon I was lying on my bunk in the barracks when this sergeant major comes in. "I don't know if you're busy tonight," he said, "but I'd sure like you to come and have dinner with my wife and my daughters tonight."

"No, thank you," I told him. "Previous engagement."

That was a lie; I just didn't want to go. My image of a career army guy was that they were lumps: they beat their wives; they threw their kids against the wall. I didn't want to have any part of his world.

Next weekend he came by again, with the same invitation. "Look," I said, "I appreciate it, but I'm not interested." But the following Saturday he showed up again and said, "Just come to dinner one night." So I went.

Boy, had I been wrong about him. His name was Ed Masalonis, and he came from the Mesabi Iron Range in northern Minnesota. He'd enlisted in the army at age seventeen in 1940 and was stationed in Scotland. While he was there, his commanding officer asked for volunteers to be trained by British commandos. Three thousand men volunteered, and the commandos told them to start running—wearing jump boots and carrying all their gear on their backs. The last five hundred who were still running after a few hours were chosen as the first-ever army rangers. Ed was one of them. He went to Ranger School, fought in some of the major battles of World War II and Korea, served in Laos. Now he was running army recruiting for the Fort Bragg–Fayetteville, North Carolina, area. His wife, Pat, worked in the post library at Fort Bragg. Ed and Pat had two sweet daughters, and all four of them were the nicest, kindest, politest people I've ever known in my life. Ed was not just my student; he became one of my best friends.

That February—Elaine was now pregnant again—we decided to get a little apartment in Fort Bragg, and she and Kenny came down to live for a couple of months. We used to go to Ed and Pat's house, and they'd make us barbecued chicken and ribs. As nice as that was, though, I was still eager to get out of the army and back to my life.

NYU told me that if I could get out by June, they would let me teach that summer. So I put in for an early discharge, and it was approved. I mustered out in May. And that same month, May 1962, the stock market had its biggest crash since 1929. "This is it," I said. "I'm going to Wall Street."

It was strictly counterintuitive. Investment banks were cutting staff like crazy: to me that meant it was a golden opportunity to get my foot in the door.

My father-in-law disagreed, to put it mildly. Elaine's dad was really upset. Here's his beloved daughter living in a little rented cottage out in Brookville with a toddler and another baby on the way, and his crazy son-in-law wants to quit a secure position with solid benefits and a good salary; I was making almost $10,000 a year at the Equitable Life, the equivalent of about eighty grand today. He said, "Look, you've got a great job, you've got a family. Please don't do this."

I said, "Babba"—that was what I called Mr. Abbe—"I'm sorry. I've got to go to Wall Street; it's what I've always wanted."

And to his great credit he said, "Okay. I'll see if I can get you some interviews."

Now, I knew that nobody on Wall Street would talk to me as long as I was still at the Equitable Life. Many investment banks did business with the Equitable, and if one of them hired me away, it would risk retribution. I had to quit before I got a new position, not after. I had to step out into the yawning void.

I went to Bill Cowie, who was the head of the Equitable's industrial companies department, and said, "Mr. Cowie, I'm going to Wall Street."

"Do you have a job?" he asked.

I told him I didn't.

"Why aren't you coming back to work for us? You were doing so well."

"I know, Mr. Cowie. But I want to go to Wall Street; it's just something I've always had in my head."

"Look," he said. "You can't *get* a job now. I left Wall Street in the '30s to come up here. Things were so bad during the Depression that the investment banks used to have what they called Scotch Weeks; two guys would split the workweek so the firm wouldn't have to let one of them go. Things aren't looking much better now."

"There's no way anybody is ever going to talk to me if I'm still attached to you," I told him.

"Okay," he said. "I'll tell you what I'm going to do with you. I'll accept your resignation, but I want you to promise me you'll come back if you can't get a job."

"Mr. Cowie, all due respect, I'll never come back," I told him. "Because if you were that good to me and I did come back, my conscience wouldn't allow me to ever leave here again."

He looked at me. "You're going to have a tough time," he said.

Boy, did I have a tough time.

It was like my first Wall Street job search, only worse. The WASP firms didn't want me; the Jewish firms didn't want me. Nobody was hiring; they were throwing people out the window. Finally, I found my way to a sleepy backwater of a firm called R. W. Pressprich, which specialized in railroad bonds; they had a very good railroad research department. And the head bond trader there, Eddie Rowan, was a good friend of my father-in-law's. Rowan introduced me to the head of institutional sales, Jack Cullen. Institutional sales was the department that talked to the Equitable Lifes of the world, showing them investments they might be interested in.

Cullen was a partner at Pressprich, a man in his sixties, a former bond trader. I remember he was a sharp dresser: he wore a little flower in his lapel and smoked with a cigarette holder. But what really impressed me was his interpersonal skills: he was a better interviewer than anyone I'd ever encountered before. We hit it off right away. After we'd talked awhile, he said, "You know, I think you can be a great salesman. But I can't afford you."

"How do you know I can be a great salesman?" I asked.

"I can tell," he said. "You listen. You're sensitive to the person you're talking to. You'll know when to go in for the kill and when to back off. That's something most salesmen don't do—*can't* do. They want to just charge, charge, charge in, and they wind up pissing everybody off."

We talked for a little while longer, then he said, "I'd like to hire you, but I just can't. But I know I'm going to hear a lot more about you. So good luck, and all the best."

Pressprich's offices were at 80 Pine Street. I took the elevator down to the lobby, and suddenly I stopped where I stood. "Wait a minute," I said to myself. I got back in the elevator and went upstairs.

"I just left Mr. Cullen," I said to the receptionist. "Could I see him again for a minute?"

Jack came out. "Did you forget something?" he asked.

"No," I said. "Can we talk again?"

We went into a little conference room. "How much do you pay a secretary?" I asked him.

"A hundred fifty bucks a week."

"Pay me what you pay a secretary," I said, "and I'll come to work for you."

"You can't make ends meet on that," Jack said.

"Yes, I can. I'm teaching at NYU at night. Believe me, I'll make ends meet. That's my problem, not yours."

He took a puff from that cigarette holder and thought about it. Finally, he said, "I'll do it."

"Jack, there's only one condition," I said.

Now he smiled. "You have a condition?"

"You have to give me every account you're not doing business with," I said. "If you're not doing business with an account, I have a right to call on them."

"Sure," Jack said. "That's great."

I started work at R. W. Pressprich on Monday, August 13, 1962. I remember the day well: everybody there was in mourning because the previous Friday their senior partner in charge of municipal securities, a fellow named Cushman McGee, had dropped dead of a heart attack. But work went on. Jack Cullen put me in his unit, institutional sales—they called it Unit 15—with three other salesmen at a desk in the middle of the trading room. The most senior salesman was Vincent Banker; Bindy was his nickname. Bindy Banker was the stepson of the head of the firm, W. Barrett Brown; he was an ex-marine officer and very much to the manor born. I liked him, but for all those reasons I was intimidated by him at first. The other two guys in the unit were Charlie Benedict and Silas "Bud" Canaday. I was very much the low man on the totem pole. For Christmas that year, I got a $300 bonus. I went to a bank and borrowed $200 for Christmas presents.

Here's how I got my start at Pressprich. The firm had a research department that covered every industry: retail, consumer products, steel, chemicals, automobiles, and so on. For any stock that was listed, the research department would have an analyst who made it his business to know about the fundamentals of the industry. All the research analysts had investment recommendations: Buy U.S. Steel. Sell General Motors. Buy Procter & Gamble. The model on Wall Street was that the analysts would give their recommendations to the salesmen, and the salesmen would try to sell the idea to institutional investors and what was known as the carriage trade: rich people.

Stocks had been in the doghouse for years after the Depression, but in the booming economy of the late 1950s institutional investors began to get serious about buying equities. In the wake of the crash of 1962, with stock prices low, we were telling the pension funds and insurance companies and banks we serviced that the market could only go up.

I made my first road trip for Pressprich in January 1963, to Cincinnati; Jack Cullen went along with me, to show me the ropes. And Jack didn't like to fly, so we had to take the damn train. It was a long haul, an overnight ride from Penn Station to Columbus, where the train split and became two trains, the Spirit of St. Louis and the Cincinnati Limited, going on to those respective cities. Jack and I had scheduled meetings with the analysts in the bank trust departments, the people who were looking for investment ideas. Our first stop was the First National Bank in Cincinnati; Jack introduced me, then let me lead. I said to the guy who was the head of research there, "Look, we like U.S. Steel, and here's why we like it." My research background from the Equitable, plus the fact that I was teaching at NYU, put me a few cuts ahead of the typical salesman, because I could talk quite knowledgeably about what I was selling.

Soon I was traveling a lot around that region; I was gone at least a week a month, which meant I had to give up teaching. I was developing accounts in Cincinnati, Louisville, Cleveland, Columbus, Toledo, Detroit, Pittsburgh. As I'd requested, these were accounts that nobody had been doing business with, which meant that whatever business I did was brand-new: I would make more money because I wasn't competing with anyone. I didn't give a damn about the size of the accounts: I worked my ass off. And over time I picked up the Fifth Third Bank in Cincinnati, the Union Commerce Bank in Cleveland, the Western and Southern Life Insurance Company, the Union Central Life Insurance Company, the School Employees Retirement System of Ohio.

But I was already starting to think beyond security sales. One night over Christmas just before that first trip to Cincinnati, I'd been putting away the kids' toys (Kenny had just turned two, and Bruce, who'd been born in September, was three months) when I noticed something. My in-laws had given the baby some Flintstones building blocks, and on the blocks was stamped "Kenner Products, Cinti, Ohio"—an abbreviation for Cincinnati. That intrigued me, because the *Flintstones* TV show was very big then: there was Flintstones marketing all over the place. My natural curiosity about supply and demand made me wonder how big a piece of the pie this Kenner Products was getting.

I went into the office and looked the company up in the big Moody's and Standard & Poor's manuals; that was what we had before there were computers. I found out that Kenner Products had been planning to do an IPO of its stock through Kuhn, Loeb in the spring of 1962, but then because the market collapsed, the offering was canceled. So I dialed information for Cincinnati and got the number for Kenner Products. I called it up and asked if I could talk to the CFO. The woman said, "We don't have a CFO."

It turned out Kenner Products' management structure consisted of three people: three brothers named Al, Phil, and Joe Steiner. They'd come up with the company name one day when they were sitting in their office and looked out the window and saw a street sign that said Kenner Street. Al Steiner took my call. "I'm going to be in Cincinnati next week," I said, "and I'd love to stop by and see you."

"Why do you want to see us?" he asked.

"I'm with R. W. Pressprich, an investment-banking firm," I said, "and I have an idea about financing for your company."

Al was a nice man. "Sure," he said. "Stop by when you're in town."

When Jack Cullen and I got to Cincinnati, I had two hours to kill the afternoon after our first meeting. I told him about my call to Steiner and asked if he wanted to go over with me to see them.

Jack gave me a funny look. "I don't know shit about the toy business, and neither do you," he said. "I think you're chasing butterflies."

"Jack, look," I said. "It's simple: they were going to go public, and every cent they raised would have gone into the company. It's got nothing to do with taking money off the table for themselves."

"I still think you're wasting your time," he said.

Now it was my turn to stare at him. He was very good at what he did, I realized, but he was a salesman. His world stopped at that horizon. "Okay," I said. "We agree to disagree. I'm going to stop by there before our next meeting."

So I went over and sat down with Al Steiner and his brother Phil. They were two rather elderly gentlemen (that's how they looked to me at the time), around sixty-five and fifty-five, and they were frankly puzzled by my visit. "Why are you here?" Al asked.

"Well, I assume you need capital," I said.

"Why do you assume that?"

"Well, I know you were going to go public last spring, and then the market blew up and you didn't raise the money."

They looked at each other. "In fact, we would like to raise some money," Phil Steiner said. He told me the story. They had just gotten a license deal with Hanna-Barbera for *The Flintstones*, they were bringing out a line of Flintstones products, and they were going to build a new plant. It was very straightforward, they wanted to grow the company.

"I don't know what your balance sheet looks like," I told them.

"The balance sheet is very good," Phil said.

"Would you ever be interested in a loan?" I asked.

"What kind of loan?" they asked.

I knew exactly what to say: this was where my four and a half years at the Equitable paid off. "How about instead of doing an initial public offering, you issue a bond?" I said. "With a public offering, you've got to file with the SEC, you're subject to the vagaries of the stock market, you're beholden to stockholders. A bond would be simpler; you could deal with just one or two investors."

The brothers looked at each other.

"If you just sold, say, $5 million worth of stock, all five million would be stock eventually," I told them. "But if you sold a bond with a warrant attached, you might do a one-to-two ratio—for every $2 you owe, the purchaser has the right to buy $1 of equity. You cut your equity dilution in half."

"Pretty interesting," Al said. "Who would be interested in such a bond?"

"I don't know," I said, because I didn't know. The last thing I wanted to do was bullshit these totally honest guys.

"What do you mean you don't know?"

"I don't know," I repeated. I knew there were bonds out there with warrants like this. But I didn't know which insurance company or pension fund or investor would be interested in buying on that basis. "If you want me to explore it, I'll make some calls."

They thanked me for coming over. "Let my brother and me talk," Phil said, "and we'll get back to you."

After the meeting, I called a couple of the banks Jack and I had met with in Cincinnati and asked about the Steiner brothers and Kenner. Their reputation was spotless. And when I returned to New York, I didn't wait for Al and Phil Steiner to call me: I phoned them as soon as I got back to the office. "What do you think?" I asked.

"We've been thinking about it," they said. "What would be the terms?"

"Well, you're going to probably pay 6 percent, and it's going to be for a ten-year term," I told them. "I can probably get the bondholder to take no repayments for the first two years, and then eight equal payments for the last eight years, fully amortized."

"What's your end of it?" they asked.

I asked how much they wanted to raise. They said five million.

"If I don't get the deal done," I said, "you owe me nothing. If I get the deal done, you pay me 2 percent—a hundred thousand. You'll also have to pay your legal expenses, and probably whoever buys the bond is going to make you pay their legal expenses, with a cap on them."

"Do you have somebody at Pressprich who's a specialist in this?"

I said, "No, we have a guy at Pressprich who runs the investment-banking department, where we raise money for companies. He would get involved in the details. My role will be, hopefully, to get a deal with you and then take that deal and go out and sell it to institutional investors that we know."

"Let's do it," they said.

So I went over to the investment-banking department. Now,

the fellow who was running it—call him David G.—was a stiff: a real stuffed shirt. Harvard Law, the whole nine yards. When I told him I had this deal, he got all edgy about it. Here I am, this punk kid from Roslyn Heights, twenty-seven years old, stepping outside the bounds of my department and right on his toes. "What do you mean, you've got this deal?" he said.

"I have an Ohio company that wants me to go raise money for them, and I'm going to show the deal to all the Ohio insurance companies I've been selling to."

He looked suspicious. "This sounds like a lot of work," he said.

"No, no," I said. "All I need is documents to be signed by them and us saying that if we succeed in raising five million, on terms acceptable to them, they owe us $100,000."

He says, "What about our out-of-pocket expenses?"

"Don't be so damn cheap," I told him. "What the hell are my out-of-pocket expenses? I go to Cincinnati anyway. I'll make a few phone calls. I'm not going to hit them for out-of-pocket expenses. That's nickel-and-dime shit. I want these guys to trust us." I didn't give a damn that this guy was senior to me. He was the head of the corporate finance department, and I didn't work in that department. The way I thought about it then was the way I still think about it today: I had only one boss—the customer. You treat a customer right, and you never have to worry.

But David got all huffy. "Well, we have standards to maintain," he said.

"You don't want to do the deal?" I asked him.

"No, no, no, I want to do the deal."

"If you want to do the deal, you do it on my terms, not yours," I said. "And if you don't want to do the deal, I'm going to quit and go do it myself."

This guy was nervous because I was doing what he was getting paid to do. Because I'm bringing in the deal that he doesn't know how to bring in. This guy couldn't sell girls in a logging camp. And so he ran and tattled on me to the head of the firm, W. Barrett Brown. Brown called me in while David was sitting with him. He was a Waspy old guy who smoked a pipe. "Well, fella, nice piece of business," he said to me, squinting through the pipe smoke. "But we have ways of doing business around here."

"I understand that, Mr. Brown," I said. "What I don't understand is how anything I've done on this deal goes against the customs or the values of this firm. Can you tell me?" I turned to David G. "David, can you tell me?"

David wouldn't even look at me. "Well, Barry," he says to the old man, "there's the question of out-of-pocket expenses."

"I'll tell you what, David," I said. "I'll pay any out-of-pocket expenses we have, other than phone bills. If there's any special reason to go to Cincinnati, I'll pay my own way. So there goes that objection. What else you got?"

"Well, we want to make sure we're dealing with good people."

"You pick up the phone and call all the banks in Cincinnati," I told him. "I've already done it. These are solid people. They are upstanding members of the community. They are very philanthropic. This company has been around forty years."

I turned to the old man. "Look, Mr. Brown. I'll tell you what I'll do—no hard feelings. I'm going to leave Pressprich, and I'll go do this deal myself. If you want to hire me back, you'll hire me back."

"Wait a minute," the old man says. He's puffing on the pipe like crazy. "We don't want that; we don't want that."

I looked at David. "You can't have it both ways," I told him. "If you want to put obstacles in the path of this deal, you're going to scuttle the deal. I don't have any trouble if you want to get audited numbers on Kenner, which you'll have to have anyway for the insurance companies." By the way, it turned out that Taft Stettinius & Hollister, the finest law firm in Cincinnati, was representing the Steiners. These were solid people.

Brown grumbled a bit, but he knew I was right. I was bringing in a significant piece of business, while David, by comparison, was producing very little. He okayed the deal.

I made two phone calls, one to a guy I knew at Ohio National Life Insurance Company and the other to a guy at Western and Southern Life Insurance, both Cincinnati companies. Both guys said the same thing: "Why didn't they come to us in the first place? They're right here in town."

"I don't know why they didn't come to you," I told each of them. "But they've hired us, and I think we can make a nice deal here." The guy from Western and Southern said, "We want the whole deal." I said, "No, I've offered it out to somebody else too. If he wants in, let's see what we can do."

Within a week, they both wanted to do the deal: both firms took $2.5 million. Within thirty days, the deal closed, and the $100,000 commission came in. I went to the old man and said, "Look, Mr. Brown, I don't want to go through this every time. We now know all about the Steiners; they're solid as a rock. They're highly respected by all the retailers who are their customers; they're respected by all the bankers and they are solid citizens in Cincinnati." I said, "Mr. Brown, it's hard enough to sell a deal in the first place. I'm willing to work my ass off, but I don't want to have to sell a deal, then come back and have to sell it to you guys all over again. I want you to know that if you have a question of ethics or integrity or values, or there's the slightest chance we're dealing with people we shouldn't be near, I'll be the first guy to kill the deal."

He took his pipe out of his mouth and got straight to the point. "What do you want?"

"Thirty percent," I told him.

"All right, fella," Mr. Brown said. "The firm gets 70 percent, and 30 percent goes into Unit 15. Fifty-five percent of that goes to you; the rest is divvied up among your partners."

My three partners, who were strictly salesmen—they wouldn't have known a deal like this if they tripped over it—each got a nice gift of four and a half grand. I netted $16,500 (which was over twice my annual salary) and bought our first house. In Manhasset. On the right side of the tracks. Elaine and I and the boys moved out of that rented cottage in Brookville, and we never looked back.

———

A couple of months later, I got a call from Warren Cavior, whom I'd met through my office mate at the Equitable, John Turner. Warren was doing PR work for a company in the Garment District called Colonial Corporation of America—they made shirts and pajamas. He said, "Colonial's CFO is a guy by the name of Lou Epstein. You ought to meet him."

I went up there and had lunch with Epstein. After we ate, he lit up a big cigar. It seemed Colonial was doing very well. They worked the way the *schmatta* business often does: they would make a pattern—a sample—and then go out and get orders for the garment, then get the thing manufactured. They sold to Sears and all the big discount stores, because they had good price points. The stores would sell the clothing under their own house brand names. And Lou Epstein told me that Colonial needed to raise $10 million to build a new plant in Tennessee.

So I went back down to Pressprich, and I walked into David G.'s office and said, "David, I've got another deal—Colonial Corporation of America."

"What do they do?" he asked

"They make pajamas," I said.

"That's a tough business."

"Yeah, it's a tough business," I said. "They need a substantial sum, and we're dealing with sophisticated investors. So we're going to have to do some substantial due diligence. Colonial is going to have to give us audited statements; they're going to have to give us all kinds of documentation. We have to find out if there are any problems here before a nickel changes hands."

"What will you tell them about our fee?"

"I'm going to say 2 percent," I said.

"Why don't we do the Goldman Sachs fee?" David said.

"What's that?"

"Five-four-three-two-one," he said. "Five percent on the first million we raise, 4 percent on the second million, 3 percent on the third, 2 percent on the fourth, 1 percent on everything five million and over."

"David," I said, "you know what I don't like about that? It's too damn complicated. I'd rather just go for 2 percent." I said, "It's my deal; I'm going to do it the way I want to."

He gave me a grudging nod. Still, David and the rest of his department couldn't stop being nervous about the *schmatta* business, which, after all, lives on credit. Garment companies have to borrow money every quarter to finance the next season's line. So I did a lot of checking up on Colonial Corporation. And what came back loud and clear was that Colonial was crushing everybody on price and quality and making big money. So we did the deal.

Now, once I did a deal, I'd always stay in touch with the company. I'd always call the Steiners out in Cincinnati, for example, and ask how they were doing. So one day I phoned Lou Epstein. "Lou, how are you?" I said. He said he was doing fine.

"Anything going on?" I asked.

"Well, nothing more than what we're doing with you right now," he said.

I said, "What do you mean, what you're doing with us right now?"

"Yeah," he said, "we have this customer, Wigwam stores out in Arizona, and they needed money, so I called up and told your guys."

It was news to me. "Really," I said. Then I got off the phone with Lou and went into David's office. "I understand that Lou Epstein gave us a referral to a company called Wigwam stores," I said.

He went white. I said, "That's my fuckin' deal. Don't forget that." I looked David in the eye. "Is the deal done?" I asked.

"It's done," he said.

"Let me tell you right now," I said, "anytime I bring a corporate client in, you come through me."

I instantly knew what he was up to: he was going to pocket the fee and claim it for his own. But as wrong as he was, he was ready to fight me on it. "We've got to go see Barrett Brown," he said.

"Great," I said. "Let's go see him."

We walk into the old man's office. He's smoking the pipe. "Mr. Brown," I say, "we talk about ethics in this firm. We talk about integrity, and we talk about values. The way I see it, all those things are like charity. They begin at home." I said, "I brought this relationship in. I maintained the relationship. This is my due. Mr. Brown, if I have to worry that I'm going to get picked off inside this firm, I don't need that. I can go outside, and all I'll have to worry about will be one thing—getting the customer and making him happy. And as we've seen"—I looked at David—"I'm pretty good at that."

"Oh, absolutely," the old man said. "David, how did this happen?"

"Well," David began, "I was talking to Lou one day, and Lou—"

I broke in. "David. David. That's not the way it happened. Lou tried to reach me first, and then, when he found out I wasn't in the office, he called you." I said, "Now, David, this deal is my deal, and Unit 15 gets 30 percent of the commission. If that's not the deal, Mr. Brown, then I'm working under false pretenses."

"All right, fella," Brown said. "We're with you. David, are you agreed?"

Another grudging nod from David. I knew—and the look on his face confirmed it—that I'd made a serious enemy out of this guy. I was doing part-time what he was doing full-time, and my labors would soon bear fruit. Big-time.

———

Jack Cullen might not have known much about chasing butter-flies, but he once taught me a lesson I would never forget. When one of our analysts came up with a buy recommendation for a company called Harbison-Walker Refractories—they made re-fracting brick with super-high heat tolerance, the kind they lined steel furnaces with—I told Jack about it, and he made an appointment for him and me to go try to sell the stock to a man by the name of I. C. Mahanna, at Elfun Trusts.

GE managed its own pension fund for its employees; Elfun was the mutual fund the company ran for its officers. Shorty Mahanna—they called him Shorty because he was only about this high—was a legendary fund manager, the guy who had bought Xerox at nineteen cents a share in 1957, just a couple of years be-fore it went through the roof. Xerox was so successful that Shorty kept having to sell the stock off as it rose because Elfun's rule was that no single holding could exceed 5 percent of the fund's total assets. A meeting with Shorty Mahanna was a very high-level one, and I was nervous. And in the cab on the way uptown, Jack said to me, "Listen to me. You're going to walk in there, and the first thing you're going to do is tell Shorty all the negatives—all the reasons why he shouldn't buy Harbison-Walker Refractories. What's wrong, what could go wrong, what needs to be fixed but can't be fixed."

"What the hell are you talking about?" I said. "I'm going up there to tell him to buy it."

Jack looked me in the eye. "You just remember," he said. "Give him all the negatives first."

"Why am I doing this?" I asked.

"You just do it, and I'll tell you after we leave."

"Okay," I thought. "This is my boss. I'm not going to screw around."

We got to GE and were shown into Mahanna's office. I was immediately intimidated: the only thing on his desk was a telephone. And when he stood to greet us, he really was short! We sat down. And I said, "Mr. Mahanna, I'm here to sell you on a stock, but let me tell you all the reasons why you shouldn't buy it."

"What do you mean?" he said.

"Well," I said, "nothing is perfect." And I proceeded to go through a list of every downside to Harbison-Walker. The company had a very limited product line, I told him, and faced strong competition in a limited market. A recession could impact it badly. And there were a couple of problems with its current management.

Mahanna looked thoughtful. "Now," I said. "Let me tell you why I like it."

I said that because the economy was picking up, demand for steel looked like it was going to take off. I told him that Harbison-Walker was the Cadillac of the industry; everybody respected the quality of what they did, and they were also the lowest-cost producer of their product. And the company was based in Pittsburgh and had deep and strong relationships in the steel industry.

"Well," he finally said, "do you like it more than you don't like it?"

"Yeah, a whole lot more," I said. "I think this is a great stock."

"Okay," he said. "Let me think about it." And Jack and I left.

In the cab downtown, I said, "Jack, why did I just do that?"

"I'm going to tell you why you did it. This afternoon he's going to call up all of his buddies on Wall Street, and he's going to ask them, 'What do you think of Harbison-Walker Refractories?' He's going to have a checklist on that nice clean desk of his. And if his pals tell him anything negative about the company, he's going to tick off the list. He'll say, 'Well, Ken told me that, Ken told me that, Ken told me that.' Your trust is going to go through the roof with him."

And sure enough, that's exactly how it happened. Shorty Mahanna bought Harbison-Walker through me, and then he bought a lot more.

Lesson learned.

————

My father-in-law at Shearson, Hammill did nice business with Standard Oil of New Jersey and knew the guys there very well. He said, "This is a good account; they're honorable people. You should try to get something going there."

The head of my unit, Bindy Banker, was covering Standard Oil but doing nothing with them. "I think I can do business with them," I told him. "Fine," Bindy said. "I'll arrange a lunch."

Oh boy, did he arrange a lunch.

Three guys from Standard—New Jersey—Webb Williams, Bud Cone, and their boss, Ted Lilly—accepted our invitation to lunch, and Bindy made the reservation at the Pinnacle Club in the Mobil Building on Forty-second Street. And I'm saying to myself—but not to Bindy—"Is that smart, to take guys from that company to a meal in their chief competitor's headquarters?"

We went to the Pinnacle Club. We were seated in a private room. Bindy ordered for everyone, and he was like the lord of the manor. "Want a steak? How about a shrimp cocktail to start? Drinks all around!" We ate our fancy meal, and the conversation was pleasant. But then, suddenly, Bindy turns to our guests and says, "Look, I bought you guys lunch; now you tell him why you don't do business with us." Bindy's pointing at me, and I'm squirming. "This kid wants your account," Bindy says. "I don't know what the hell we need to do to get business out of you guys."

Radio silence. Pin-drop silence. I'm bright red with embarrassment. I figure it's all over with Standard Oil–New Jersey.

But these guys were polite and gracious in spite of it. They said everything except, "Bindy, you don't do anything for us; you don't help us do our work." They didn't say that, but it was clear.

In the cab back to the office, I said, "Bindy, do me a favor. Let me have this account. I don't know if I'm going to be able to do business with these guys after the way you've just put them through the wringer. But I want you to give me one year to try; if I can't do anything with it, you can have it back.

"You get a piece of what I do," I argued. "You've got 100 percent of nothing now; at least you'll have some percentage of something if I'm successful."

He saw my logic. "Okay, kid. Give it your best shot," Bindy said.

The next week, I went to see Standard's point man, Webb Williams, at its headquarters in Rockefeller Center. Webb was a real gentleman, and I still felt embarrassed about that lunch. "Webb, I want to tell you first of all that that's not my way of doing business," I said. "I think I can help you guys, but I need to know what your definition of 'help' is."

He said, "Let me tell you how we work." And he laid it out.

Standard Oil–New Jersey had a very large pension fund—so large that it was spread among several different asset managers (the shorthand for them was "banks," even though only some of them were also commercial banks) like Scudder Stevens, Continental Illinois, Chase Manhattan, and J. P. Morgan. Those money managers would buy and sell stocks for Jersey's pension fund through investment firms like Goldman Sachs and Morgan Stanley, using the pension fund's money, rather than their own, to pay the investment firms' commissions.

In those days, a bank like Continental Illinois could say to an investment firm like R. W. Pressprich, "Okay, Pressprich, you want some of that business? You want some of those commissions? You have to deposit a substantial sum"—say $100,000—"with us."

It was very clever: the bank would make loans with the investment firm's $100,000 and keep the interest for itself. The only money the bank would pay the investment firm—in the form of commissions—came out of the pension fund's pocket. This used to be legal; it no longer is.

Standard Oil–New Jersey didn't like that system. They said to the banks, "Wait a minute, guys. Those are our assets you're using to pay commissions with. We're going to decide who gets the commissions, not you."

Webb Williams and his people met semiannually with the asset managers, he told me. If they could go into those meetings thoroughly versed on current business trends and investment sectors, they'd be way ahead of the game.

So I began to cultivate Webb. I took him to lectures at NYU Business School by famous economists like Theodore Yntema and Marcus Nadler, and we'd have dinner afterward. I started to go up to Standard Oil–New Jersey once a month, and every time I went, I took an analyst with me, a guy who was covering a specific sector of the stock market. We would talk with Webb and the other guys in his department about the economy and certain areas we thought were good buys at the moment. Whenever they called with a question, I had an analyst make up a detailed report. Williams and his colleagues were always receptive, always interested. They weren't sending any commissions our way, but I felt it was just a matter of time.

A few months went by. It was early 1964. One day, Bindy leaned across the trading desk and said, "You see? All that damn time you're spending with those guys, all that money you're spending with those guys! They're takers. They'll never do a thing with you!"

I said, "Bindy, what do you want me to do?"

"You ought to nail them," he said. "You ought to say, 'Where's my business?'"

"No, Bindy, that's not how I operate. I would never do that, and I'm not going to start now."

"So what are you going to do?" he asked.

"I'm going to keep servicing them. If I've overestimated our usefulness, they're going to tell me one day, 'Look, we've tried you; you don't add value.'"

One day in May 1964, I got a call from Webb Williams. He said, "I'd like you to come up and talk with Bud Cone and me. Bud manages our relationships with all of our banks."

I took a cab up to Rockefeller Center and met with Webb and Cone. "First of all, Ken, I want to apologize," Bud said, in his nice Texas accent. (They were all from Texas up there; it was the oil business!) He told me which investment firms their banks had been dealing with, then said, "I didn't realize we hadn't done any business with you guys yet, but we're going to fix that today."

I thanked him, and he said, "No thanks necessary, Ken. We just want you to keep doing exactly what you're doing for us, nothing more and nothing less."

I got back to the office an hour later. The equity-trading desk was one side of this big block-long desk; Harry Seaver was the head trader. Harry used to call me "Languadeuce." Why? I have no idea. He probably just liked the sound of it. "Languadeuce!" he called across the desk. "I just got a call from Continental Illinois. Three orders for Standard Oil–New Jersey—big orders." They were buying a hundred thousand shares of one stock, fifty thousand shares of another stock, and ninety thousand shares of a third stock.

I was just standing there with my mouth hanging open. This was over $75,000 of commissions in one day.

Harry said, "The guy in Chicago told me, 'Don't worry, we've got some more to make up with you guys. We're calculating what it is right now, but we'll get back to you, because now you're on our list, and we haven't come anywhere near paying you.'"

I picked up the phone and called Bud and Webb. "Guys," I said, "you could have knocked me over with a feather. I've never seen that much business in my life."

Bud said, "Let me tell you right now, Ken. We deal with a lot of people on Wall Street. Your firm is more professional with us than anybody else we do business with."

I went to see the old man. I used to call the partners' office Sleepy Hollow; every day they would go out and drink at lunchtime, then come back and go to sleep in their chairs. "Mr. Brown," I said, "I just got a wonderful surprise from Standard Oil–New Jersey."

"What's that, fella?"

"I got over $75,000 in commissions."

"Today?"

"This morning. Harry just executed it now."

He puffed on the pipe, looking impressed.

"Mr. Brown," I said, "I want to do something, and I'd like you to agree to it. I want to allocate a certain percentage of those commissions to the research department for the analysts who helped bring in this business. Mr. Brown, these guys downstairs are great; I don't think you understand the quality of talent you've got down there."

Brown wrinkled his nose. "Well, they're all right."

"Mr. Brown, they're a lot better than that. Maybe it's how we use them that's not all right. But I can tell you right now, I can take these guys anyplace and do a lot of business."

He shook his head. "Well, if you want to give them bonuses from your end, go ahead."

I shook my head back. "I've got another idea, Mr. Brown. Let's you and I pick a total dollar amount off the top of whatever I bring in from Standard-Jersey, or any other company going forward, for analyst bonuses. Now, you're going to only have to pay 70 percent of it because I'm going to pay 30 percent. I'll tell you which analysts are higher on the approval list at Standard–New Jersey, and you can decide how much you want to allocate to each analyst. It's completely fair," I said.

He took the pipe out of his mouth. "I don't know if I like that, fella."

"All right, sir, then let me do it a different way," I said. "I'm going to take a portion of Unit 15's 30 percent and give it to them directly. It'll cost you nothing."

"Why would you want to do that?" Brown asked.

"Because, Mr. Brown, when I pick up the phone and call the research department, I want those guys to jump *through* the phone. I want these guys to keep doing as great a job as they've been doing, and I want them to be excited about it."

"Well, let me think about it," he grumbled.

He called me back into his office the next day. "Fella, I don't know what you're up to, and I'm not sure I like it," he says. "But I'm going to go along with it."

I'd given it some further thought. "Fine," I said. "And what I'd like to do is allocate points every quarter to each analyst on the basis of how much they've done. Then we'll take 20 percent of the commissions we generate from Jersey or any other account and give out bonuses based on point totals. I want every analyst who's been instrumental to have a piece of that pie."

"That's complicated," the old man said.

"No, Mr. Brown, it's not complicated. It's fair." As I was leaving his office, I turned around. "By the way, with the extra business I'm doing, I'm shorthanded," I said. "I'd like to hire a couple of kids; I want to train them to be salesmen."

That got the pipe out of his mouth. "No, no, no, no," he said. "We don't want any overhead."

"Let me see what I can figure out," I told him.

I went and talked to my three partners, who as a result of what I was now bringing in were making so much damn money that if I'd told them to jump out the window, they would have jumped out the window. They'd never seen business like this, and they knew they were going to get a piece.

They also knew that it wasn't going to last forever. Each of them understood that at a certain point—and it wouldn't be long—I was going to come to them and say, "Hey, guys, this isn't fair. This is what I'm bringing in. Charlie Benedict, this is what you're bringing in. Bud Canaday, this is what you're bringing in. Bindy, this is what you're bringing in. And I'm bringing in a hell of a lot more. But you guys are taking out as much as I am. What's wrong with this picture?" They knew that was coming.

I told them about my plan for hiring some young guys, and I

told them I wanted to pay these kids well; I wanted to start them at $20,000 a year, which in 1965 was a lot of money. We would teach them, I said; we would take them on trips with us. And by the way, their salaries and expenses would all come off our, Unit 15's, gross.

To his credit, Bindy agreed to it right away. He was and would continue to be very receptive to bringing new young guys into the firm: he understood just why it was so important. As a matter of fact—since less than two years earlier *I* had been the new young guy at R. W. Pressprich—I'd like to say now what a real debt of gratitude I owe to Bindy Banker.

Bindy might not have known an asset from a liability, but he was smart and he was street-smart. He not only taught me many crucial lessons in business and in life; he also instilled confidence in me at a key moment in the beginning of my investing career.

Wall Street was a closed, Waspy world back in those bad old days. Nepotistic. Bloodlines and family connections still meant a lot. And if I look deeply into myself, I see that even at the ripe old age of twenty-seven and twenty-eight I was still carrying some of the self-consciousness about my origins that I'd first taken to Bucknell. Here I was, a plumber's son from Long Island, a rough-and-ready Italian American kid—what business did I have rubbing elbows with the high and mighty, let alone making big deals with them?

Bindy Banker felt no such hesitation. He had all the social confidence that I lacked at that age: he came from the right WASP background; he'd been a marine officer; he was the boss's stepson. He was a bon vivant and man-about-town. He knew just how to dress and how to act; he knew all the right things to say to the right people. And he belonged to all the right clubs: the National Golf Links, Piping Rock Club, Racquet and Tennis, the Down Town Association. By night, he haunted El Morocco and Le Club and 21, where he knew exactly what to order and whom to tip; the headwaiters loved him.

He was equally masterful at playing his connections and his relationships. And he took me under his wing. He encouraged me, and he exposed me to a life I never knew existed. He got me involved in the Investment Association of New York and the Bond Club of New York.

I guess Bindy saw from the jump that he and I could be each other's business other half. He was perceptive enough to realize I had the investing savvy he lacked, and he was generous enough not to try to pick my brain and keep me in my place. He made damn certain that I was recognized, both in the firm and outside. Not everyone would've been so kind, believe me.

The first big lesson Bindy taught me was one he taught by example. I'd begun encountering some of the big, big guys on Wall Street, legendary guys, men I'd read about in *Fortune*. These men were gods to me, and I saw right away that Bindy simply wasn't in awe of them. In short order, he taught me to understand that a man's public persona usually has very little to do with his private persona. Without that lesson, I would have felt subservient toward these muckety-mucks, but with that lesson under my belt I felt completely equal to anyone I dealt with. And without Bindy in my life, I don't think I would be as certain of myself as I am and as outspoken as I am.

———

Unlike Bindy, Charlie and Bud were resistant to my plan to bring new young guys into Unit 15—probably because they smelled what was coming. But finally they agreed, and I went back to Mr. Brown. "Okay, here's what we want to do," I told him. "When we hire these young guys, we want to pay them out of our commissions. That way all the business they do will have Unit 15's number on it."

"Well, who's going to pay their fringe benefits?" Brown asked. "FICA, medical?"

I thought about it for a second. "I guess we'll pay it all," I told him.

He nodded. Done deal.

So we went ahead and started interviewing, and oh boy, did we find some terrific kids. The first two we hired were Tom Kane—T. F. Kane—a marine fighter pilot just back from Vietnam, and his cousin T.W., who was a preferred-stock trader at Kidder, Peabody. Like me, they had grown up in households that were far from wealthy. Both their fathers worked on Wall Street, but as traders. Tom had gone to Fordham, and T.W. had graduated from St. John's.

One led to another and then another. We made an art form out of finding these kids, and they would bring other kids to us. They were all cut from a certain cloth: young and smart and hungry as hell, and not one of them to the manor born. We hired a kid named Bruce Shroyer, and he brought in a Montana guy named Bob Potts who had been with him at West Point. T. F. Kane brought in Gene Kirkwood. We hired Frank Dunne, who brought in his brother Bill; then they brought in Frank Martucci and Bob Kelly. All hungry, hardworking, decent kids. We placed them all around us at the Unit 15 desk and instructed them to always pick up the phone when we were on sales calls so they could listen and learn.

One day T. W. Kane came to me and said he had a friend, a fellow St. John's University graduate who he thought would really be a great salesman on Wall Street. "Sure, bring him in," I said.

I was headed out for a late lunch at the Bankers Club when T.W. introduced me to Ed Braniff. I took the two of them to lunch with me, and Eddie blew me away. Like me, he was a little rough around the edges—his old man was a lieutenant in the NYPD, he told me—but he was smart, he was aggressive, and I could tell he had a lot of common sense. Eddie's current job was selling electrical products for a big company called Graybar Electric, and he was doing well.

"You're gonna take a pay cut if you come to work for us," I told him. He smiled.

Eddie Braniff wound up becoming a phenomenal salesman; he would eventually leave Pressprich and go on to Drexel Burnham, Oppenheimer, and then Prudential Bache, where he became head of institutional sales. To me, Eddie was really the prime example of the democratization of Wall Street.

These young guys traveled with us; then they started going out on their own the same way I had at first, covering accounts no body had covered. They went to Canada; Des Moines, Iowa; Springfield, Illinois. They were bringing in business, and of course I was out on the road too, bringing in more and more. And over the next two years, business just went through the roof.

All from one bad lunch at the Pinnacle Club.

4.

MAKING WAVES

arly in my career at Pressprich, I happened to remark to a colleague that I thought pipe smokers were slow thinkers. Word somehow got back to W. Barrett Brown.

"Oh, fella," he said to me one day, "I understand that you think I'm a slow thinker."

I thought as fast as I could. "No, sir," I said. "What I said was that *most* people I know that smoke pipes are slow thinkers. That doesn't mean *you're* a slow thinker."

"Humph," he said. I could tell he was pissed. Then I thought about it for a second and realized I didn't especially care.

———

By 1965, I was spending less and less time selling securities and more and more on my first love: corporate finance, mergers and acquisitions. One day Larry Victor, one of our research analysts, came to me and said, "There's a company I know that looks very interesting."

Evans Products was a company in Portland, Oregon, that sold building materials and manufactured railroad-car equipment, among other things. For boxcars that transported manufactured goods like refrigerators, they made a damage-control system called Evans DF, an array of boards fastened across the width of the car that kept the contents from shifting and colliding if the train stopped short. Larry Victor introduced me to the CEO of the company, a guy named Monford Orloff.

Orloff had taken over the company from the Evans family when it was in rough shape, then steered it to profitability. He wanted to expand the company's railroad-equipment business, so he bought a company, U.S. Railway Leasing, in Blue Island, Illinois, that purchased old railcars, reconditioned them, and leased them out to railroads. But now he wanted to buy more railroad cars, and he needed a substantial amount of money.

One day when Larry and I were out in Portland, we got to talking with Orloff and his CFO, Luke Wygal. "I think we can get you financing for those railroad cars," I told them. "How much do you need?"

"Around fifteen million," Wygal said.

I thought for a moment. "You're leasing out the cars, so whatever financing you get depends on the strength of your lessees' credit," I said. "The stronger their credit, the higher quality your debt. And since you have lessees like the major railroads, I think this financing is eminently doable."

I went back to New York and started putting the paperwork together: an offering sheet, a list of the equipment Evans wanted to buy, the terms on the leases. One day, one of the senior partners at Pressprich, Charlie Bergmann, called me and said, "Well, you really messed this one up. You've made Blyth and Company angry as all hell." Blyth and Company was another investment-banking firm but, unlike Pressprich, a very big and powerful one. When the people at Blyth did a major underwriting—say a $50 million bond deal for Georgia-Pacific—they'd typically put together a syndicate of investment firms to handle it along with them. Pressprich was small enough that we'd basically have to go begging to be included in deals like that.

"You know that Evans Products is a client of Blyth and Company, don't you?" Charlie asked.

"So what?" I said.

"Well, you can't do what you're doing."

"What are you talking about? What am I doing?" I said, "I went to Evans Products. I knocked on their door. I brought the business in."

"Do you realize how many other underwriters Blyth can go to besides us on any given deal? If we take business from them, they won't invite us in anymore."

"Charlie," I said, "I'm going to make more money on this deal than you've made on all the underwritings you've ever done with Blyth, all the way back to when they gave you a piece of their first deal." I said, "I don't understand what you're upset about."

"We've got to go over there and make peace," he insisted.

"I don't need to make any peace, Charlie," I told him. "I won, fair and square. If you feel you've got to go over and kiss their ass, you go right ahead. But I'm not going." And I said, "Better than that, Charlie, I'm doing this deal."

And I did the deal. And brought in another big commission. And I tucked away a thought in the back of my mind: Was a firm this stuck in its ways really the right place for me?

I was now beginning to get some real economic clout at Pressprich. It wasn't just the deals: I was still selling stocks and bonds, and these kids we'd hired and trained—almost all of them were twenty-six, twenty-seven, twenty-eight (and I was just twenty-nine!)—were doing fabulous. The firm's brokerage business was growing nicely because of us. By the spring of 1965, I was earning $100,000 a year on commissions alone, the equivalent of about three-quarters of a million today.

And I was being given broader responsibility all the time: we now had branches in Buffalo, Rochester, Syracuse, Albany, Hartford, Philadelphia, Chicago, Dallas, L.A., and San Francisco, and I was overseeing a lot of what they were doing—stopping in, spending time. Ushering some old staff out of the firm and a lot of new staff in.

Our third son, Stephen, was born in April 1965, and suddenly the house we'd bought just a couple of years before—337 Ryder Road, Manhasset—was starting to feel a little bit crowded. Part of it was psychological, I'll admit. Because I was doing so well, suddenly it was easy to imagine living in a grander style.

Elderfields Road, in the Flower Hill section of Manhasset, was the finest street on the North Shore of Long Island. I'd always dreamed of living there, and now I realized the dream was within reach.

Jack Clapp, a senior partner in charge of the municipal bond department at Pressprich, lived on Elderfields Road. Of course Jack was middle-aged and I wasn't thirty yet. But I wasn't thinking about that; I had this bee in my bonnet. And one morning Jack told me that the man across the street from him had died, and his widow was living alone in the house, a big, beautiful Georgian at the top of a wide, sloping lawn. Jack didn't know whether she was going to sell the place or not. So Elaine wrote a letter to the owner— her name was Ruth Riebow; her late husband had been CFO of S. H. Kress & Company, the five-and-dime chain. "We don't know if you're ever interested in selling your home," Elaine wrote, "but if you are, we'd like to buy it." And Mrs. Riebow phoned Elaine and invited her to come by.

We both drove over. Mrs. Riebow, a nice-looking older lady, told us that she was probably going to leave the house—it was too big for her to live in alone—and that the estate was in the hands of Chase Bank. And she gave me the name of the officer at the bank who was handling the estate.

So I went to a real-estate broker in town and said, "What's that house worth?"

"Oh, I'm going to guess it's around $75,000, $80,000," he told me.

I called the trust manager at Chase Bank and said I would like to buy that house, I was prepared to bid $77,000 for it, and there wouldn't be any brokerage commissions involved. If the offer was accepted, I said, the late Mr. Riebow's estate would receive $77,000—net.

I took a deep breath while I waited for his response. Seventy-seven thousand dollars was a lot of money for a house in 1965, and it was a lot of money for me. The man said he would look into the matter and get back to me.

One day that summer, Elaine and I took Kenny and Bruce to the World's Fair out in Flushing. When I called in to the office from a pay phone to see if I had any messages, the secretary said to me, "Chase Bank called to tell you that you bought a house." I went back and told Elaine that 83 Elderfields Road was ours.

She was thrilled. I was thrilled. But the truth is that buying that house for seventy-seven thousand bucks was a big risk for me, relative to my net worth at the time. Any number of things could've gone wrong; I could've wound up not being able to swing the payments. It's not the kind of bet I would make today; I can name too many people who were wealthy, very wealthy, even enormously wealthy, and wound up literally going broke.

But I was young, and I had a lot of—well, "pluck" is the fancy term for it. And a lot of luck.

That August the old man called me into his office. "I'm not offering you anything, fella," he said, "but I just wanted to tell you that a partnership could be in the offing for you."

"Thank you, Mr. Brown, but I'm not sure exactly what you mean," I said. "You're not offering me a partnership?"

"That's right. I just want to sound out your level of interest."

"I think I am interested," I said. "But what would it mean, exactly?"

"Well," he said, "you wouldn't get commissions anymore. Instead, at the end of each year you'd get a percentage of whatever the firm makes overall."

"Hmm," I said. "How do I live in the meantime?"

"You'd get a draw of twenty thousand a year," he said, "but you wouldn't pay taxes on it, because it's a draw. You don't pay your taxes until the partnership returns are filed."

"Hmm," I repeated.

"Well, are you interested?"

"I think so," I said.

"Okay, fella, I'll be back to you."

A couple months later—it's now October—Brown calls me in and says, "Come in and see me." I go in. "Here's the deal," he says to me. "We're offering you a partnership. You'll run your sales operation. We hope you'll keep doing deals if you can, but any deal you bring in has to go through the corporate-finance department."

"I can't do that," I told him.

"Why?"

"Because they don't know how to bring business in," I said. "I don't need them to process my deals. You're wasting your money."

"That's not true," he said. "We've got to be mindful of correct procedure here."

"Okay," I said. "But I want to warn you: If I put together a deal, I'm going to get the deal done. I don't care what corporate finance does."

He frowned and puffed on the pipe, but he didn't say no.

"Where do I come in?" I asked. Meaning, where among the twenty-three partners at Pressprich would I be ranked?

"You'll be ranked twenty-four," he said. "But every year we reevaluate who does what, and you'll move up if your performance merits it."

"I don't want that deal," I told him.

He looked a little shocked. "Why not?"

"I don't want it," I repeated. "I'll stay on commissions." I could see now exactly what this was all about. It was killing them how much I was making; none of the partners were earning that kind of money. They wanted to cut my pay, put me on a leash. This was an offer for them, not for me.

"Mr. Brown, look," I said. "You know what we call the section of the trading room where the senior partners sit? We call it Sleepy Hollow."

"Why do you call it that?"

"Because those partners go out and get drunk at lunch, and they come back in the afternoon and sleep until it's time to wake up and go across the street to the bar and get drunk again." I said, "I'm not going to wade through that group. I want to come in at number twelve, or not at all."

He takes out the pipe. "How'd you come up with that number?"

"My numbers easily put me in the top half," I told him. "I am not coming in at the bottom. I haven't got that many years left."

"I don't know if I can do that," the old man said.

"That's fine," I said. "I'll stand away and make deals. You're making a lot of money off me. I'm not going anyplace; I'm doing very well. I'm happy."

"Well, we really feel you've got a lot of potential."

"I appreciate that," I said. I was doing my best to be diplomatic. It had been a little more than eight years since I'd started at the Equitable for $82.50 a week, bringing my lunch and eating it in the public waiting room in Grand Central Terminal, and now I was earning well into six figures. Potential!

But in a certain way Brown was right. I knew my biggest days were in front of me.

He called me the next day. "Well, we're going to do it," he told me. "But there are going to be a lot of unhappy people."

"Mr. Brown, I don't want anybody unhappy," I said. "But it would be crazy for me to have to slog through eleven people when I know I'm going to do more in my first month than they're going to do the whole year. If you want to keep them as your partners, that's your business."

"Don't you want to know what your percentage would be at number twelve?"

I shook my head. "That doesn't matter to me," I said, and I was telling him the truth. "I'm more concerned about where I'm going to be in five years. I'm happy to start in the middle of the pack."

W. Barrett Brown told me that I would start at 3.5 percent of the firm's earnings per annum, and I told him that that was just fine with me. So I did it. I became a partner at R. W. Pressprich on January 1, 1966. I had turned thirty just three and a half months before. Word got around.

———

Soon after that I got a call from, of all people, my old boss at the Equitable, Bill McCurdy. McCurdy, you'll remember, was the prick who called me a square peg in a round hole. The guy whose nose got out of joint when his boss told him he was going to have to find a place for me. Now he wanted to have lunch with me.

We went out for lunch. And he sits down across from me with a big grin on his face. "I always knew you were a winner," he tells me. "I always knew you were going to be somebody in this business."

I gave him my best fake smile. "Why, thank you, Bill," I said.

He leaned across the table, looked around to make sure nobody was listening, and lowered his voice. "I just wanted to say, if you ever see any especially good deals, anything I should be interested in, I hope you're going to give me a call."

"Sure, Bill," I said. "I'll be happy to give you a call."

Three years later, in one of the earliest leveraged buyouts in American financial history, Pressprich bought the F. & M. Schaefer Brewing Company, taking it public in a $106 million stock offering. David G., who was friends with the lawyer who represented the Schaefer family, had brought in the deal. The Equitable participated in the financing, and McCurdy was the officer on the account. And he called me up and asked me to keep in mind opportunities that he could invest in personally.

"Bill," I said, "I don't feel good about a personal investment relationship as long as you are responsible for the relationship between Pressprich and the Equitable."

I didn't hear from Bill McCurdy again after that.

————

Not long after Shorty Mahanna of GE followed my recommendation on Harbison-Walker Refractories—and was very pleased at the outcome—I took him to lunch at the Bull and Bear in the Waldorf Astoria. Shorty was a straight shooter and a good guy, and I wanted to cultivate him as an adviser and a friend. He became both, and by the way I never called him anything but "Mr. Mahanna."

While we were eating lunch that day, the subject of Rudy Smutny came up. Rudy was a senior partner at Pressprich, an old Wall Street hand who was head of the firm's railroad-equipment-financing business. "You know," Shorty said, "I like Rudy; I just don't trust him." I tucked the remark away for future reference.

Smutny had come to Pressprich in the late 1950s after being forced out of Salomon Brothers, where he'd been a senior managing partner. He was a tough little guy with a long nose, cold eyes, and a bald dome. And he didn't just look tough: he'd been a marine officer in World War II. In 1968, when the firm incorporated, the partners elected him president.

Rudy Smutny had a reputation for being ruthless; he scared a lot of people. One day soon after he became president, he came up to me and said, "You know, I can't tell you how much I admire you. You get things done. You *really* get things done." He began walking away from me, then he turned around. "But stop producing," Rudy said, "and see how quick I stop liking you."

Now, another guy might have said, "Oh my God, what am I going to do? The guy's telling me he's going to fire me!" But that wasn't me, and not because I was so tough or brave. I was just realistic. I knew exactly what I had to do. I had three kids to feed and educate and provide a home for, and all I knew was I had to go out and kill every day to eat. So I wasn't producing for Rudy Smutny. I was producing for my family.

———

And I was producing, big-time. By 1968, I was the number-five partner at Pressprich, and the firm had a really hot hand; we were doing business all over. Now, four years earlier Bindy and I had hired a former Davis Cup tennis player named Hamilton Richardson to run our Dallas office. Ham came from Baton Rouge, and he'd once worked as an aide to Senator Russell Long. Every year, the Louisiana delegation in Congress held a Mardi Gras ball in Washington, and early in 1968 Ham Richardson got Elaine and me invited to the party.

We were seated at a very interesting table. Across from us was Gus Levy, the number-one guy at Goldman Sachs, who was also from Louisiana. And next to me was a friend of Ham's from Dallas by the name of Jack Hight. Jack and I got to talking, and he told me that the company he'd co-founded was ready to go public and they were talking to underwriters now. The company, Electronic Data Systems, or EDS, was doing big business in Texas in a new field, computer-facilities management. Among its clients were several big banks, Frito Lay, and Texas Blue Shield and Blue Cross. "Gee," I said, "is there any chance we can get in to make a pitch?"

"Call me on Monday and I'll let you know," Jack said, and we went back to drinking and raising hell and having a great time.

I called first thing on Monday morning. "Jack, how did I do?" I asked.

"You've got an appointment at eleven thirty Wednesday morning in Dallas with my partner, Ross Perot," Jack said. "You've got to be there on the dot of eleven thirty, and you've got to be out exactly at twelve o'clock. I'm going to tell you two things. Be on time and leave on time, and don't swear. Perot hates profanity."

I made a mental note to temper my customary conversational style.

I flew down to Dallas with two people we'd just hired in the corporate-finance department at Pressprich, Duke Glenn and Roger Green. We walked into Perot's secretary's waiting area, and even though I don't scare easily, there was something intimidating about the place. There was a big clock on the wall, for one thing. And as soon as that second hand hit twelve on the dot of eleven thirty, BAM, the door opens, and we're shown in.

Perot had his desk catty-corner—don't ask me why—and he was

such a little guy that he barely came over the top of it. He might've even been shorter than Shorty Mahanna. Perot at his desk reminded me of one of those old "Kilroy was here" cartoons from World War II, with the guy's eyes just peeping over the top of a wall.

"Hi!" he yelled out, in a Texas accent. "Ross Perot!"

"Mr. Perot, Ken Langone, Roger Green, and Duke Glenn. Happy to meet you."

"Well, let's sit down and talk a little bit," Perot said. And for the next twenty-nine and a half minutes, he did all the talking. It was impossible to work a word in edgewise through his steady monologue about all the big-time underwriters that had approached him—thirteen in all, all of them much larger firms than Pressprich, including Goldman Sachs, Merrill Lynch, Salomon Brothers, Allen & Company, and G. H. Walker.

"This is what Goldman Sachs told me," Perot said, and he told us just what Goldman Sachs had told him. "This is what Kidder, Peabody told me; this is what Merrill Lynch told me." On and on, for twenty-nine minutes.

After what felt like forever, he turned to me. "Okay, now what have you got to say?"

I glanced at my watch. "Mr. Perot, Jack Hight told me I had exactly thirty minutes, not a second more," I said. "I see I just have enough time right now to say good-bye. Maybe you can see me some other time."

"What do you mean? What do you mean?"

"Jack said I had just thirty minutes."

"Ah, forget that," Perot said. "What do you think of what I said?"

I figured I'd already blown the thirty-minute rule; I might as well break the other one too. "Mr. Perot," I said, "that's the biggest pile of horseshit I ever heard in my life."

He reared back in his chair. "Whoa!" he yelled. "What do you mean?"

"Well, Mr. Perot, these firms are telling you all kinds of things. What I'm telling you is I'm going to value your stock at the highest possible price consistent with having a successful offer. It's that simple. All the stuff in the middle is bureaucracy. You want to sell at that price, I gotta find a buyer at that price. That's it."

He looked at me. "I've got to talk to you some more," he said.

"Sure," I said. We'd been planning to return to New York on a three o'clock plane: instead, we stayed with him until one o'clock in the morning. We just talked and talked and talked, for thirteen hours. It turned out that Perot and his wife were married the same hour, the same day, the same year as Elaine and I. His father was a cotton broker and my father was a plumber. At 1:00 a.m., he was driving the three of us around Dallas looking for a motel with a vacancy and a drugstore where we could buy shaving gear and underwear.

We finally found a motel. "I have a lot to think about," Perot said when he dropped us off.

I went back to New York on the first flight in the morning. That afternoon, Thursday afternoon, I got a call from him. "I haven't made my mind up," he said. "I want to get to know you better, and I want to learn some more about this whole process."

"How can I help you know me better?" I asked

"Well, when you get a chance, come on down here again."

"No, Mr. Perot, I'm not going to take a chance on this. When do you want to see me?"

"Well, what about next week?"

"I'll be there Monday morning," I said.

"Hey, Ken?" he said.

"Yes, sir?"

"Do me a favor when you come down. Bring down the prospectuses of all the offerings you've done."

"Yes, sir," I said. But the fact was I didn't have any, because we hadn't done any. I'd put together deals all over the place—corporate-financing deals, corporate-purchase deals. But I'd never done an IPO. I was hoping he'd forget about the prospectuses.

I went down to Dallas and we talked some more. It went well. Perot introduced me to his people, including his number-two guy, Mitch Hart. I liked Mitch a lot, and over the years we would become very close friends. He had graduated from Annapolis, the year after Perot; then he'd gone into the marines. He prided himself on his nose for people, he told me, and he smiled at me when he said it.

Then Perot drove me to the airport. "By the way, Ken," he says, "do you have those prospectuses?"

I said, "No, sir, I don't."

"Forget 'em?"

"No, sir, I didn't forget 'em."

"What you mean?"

"There aren't any," I said. "You're it."

"What do you mean, I'm it?"

"You'll be the first one I'll do."

He gave me a long look.

"Ross," I said—by now we were on a first-name basis—"your deal is going to get done, because you've got a great company and investors are going to want it. An idiot could do your deal. I've got a bigger risk in this than you do: If I mess up your deal, my one chance of success is gone. But if I do a great job for you, Pressprich's reputation is enhanced. We have every incentive, and I promise you I will handle every detail of this deal personally."

I later found out that after I returned to New York, Mitch Hart told Perot, "That's the guy."

This was March, and Perot and I kept talking for three months. One day, he wanted to know what I thought his company was worth. I said, "Look, I'm going to be honest. Your company is one of a kind. I've never seen one like it before, ever. I'd be very comfortable putting a valuation of 160 million on EDS."

"A hundred sixty million!" he said. "I'm going to make about a million and a half dollars this year—160 million is more than a hundred times earnings."

"Right," I said.

"You can really do it for a hundred times earnings?" he asked. That meant if the current earnings were $0.15 a share, EDS would sell for $15 a share. It was a stratospheric number; all the other firms were coming in at thirty and forty times earnings.

"I think so," I said. I meant what I said. It was a unique company. I'd never seen anything like it, and I thought it was going to grow like a weed. I was willing to bet on the future. At a hundred times earnings, it would be way overvalued. But it would only be overvalued until it grew, and then it wouldn't be.

"Okay," Perot said. "Let me think about it."

One day in the midst of our discussions—it was late May or early June 1968—a strange thing happened. Perot called me up and said, "How do you feel about having a partner?"

"What do you mean?" I asked.

He started telling me about a guy he'd gone to Annapolis with who was now a partner at G. H. Walker—a firm that, incidentally, had been founded by George Herbert Walker Bush's grandfather. "My friend Gerry Lodge at G. H. Walker called up and said if you do it at a hundred, he'd do it at a hundred," Perot said.

"Ross," I said, "let me ask you a question. How comfortable would you be if I'm driving a car and we're going 150 miles an hour, and I have the steering wheel and you have the brakes?"

"What do you mean?"

"All I've got is the steering wheel and all you've got is the brakes, and I'm going 150 miles an hour."

"I get your point," he said.

"Ross, look," I said. "If you feel so strongly about wanting G. H. Walker in on this deal, I'm not going to cut my wrists. Why don't you do the business with them? And you and I will do business another time. Now we know each other and I think we have a good relationship. No problem."

"I'm not doing that," he said. "I'm not doing that. They wouldn't have come to me with that number unless you had first."

"Well, that's probably right," I said.

And for the umpteenth time he says, "I'll call you back."

A couple of hours later, he calls me back. "You know, Ken," Perot says, "Mitch Hart and I were just saying, the only thing that scares the hell out of us about doing business with you is you don't show much enthusiasm."

"What?"

"Yeah," Perot said. "I don't feel the passion."

"Ross," I said, "what are you doing tonight? I'm coming to Dallas."

He gave a dry chuckle. "Ken, we Texans think anybody that's from Texas has a good sense of humor, and nobody from outside Texas knows a good joke when he hears one."

"Well, I didn't think that was particularly funny," I said, "but if you want me to come down there, I'll be there in a few hours."

"Langone, you can stay right where you are. Let's do business."

And we did it. The world thought I'd gone nuts. But we did the deal.

———

That was June. It took three months to get all the paperwork done, and then it was time to complete the actual transaction, which needed to occur in New Jersey, because the process of Pressprich, the managing underwriter, buying EDS shares, then selling the shares, would have incurred a transfer tax in New York. The way the firms customarily got around the problem was to go to New Jersey, which didn't have a transfer tax, and sign all the papers there.

The night before the underwriting, Ross and his wife, Margot, and Elaine and I—by now we'd gotten to be good friends—were having dinner at 21. It was Wednesday, September 11, 1968. After dinner Elaine had to go back home because the kids had school in the morning. So Ross and Margot and I were going to drive through the Holland Tunnel to the first pull-off in Jersey City to sign the papers, then turn around and come right back in. It was customary to have the limousine driver be the witness.

We're driving through the Holland Tunnel; Ross and Margot are in the backseat and I'm in a jump seat facing them. Perot looks me in the eye. "Well," he says, "they tell me this is when you're gonna admit you can't do the deal you said you'd do."

"What do you mean, Ross?"

"Well, all those guys that you knocked off at White Weld and Goldman and Merrill Lynch and Kidder, Peabody, they're all telling me there's no way you can do it at a hundred times earnings, and you won't do it at a hundred times earnings."

"Ross, they're right," I said.

That caught him by surprise. "What do you mean?"

"They're right," I said. "We're not doing it at a hundred times earnings."

He pointed his finger at me. "I knew it!" he said. He turned to his wife. "See, Margot? They're all alike up here. They're all the same. They get us up here, and they pick the skin off our body."

Now, Margot was sitting directly across from me, and as we went through the tunnel and the lights flashed on our faces, I gave her a wink. Ross didn't see it, but she caught it; I could see just the hint of a smile on her face.

Meanwhile, Perot is still raising hell. "You're all the same!" he's yelling. "You guys have no idea what giving your word means!" On and on.

I held up my hand. "Ross, wait a minute," I said. "Hold it. If a hundred times earnings means that much to you, I'll do it at a hundred times earnings."

That calmed him down just a little. "Damn right it means something," he said. "Because you Wall Street fellas have got to learn something: Your word is your bond. When you say you're going to do a thing, then, by God, you've got to do what you say!"

"Ross, please. I'm very, very happy to do it at a hundred times earnings."

Then Margot—God bless her, a great lady—turned to me with a twinkle. "What were you going to do it at?" she asked.

I said, "Well, I was going to do it at 115 times earnings. But if Ross only wants 100 times earnings, it's okay with me."

A moment later Perot was laughing, hard. But that was the closest I ever saw him come to uttering a profanity.

So we brought EDS public at 115 times earnings—$16.50 a share—instead of 100 times earnings. I was following one of the first rules I learned in business: "Under-promise and over-deliver." Let me tell you how I learned it.

There used to be a bond broker in Philadelphia named Blaine Scott. Let's say you were selling some bonds, and their market value was ninety cents on the dollar, based on interest rates, the maturity of the bond, and the coupon rate on that bond. Blaine Scott would call the company that was interested in buying and say, "I think I can get them for you at eighty-two."

Well, that sounds great to the company. "Go get 'em," they say.

Scott then calls the guy who owns the bonds, who thinks they're worth ninety, and says, "I think I can get you ninety-three for those bonds."

The guy likes that a lot. "Go sell 'em for me at ninety-three," he says.

Blaine Scott then calls the buyer and says, "Look, I was a little too aggressive; we may have to pay more."

"How much more?"

"Well, let's try eighty-six."

"Okay, buy 'em at eighty-six."

Scott then goes back to the seller and says, "Look, I guess I was a little too optimistic; we should probably bring the price down a little bit."

"How much?" the seller asks.

"Let's try ninety-one and a half," Blaine Scott says.

After a couple of more back-and-forths, the trade ends up where it should've in the first place—at ninety cents! And the buyer and the seller are both pissed off. Scott over-promised to get them on the hook, to get them to bare their chest to him. And he made the trade, but they never trusted him again.

I've always tried to do the opposite.

EDS's stock went to $25 a share the first day it was issued, and by mid-1969 it was selling for $75. Within eighteen months it was selling for $162.50 a share. Not long after the initial offering, *Fortune*—my favorite reading material since my freshman year at Bucknell—did a big feature story on Perot, "the fastest, richest Texan," calling the IPO "the greatest personal coup in the history of American finance." In the piece, Ross said extremely generous things about his relationship with me. My reputation as one of the hottest hands on the Street was cemented.

———

One day in January 1969, Perot called me and said he was bringing a guy to New York that he wanted me to meet. We made a lunch date at the Wall Street Club, on top of the Chase Bank building downtown. I got there at the appointed hour, and when I walked in, I saw Ross standing with another short guy, also with a military haircut. "Holy shit," I said to myself. "That's Frank Borman."

Just three weeks earlier, Borman, one of NASA's second group of astronauts, had commanded Apollo 8, the first manned flight to orbit the moon. He was a genuine American hero—he looked like a damn hero—and he'd been all over the news ever since. I was proud to shake his hand, and as the three of us started talking, I liked him right away.

It turned out Frank was considering running for public office sometime and Perot wanted to help him. Ross's idea was to stake him to a couple hundred thousand dollars and to have me open an account for Borman at Pressprich and invest the money for him. As the account grew, Borman would gradually pay Perot back. "I want Frank to be rich independently so when he runs for office he owes nothing to anybody," Ross said.

I said, "I'll be happy to do that." So I opened an account for Frank, and we got to know each other and become close friends. Within a short time, he was really like a member of my family. Funnily enough, a couple of years later—it was in 1971, when my son Bruce was nine—Elaine got a call from Bruce's teacher, saying, "Mrs. Langone, your son Bruce—"

Elaine immediately thought Bruce had done something terrible. "What happened?" she asked.

"Well, he's telling everybody he's a friend of Frank Borman's."

"I don't know if Bruce could call him a friend," Elaine said, "but he does know him well because Frank has been to our home and stayed with us."

Needless to say, Bruce's teacher was very impressed. When Elaine told me about the call, I phoned Frank and said, "Frank, is there any chance you'd be willing to come and talk to these kids in my son's class?"

"I'd love to," Frank said. And they had a big assembly at the school with Frank as the speaker, and Bruce walked him up to the stage. They made a little badge for Bruce that said "Astronaut's Guide." A very big day for Bruce.

Anyway, after I'd been investing for Frank for a while, I called Perot and said, "Ross, the way we really can help Borman get rich is if I can figure out ways to put him into some of these deals without any financial risk."

My idea was to get Frank onto the board of a corporation that would give him founders' shares. He clearly would add value to a business in all kinds of ways, not least through the power of his name. The first board we put him on was of a company called Automated Environmental Systems, which manufactured remote telemetry equipment for monitoring smoke and water discharge from factory smokestacks and waste pipes. The business didn't work out, but when we sold it and put the proceeds into a textile company I was taking public, Frank switched his board membership to the new firm, which prospered. Soon after that initial meeting with Perot and me, Frank put aside his political ambitions and took a job as a special adviser to Eastern Air Lines, whose CEO he became in 1975. As he got deeper into the business world, he took on a number of board positions, including one at the company that changed both our lives.

————————

Not long after the EDS IPO, Ross Perot got interested in buying a company called Collins Radio. Collins, which manufactured avionics and information-technology systems for the CIA and the military, had been founded by an electronics wizard named Arthur Collins, and Arthur Collins, who had taken a particular dislike to Ross Perot, didn't want to sell. So Perot decided to do a hostile takeover of the company by buying up 51 percent of its stock—only instead of paying cash, he wanted to trade shares of EDS for shares of Collins, a very unusual approach for an unfriendly deal.

The deal hadn't happened yet, but while Ross was in New York, we went to meet with Dick Clancy, one of the principals of a hot investment-management firm called Brokaw, Schaenen & Clancy. Perot and I were trying to get Dick interested in investing in EDS: I thought we had a potential bonanza on our hands. Dick seemed interested, but not 100 percent interested. I was puzzled.

As we were on our way out of the office, Clancy pulled me aside. "We don't like this Collins deal," he told me. "But I'll tell you this much: if you ever broke this deal up, we'd give you an order to buy as many shares of EDS as you can buy."

Early one Friday morning in the spring of 1969—I was in Los Angeles, doing some business—I got a call from David G., the head of Pressprich's investment-banking department and our general counsel, saying that the SEC had been investigating the EDS attempt to take over Collins Radio and that the investigators wanted to see me personally on Monday morning. I knew about these people: when they think there's something bad going on, they do an investigation, and if violations have occurred, they recommend corrective action and possibly punishment.

A phone call like that would've put the fear of God in most people, but this was one of those moments when my arrogance kicked in. Was I scared? I guess you could say I was too stupid to be scared. Or too full of myself. After the EDS IPO and that big Perot story in *Fortune,* companies had started calling me up right and left, wanting me to do their deals. This was a time in my life when I was starting to believe my own shit.

Our plan to buy Collins with EDS shares was tricky, because even though EDS stock had ridden a skyrocket since the IPO, it—like all stocks, even hot ones—was subject to ups and downs.

Therefore, we were using something called a stabilization mechanism to avoid volatility while the deal was in process.

When you're doing an underwriting for a company, either an IPO (bringing it to the market for the first time) or a secondary (if the company is already public and is selling more shares), there's a period before you sell the shares to the market: you've announced the issue; you're doing the road show, you're out selling the deal, but you haven't yet gotten clearance from the SEC. In the case of a secondary, the stock goes up and down during that period. So the SEC allowed underwriters to go into the market and put a stabilization bid in—to literally lock the price in at a certain level—in connection with an offering.

We were using a stabilization mechanism, which was intended for secondary offerings of stock, to do the Collins Radio deal, but the Collins deal was not an offering of shares to the market. However, our lawyers and EDS's lawyers assured us that what we were doing was permissible.

It seemed the SEC felt differently.

David G.'s call to me had followed a meeting he and my lawyers had with the SEC's Trading and Markets Division. He and the lawyers had cited regulation this, rule that; this paragraph, that subsection. They were fuckin' dancing around the stabilization rule. And finally, the SEC guys said, "Enough of this shit—we know the rules and regulations, guys. We want to know what the hell you guys are doing! You've been frustrating us. We want you to get the guy in here who's pulling the trigger, doing all these things."

That trigger puller, of course, was me.

I called Perot and told him about the SEC's summons. "I'm very worried about this, and I'm coming to Washington," he said.

"Okay—come on up," I told him. "I'll meet you Sunday night."

In the meantime, he called his lawyers, the Washington firm of Leva, Hawes, Symington, Martin & Oppenheimer, and told them he wanted to talk to them about this deal. And his lawyers said, "We don't know anything about all that; we think you ought to get somebody who knows what they're talking about in this area. You should get Manny Cohen."

Manny Cohen, until very recently, had been chairman of the SEC. If anybody knew the ins and outs of a case like this, it would be Manny Cohen. So Ross hired Cohen—for a fee of $5,000—and he and I agreed to get to Washington on Sunday afternoon and have a meeting with Cohen in Perot's suite at the Madison Hotel.

Cohen comes in around five o'clock, and we sit down: Perot, Mitch Hart, and I; my lawyers, Perot's lawyers, Manny Cohen. And we explain the deal to Cohen, and he says, "Excuse me, fellas, I have to make a call." And he picks up the phone and calls his wife. "Where do you want to have dinner?" he asks her. I'm thinking to myself, "I've got this mess all around me, and this guy's only worrying about where he's going to take his wife to dinner!"

Cohen hangs up. "Okay," he says. "I'm going to tell you fellas what you've got to do."

"What do we do?" Perot asks anxiously.

"Go in there and tell the truth tomorrow," Cohen says. Then he stands up. "That's it," he says. "I've got to go."

I thought, "Holy shit. If I could make five grand just for telling people to tell the truth, I'm in the wrong damn business!"

I reported to the SEC first thing the next morning, greeted a very nervous Ross Perot, who was sitting in the lobby waiting area with Mitch Hart and their lawyers, then went upstairs to have my interview. I had David G. with me and two of my lawyers from Winthrop, Stimson, Putnam & Roberts. We walked into the meeting room.

In the room was a big T-shaped table, with five SEC guys sitting across the horizontal stem of the T. David G., my lawyers, and I sat down at the end of the vertical stem. The lead SEC investigator was named Larry Williams. At 9:00 a.m. sharp, the SEC guys started firing questions at me.

They started by scolding me: They didn't want to be frustrated having all these rules and regulations thrown at them. They knew the rules very well, they told me.

"Stop!" I said. "Fellas, I'll make it easy. I'm going to tell you every single thing we're doing, and did, and plan to do. And I want you to know something. The guys on my right and the guys on my left"—David G. and my lawyers—"before we did anything, we went to them and asked about it, and they said, 'Yes, you can do it.' So if I broke the law, I want you to know something: they told me it was okay. That's what I pay them for! So let's go from there."

The SEC guys continued their grilling. And with every question they asked me, my lawyers were cringing, because every answer I gave was just repeating what they'd told me I could do.

This meeting was supposed to be over by 10:30 a.m. It got to be 11:30, and we still hadn't finished. One of the SEC guys said, "We're going to break for lunch now."

And—it just popped out of my mouth, the salesman talking—I said, "Can I take you to lunch?"

All five of them said, in chorus, "No, no, no! We can't do that!"

I cringed—nice move. Looks like I'm trying to bribe them with a sandwich.

"But we want you back here at one o'clock," they said.

"Okay," I said. And then, "Fellas, I don't know if it'll help any, but Mr. Perot is downstairs. Would it be okay if he came in after lunch?"

"Sure, why not?" they said.

When we got back at one o'clock, the SEC guys told us we were going to meet with their boss, Stanley Sporkin, in his office. Sporkin, then the associate director of the SEC's trading and markets division, later the head of its enforcement division, was known to be one tough son of a bitch. Brutal—I mean, everybody was scared shitless of Stanley Sporkin. He screamed and he yelled; he took no prisoners.

We go into his office. Sporkin is sitting at the far end of the office, with his desk catty-corner to the walls, glowering across at us, the meanest prick the world ever knew.

Perot and I sit down in two chairs in front of Sporkin's desk. And there on the wall over his desk is a big picture of Manny Cohen, inscribed, "To Stanley Sporkin, the finest regulator I've ever known, Your Friend Manny."

"Oh shit," I thought. "We just hit a fuckin' home run."

Naturally, we didn't tell Sporkin we'd met with Manny Cohen. And—as advertised—he immediately stood up and started screaming. "I'm gonna get you guys!" he yelled. "You're playin' games! You think you're fooling the world! You think you're fooling the SEC! When I get done with you . . ." Screaming! Yelling! Saliva flying out of the sides of his mouth! In the chair next to me, Perot—his feet didn't reach the floor—was swinging his legs back and forth, back and forth, terrified.

Then Sporkin stopped and turned to me.

"Okay, what do you have to say for yourself?" he asked.

"Well, Mr. Sporkin," I said, "I guess I just heard the investigation, the indictment, the trial, and the conviction; all that's left is the punishment."

"What do you mean?" he asked.

"Well, I'm just telling you what I heard," I said.

"Well, what do you think?" Sporkin asked.

"Well, I think it's totally different from that," I said, and I explained as best I could our reasons for using the stabilization rule.

Now, we were supposed to spend half an hour with Sporkin. We spent six hours in that office. Because the Collins Radio purchase was an unfriendly deal, there were a lot of things about the company that we hadn't known: Sporkin spelled those things out, and they weren't good. Collins was having big operating problems, he told us. Were we taking advantage of the fact that their sales were down? Were we aware that we had inside information? What inside information? we asked. Sporkin told us. It was the first we were hearing about any of it.

Finally, at seven o'clock, Sporkin said, "Go ahead and do your deal. But do it without stabilization."

We told him we would think about it.

Perot, Mitch Hart, and I went back to the Madison Hotel. And Perot said to me over dinner, "What do you think?"

"Ross," I said, "based on what we learned about how messed up Collins Radio is, I don't think we should do the deal. You'd have your hands full; I think this thing would blow up on you."

But it was more than the problems with Collins. The reality was that without stabilization we couldn't do the deal; the guy who owned Collins shares would have no idea what he'd be going to get for his shares, because of the volatility of EDS.

"What happens if we don't do the deal?" he asked.

"What do you mean?"

"What are my obligations?"

"Well, you've got to pay your lawyers," I said.

"What about you?" he asked.

"My fee was a success fee," I said.

"What do you mean?"

"We didn't do the deal, so I don't get a fee. Simple as that."

Ross and Mitch and I had breakfast the next morning, and we decided not to go ahead. We had the lawyers call the SEC and inform them that we were terminating the deal. The SEC was curious about why we hadn't gone ahead. Our lawyers told them that we had a great business with a great future, and we didn't want to take the chance of having a cloud hanging over us.

After lunch I phoned Dick Clancy. "Dick, I don't know if you know this, but we killed the Collins Radio deal."

"I heard about it," he said. "And I was glad to hear it." Then he said, "All right. Here's an order. We want you to buy every share of EDS you can buy in the market, and we want you to keep buying it until we tell you to stop."

"What limit?" I asked.

"There's no limit," he said. "Just keep buying the stock. We want to put it in every account."

I hung up the phone and said, "Holy shit."

Rudy Smutny, who sat right across from me at the trading desk, said, "What happened?"

"Oh my God, oh my God," I said. "I can't believe the order I just got."

Rudy looked excited. "What order did you get? What order?"

"I got an order to buy all the EDS stock I can buy, no limit," I said.

"What do you mean?"

"I can pay any price I want for the stock, and Dick Clancy says to keep buying. We don't have to put a limit on it."

And Rudy said, dead serious, "Can you hold off for a minute so I can go and buy some first?"

I looked at him. "Rudy, I can't do that," I said. "I've got to put in the order."

I couldn't believe what I'd just heard. The president and chief operating officer of our firm wanted to run ahead of a customer's order. The worst sin in the world. It's called front running, and it's illegal.

I went to Mr. Brown and said, "Mr. Brown, I've got to see you right now."

"What about?"

Brown and the other most senior partner, Clint Lutkins—

Clinton Lutkins, who'd been with Pressprich since 1930—had adjacent desks in an office just off the trading room. Brown and Lutkins were the real powerhouses of Pressprich: Lutkins was long past his prime, but he had a lot of capital in the firm. I motioned to both of them. "Can we go in the conference room for a minute?"

The three of us went in and I closed the door. "Gentlemen, I'm leaving the firm," I said.

"What?"

I said, "I'm leaving the firm."

"Why?" Brown asked.

"Because something just happened that shocked me, and I don't want to be around a place like this if that kind of behavior is tolerated." And I told them what Smutny had said.

They looked at each other. "Give us until tomorrow morning," Mr. Brown said.

That night there was a meeting at Brown's apartment—Brown, Lutkins, some lawyers. The next morning they called me in to tell me that they were going to ask Rudy to leave the firm immediately.

They asked him to leave immediately, but he didn't leave immediately. As a courtesy, they agreed to put out a cover story about why he was separating from Pressprich and gave him the chance to move to another firm. Rudy's son was working at the brokerage and investment-banking firm F. I. duPont and helped him to get a very senior position there.

Before he left, Rudy and I and the other partners went to a savings-bank convention at the Waldorf Astoria, and while we were there, Rudy was complaining to me about what Brown and Lutkins had done to him. "Rudy, stop," I said. "I made it happen."

"What do you mean?" he asked.

"Rudy, when you told me that I should hold back on that order so you could run ahead of it, I knew at that moment you and I could never do business together. Ever." I said, "I'm the guy you want to blame. Because Brown and Lutkins had a choice. You or me. If you didn't leave the firm, I was going to."

He was just staring at me. Suddenly he didn't look so tough anymore; he just looked old.

"Rudy, no hard feelings," I said, "but I couldn't not let them know. It's just not my nature."

He was gone the next week. That was June 1969. And that September the partners of R. W. Pressprich elected me president of the firm.

5.

HUBRIS AND REDEMPTION

And just like that, Wall Street took notice.

One day I was an unknown salesman at a small Wall Street firm; the next day I was Ross Perot's banker, the guy who'd made him a millionaire! And not only was I Perot's banker and president of R. W. Pressprich and Company, but I was soon elected president of the Investment Association of New York, an organization of up-and-comers aged thirty-five and under. I was invited to join the board of North Shore Hospital. I lived in a big house on a hill in Long Island. I was all of thirty-four, and I was pretty full of myself.

As a consequence of the EDS underwriting, R. W. Pressprich, this little firm that had previously done almost no equity offerings at all, was suddenly doing deal after deal after deal. Most of them were mine. In February 1970, I brought a company called Stirling Homex public. Stirling was founded by two brothers from Toronto who came up with the brilliant idea of building prefabricated housing modules in a factory, shipping them by railroad flatcar, and assembling them on-site. They had a big deal with the housing authority in Akron, Ohio.

I took that company public for $16.50, and within a month it went to almost $52 a share, an earnings multiple of three hundred. EDS was trading at a thousand times earnings, but three hundred was nothing to sneeze at. There was a very small float for both stocks, meaning that few shares were in the hands of the public. The institutional demand for both companies, on the other hand, was enormous.

Then, in April, the roof falls in.

Nixon is battling the Vietnam War protesters, soon the Ohio National Guard will kill four kids at Kent State, the market swings wildly. Suddenly the world is coming to an end. Suddenly people on Wall Street, smarter than me and more objective than me, decide they're going to put a short on every stock R. W. Pressprich is trading. Stirling Homex. Ohio Mattress. And the jewel in the crown, Electronic Data Systems.

Pressprich had been undercapitalized for a long time, thanks to my old pal Rudy Smutny. When Rudy came over from Salomon Brothers in the late 1950s, he said, "Hey, guys, I can show you a way to have your cake and eat it, too." His idea was that instead of having to put cash into the firm, the partners could make loans to the firm in the form of stocks or bonds. Pressprich could then go to a bank and borrow cash on those stocks or bonds, but the hitch was that the firm had to pay double interest: to the partners who'd loaned it the shares, and to the banks that had loaned the firm cash. Our cost of capital was over 20 percent.

And now other firms were urging institutional investors to sell off the stocks that were holding R. W. Pressprich together.

The fact that they were going after EDS was especially galling to me. That was my brand! That's what put me on the map! My hubris kicked in, and I stupidly thought we could make a stand—that we could support this stock and the others we held by buying up what the short sellers were selling. What I didn't realize was that I couldn't play that game if I didn't have unlimited funds. And I didn't have unlimited funds. These guys were selling faster than we were buying. We got wiped out. In a single day, EDS stock went from $162.50 a share to $80. We didn't go broke, but our capital was gone.

It was the biggest defeat of my career, and it hit me like a kick in the stomach. Before, I used to love coming to work every day. Now I'd walk through the trading room seeing the glum looks all around me, knowing what everybody else knew: we were wounded, maybe mortally wounded. Every day at Pressprich was the longest eight hours I'd ever spent. Every day I would stay in the office until four o'clock, leave and take the early train back to Long Island, change into old clothes, go out in the garden, and weed the garden and cry. This went on for two or three months.

One Friday night Elaine and I were getting dressed to go out. She was sitting at this little dressing table she had, and suddenly she turned to me and said, "You know, there's a rumor going around Manhasset we're going to have to sell the house."

That caught me up short. "That'll never happen," I told her.

"I just want you to know," she said, "before we have to do that, I'll go back to work."

"You'll never have to go back to work," I said. "I'll make sure of that."

That was when I said to myself, "Okay, you son of a bitch, now let's see how good you are."

The firm's partners had made me president because I was bringing the business in, but the old man himself wasn't very happy about it. Barrett Brown had been with Pressprich since the early 1930s, and he was set in his pipe-smoking, stock-and-bond, sleepy ways. I was young and brash, I made noise, and I had made him look bad more than once. He and I were oil and water, and he was looking for his chance to get rid of me.

Now he had it.

And it wasn't just Barrett Brown who resented me; it was the entire old guard of the firm. Here was this hotshot kid they'd made president; now it was "Look what he's done to our sixty-year-old firm," and on and on. One day, the old man called me into his office. He took the pipe out of his mouth and said, "Fella, you ought to resign."

"Mr. Brown, I'm not resigning," I said. "I got this horse in the ditch, and I'll get this horse out of the ditch."

"Humph. Well, I still think you should quit."

"If you want to fire me, fire me," I said. "I ain't quitting." And I walked away.

We had a real emergency on our hands, and we had to move fast to stanch the bleeding. We held a series of meetings to figure out what to do, and one of our first decisions was that we had to cut a substantial portion of our thousand-person staff. Our rule of thumb was that anyone working for the firm who wasn't producing at least as much as we were paying him had to go. This included all of our young trainees.

So everybody—the bond guys, the stock guys—did what they had to do. But the guy who ran the stock desk came to me and said, "Ken, I've got a kid working for us. I told him we've got to terminate him because we can't afford him; nothing to do with his performance. In fact, I told him we thought he had a great future in the business. And he said he's not leaving."

"Send him in," I said.

So in comes this kid; his name is Alan Schwartz. And Alan Schwartz says to me, "I understand what you're doing and why you're doing it, but I don't want to leave. I'm learning so much here."

"I'm sorry, Alan," I said. "We just can't afford to pay you anymore."

"Can you afford minimum wage?" he asked.

Minimum wage in 1970 was $1.45 an hour. "You can't afford to live on that," I said.

"That's my problem, not yours," he said.

My problem, not yours—those had been my exact words to Jack Cullen when I convinced him Pressprich should hire me for a hundred fifty bucks a week. I liked this kid.

"Okay, Alan," I said. "You can stay."

You want to know what he did? There was a restaurant in Great Neck called Maude Craig's. And Alan Schwartz (he was single at the time) got a job there as a busboy and waiter at night so he could stay at Pressprich. He turned out to be one of the most talented and able men I've ever known in this business: he went on to become CEO of Bear Stearns and is now executive chairman of Guggenheim Partners.

Back to the crisis at R. W. Pressprich.

The lease on the three floors the firm occupied at 80 Pine Street was a substantial expense in itself, but the partners did some quick calculations and realized that with a smaller staff we could fit all our operations onto a single floor. So Barrett Brown sent me to Lew Rudin, the Manhattan commercial-real-estate magnate who owned the building, to ask if he would give us an accommodation on the lease.

"Watch out," Brown warned me. "Those Jews can be tough."

I went up to Rudin's headquarters at 345 Park Avenue and was shown right into his office. And the first thing Lew Rudin said to me was "How's my good friend Barry Brown?" And I thought to myself, "If you only knew what this guy thinks of you."

After a minute of small talk, I came to the point. "Mr. Rudin," I said, "we have a problem. Pressprich is struggling. We're going to make it, but we need to lean the firm down. And in doing that, we're only going to need one floor of the three."

"Well," he said, "here's what I want you to do. Pick the floor you want to keep, clean up the other two floors, and start paying me rent on the first of next month for just the one floor."

I said, "What about the other two floors?"

"That's my problem," he said. "Pressprich has been a very good tenant, and I'll deal with the vacancies."

So much for tough Jews.

Now, fast-forward twenty-odd years. I've gone out on my own; I've co-founded Home Depot and done very well. One day I'm walking west on Fifty-second Street, and I literally bump into an old man walking east. It's none other than Lew Rudin, who I can immediately see is losing his eyesight. Instead of watching where he's going, he's been looking down at the sidewalk.

"Mr. Rudin!" I said. He squinted at me. I said, "I'm Ken Langone; you may not remember me, but I'll never forget you." And I reminded him of the whole story and told him what I was up to now.

"Do you play golf?" he asked.

"Yeah," I said.

"I want you to play golf with me on Friday at Deepdale," he said. Deepdale is a beautiful country club not far from my house on Long Island's North Shore. "I've got two other guys," Rudin told me. One was Jack Hausman, a retired textile manufacturer who was very active in charitable causes; the other was Mel Goodes, the chairman of Warner-Lambert.

"Let me see if I'm free on Friday," I said.

I was free. So I called Lew and said, "After we play, my wife and I would like to host you and your wife, and the other guys and their wives, for dinner at our home."

Friday came. We played golf and had a nice time—and some interesting conversation. While we were playing, we got to talking about medications we were taking. And Mel mentioned that he'd had a cholesterol problem, but he'd started taking a drug that his company had in clinical trials and had had very good results. The drug was eventually marketed as Lipitor, and Warner-Lambert did rather well with it.

We finished our round, and I went home and got cleaned up. At seven o'clock, Lew and his wife, Rachel, arrived. Now is also the time to mention that in 1989, after we'd lived for almost twenty-five years on Elderfields Road, Elaine had had a beautiful new place built on a big piece of property by the water on Sands Point. We'd pulled out all the stops and created our dream house.

Lew Rudin walks into the foyer of my home in Sands Point, which is a very gracious foyer. And he squints, looks around, and turns to his wife "Can you believe I let this guy off a fuckin' loano?" he says.

———

So we saved some money on the lease, and we saved some more by letting some people go. But what Pressprich really needed in order to survive in 1970 was institutional change, and the biggest change we made was to switch from the equity business back into the bond business.

It was a collective decision. Stocks were headed toward fully negotiated commissions; if we kept selling equities, our profit margins were going to be smaller and less dependable. But all the partners were strong in bonds, particularly railroad bonds, and we felt we could make a go of it if we refocused ourselves on fixed-income securities.

We did it, and we got the ship righted. But it took a while, and it was a scary ride.

———

In the fall of 1969, when I still had a hot hand, I met a San Diego entrepreneur named Richard Cramer, who'd started a company called IVAC Corporation. IVAC invented the electronic thermometer and developed the medical-infusion pump: both devices are in wide use today but were brand-new then. For decades, hospitals had used glass thermometers, but they had two big problems: they were rarely used in mental institutions because mental patients could possibly bite them, and they were dicey for rectal use because if one broke, it could puncture the colon. So electronic thermometers, plastic with a metal tip, were the wave of the future.

As were medical-infusion pumps. Until then, if a patient got intravenous medication, it was from a bag or a glass bottle. The doctor would prescribe five or six or eight drips a minute, and the nurse would literally sit and count drips falling into the drip chamber. It was easy to miscalculate or get distracted and make big mistakes, and big mistakes could be harmful to a patient, or even fatal. The medical-infusion pump was precise and foolproof, and with my love for investing in things that worked well, I wanted in.

Richard Cramer was—in my eyes, anyway—a classic Californian, with bronze skin and a slick line of talk. But even after I factored all that in, the technology he was backing had me convinced. I went out and raised $5 million from a variety of investors to buy 10 percent of his company.

Then, in the spring of 1971, while Pressprich was still on the ropes, IVAC began to worry me. I kept telling Dick Cramer, "You've got to cut your costs. We're doing it here; you have to do it out there." But Cramer wasn't cutting costs: he was pissing money away. The company's expenses were getting out of hand, and he had all kinds of people on the payroll who probably shouldn't have been on the payroll, including secretaries the executives were romantically involved with. One day when I was in Southern California on other business, I dropped by the IVAC offices, and Cramer said, "I want to show you something."

He took me out for a drive around downtown San Diego, most of which was parking lots then. And he pointed to one parking lot and said, "That's where our world headquarters is going to be."

Well, that took me aback. I thought, "What? You haven't got $2 million in sales! *What* world headquarters for *what* business? Oh my God, this guy has got delusions of grandeur."

It wasn't long afterward that I got a call from Gene Melnichenko, a stock analyst at U.S. Trust, one of the institutional investors in IVAC. "We've got a half-million dollars in that little San Diego company of yours, Ken," he said. "And our best information is that the company is going to hell in a handbasket."

"I know," I said.

"Well, that's not money we want to lose," Gene said. "So if you want to keep doing business with us, you've got to figure out some way to save IVAC."

"What do I do?"

"Start a proxy fight," he said.

"It's a private company!"

"I don't care. Start one anyway."

It was an interesting situation. Cramer was such a slick character that he'd managed to sell stock in IVAC to thousands of shareholders without ever bothering to register the shares with the SEC. He'd literally driven around with piles of blank stock certificates and a prototype of his electronic thermometer, persuading people who didn't know the stock market from a supermarket to buy in. In the parlance of the SEC, these stockholders were known as nonqualified—meaning, they were unable to assess the risk of their purchase. So we got the shareholder list, and we were able to go to them and solicit their proxies, which, when they heard what Cramer was doing with the money they'd invested, most of them were happy to give.

We won the fight, but what a prize. When we got control of the company in May 1972, it was worth $1.5 million, with $30,000 in the bank and a $60,000 payroll due two days later. "Oh shit," I thought. "I'd better lean this thing down quick." The first staff cut was easy: Richard Cramer was out on his ass. But we still had to cut overhead aggressively. We asked all the people who worked at IVAC—it had about seventy employees—for their résumés.

The first one to catch my eye was the general manager. Previous employment: San Diego Motors. Position: used-car salesman. What the hell?

It turned out that this guy was married to a very beautiful woman, and one day back when he was selling used cars, business at the car lot was slow, so the guy goes home to have a tuna-fish sandwich, and when he gets there, he finds his wife in the sack with Richard Cramer. Cramer gets up and pulls the sheet around himself. "I'm sorry," he says. "I won't do it again."

"Okay," the guy says. "Just don't do it again." It's California!

A month later—bam—the guy catches Cramer with his wife again. And unbelievably, Cramer reasons with him. "Look," he says. "You don't like selling cars much, do you?"

"No, I don't."

"Well, how about coming to work for me?" Cramer asks.

The guy just shakes his head. "What do you mean?"

"Listen, I've got to hire a guy. How about you come in and be our general manager?"

"Me?"

"Sure."

Now I can't help myself; even though I've just canned Cramer, I've got to call the guy up. "Dick, what the hell were you thinking about, handing that job to this bozo?" I ask.

Cramer starts laughing. "Shit," he said. "It was the only way I could know where the guy would be all the time."

We trimmed staff and expenses to the bare bones and moved on, but there were some major glitches. After we got control of the company and the SEC realized that the sale of IVAC shares had never been properly filed, that IVAC was owned by all these nonqualified shareholders, the SEC was contemplating a rescission: meaning, revoking all sales of the stock. Which in turn would've meant we would have had to give all the shareholders their money back—except Cramer had sucked IVAC dry: there was no money to give back. We threw ourselves on the SEC's mercy. "If you rescind our stock sales, we're going to have to bankrupt this company because all the money's gone, and we had nothing to do with it," we said, and the SEC let us go on.

Then there was the new CEO we found through a headhunter firm—a guy from New York who robbed us blind for six months before we found out. Out he went, and for a while I was IVAC's interim chairman and CEO. For almost two years, I took a flight to San Diego every Thursday afternoon to put in face time in the office and flew back home the next day. My kids were growing: they had soccer and baseball and football and lacrosse games I wanted to be at, and I made a lot of them. Still, I was away a lot.

And I'll admit it: nobody had a gun to my head; I loved what I was doing. But my young family didn't benefit from my continual absences.

One of Dick Cramer's very early hires was an industrial designer named Steve Sato, a very able guy who created the look of the electronic thermometer. But Sato very quickly grew disgusted with Cramer's business practices and found others within the company who felt the same. Steve helped me mount the proxy fight, which, Cramer argued to the shareholders, was just an attempt on Sato's part to get his job. Well, Cramer lost the fight, and after I'd spent a few months as head of IVAC, I passed the baton to Steve.

He did a great job. Under Sato's leadership, the company went from being on its ass to being highly profitable. And while that was happening, I was getting more and more excited about the health-care field.

I kept wondering if there was a way I could be in the medical business and the investment-banking/finance business at the same time. But the more I thought about it, the clearer it became that I couldn't do it as long as I was at Pressprich: the only way they could survive with their limited capital was as a bond house. That was a noble business, a time-honored business, but it wasn't a business that thrilled me. I was an equity guy, a fish out of water.

Bonds are the first claim on an issuer's assets. Stocks are the last. With bonds, the investor typically earns a fixed rate of return; with equities, the investor owns a piece of the business. The concept is simple: greater risk, greater reward. And that's where I wanted to be. I've learned over a period of years how to structure a deal in a way that mitigates risk. The risk is always there, but if the deal is right, the sky is the limit on the return. I've got a nose for these things, and my nose has usually guided me in the right direction.

I decided it was time to go out on my own.

Early in 1974, I told Mr. Brown and the other partners that I was going to leave R. W. Pressprich and start an investment and venture-capital firm of my own, with a focus on the health-care field. They all wished me well, and I know more than a few of them were happy to see me go.

The only problem was that I had no capital.

I was worth almost a million bucks at that point, but it was all on paper, in the Partners Account—in stocks that, under Rudy Smutny's structure, I had lent, at interest, to the firm. And Pressprich was never going to let me take those stocks out.

So I went out and did something I was good at: selling equities. Except that in this case the equity I was selling was my own expertise.

I'd made a lot of good connections along the way. Aside from my investment-banking role for EDS and Ross Perot, Ross had invested infrequently with Pressprich, but our relationship was such that I could go to him and offer my services as a financial adviser for $60,000 a year. I knew I could help him with some important issues: Should EDS make acquisitions? Should they start paying dividends? How should they position their company to investors?

Mitch Hart sang my praises to Ross, and Ross signed on. I made the same offer to Allen Mebane, the chairman of the North Carolina polyester-yarn manufacturer Unifi, a company I deeply believed in and whose board I sat on. Allen came on board with $35,000 per annum. I went to a young guy named Gary Erlbaum, who had a Philadelphia wood-paneling and home-improvement company called Panelrama that I'd helped take public a couple of years earlier. Gary committed to $15,000. So I knew I'd have $110,000 a year coming in—the equivalent of about half a million today—of which I would allot myself a salary of $35,000.

I also approached twenty-five select institutions—banks and insurance companies I'd done business with while I was at Pressprich—and offered, for a handshake commitment of $25,000 in commissions a year, to advise them on investments that I thought would suit their objectives and yield the greatest potential profit. They all said yes.

I also found a partner.

I'm going to call him Ted Jones, because things between us did not work out well. Ted's father was very influential in the pharmaceutical industry. Ted lived right across the street from me on Elderfields Road. He raised a very important $250,000 of our initial capital. I raised an additional $350,000 by selling shares in our start-up to people I'd done successful business with: Allen Mebane and his business partner Charlie Edwards; Ernie Wuliger, the chairman of Ohio Mattress (a company I'd taken public in 1970 and that eventually became the Sealy Corporation); and Herb Snowden, the head of Educator & Executive Life Insurance Company, in Columbus, Ohio, one of my earliest customers at Pressprich.

Like me, my partner would draw a salary of $35,000. Besides our combined income, I was determined to keep overhead as low as possible. We wanted a prominent address, and fortunately the economy was in our favor: we were able to sublet an office on the nineteenth floor of the Seagram Building, at 375 Park Avenue, for $15 a square foot. We were able to purchase all the used office furniture we needed from Ross Perot, who'd bought into the investment firm of F. I. duPont a few years earlier and was about to get out of that business. We painted the walls, but we kept the carpet that was already there.

We hired a bookkeeper from Pressprich, Dorothea Wahrburg, and two other secretaries. We hired a well-known health-care-industry analyst, Paul Standel, and after a while, an investment banker, Cris Kepner. And we brought in Dr. Austin Smith, the retired vice-chairman of Warner-Lambert. Dr. Smith was our gravitas.

Our new firm—called Invemed in honor of our investment specialty—opened for business on June 1, 1974.

But there was one more very important outlay.

Unlike the big wire firms on Wall Street, we were a small, highly specialized organization—a specialty firm, as they're called. And I felt that my budding company needed the imprimatur of a seat on the New York Stock Exchange.

Fortunately for us, in the midst of the great bear market of the 1970s, the price of a seat on the exchange had declined from almost $200,000 to around $65,000.

But the same market chaos that had made it possible for us to buy the seat on the NYSE (we also hired a floor representative from Pressprich, Jerry Bell) was tough on our new firm. Long story short, the turbulent investment climate made it very difficult to sell stocks. And that was tough on my partner, who retreated into a kind of psychological bomb shelter. He would close his office door for hours at a time and only come out to go to the water-cooler. He would drink his water from one of those little paper cups from the cup dispenser and then—I guess he felt it was a cost-cutting move—plop the damn cup upside down on top of the big water bottle. Which drove Dorothea Wahrburg bat-shit, because she thought it was unsanitary. As soon as Ted would go back into his office and shut the door again, she would throw his cup out, then, when he came back to the cooler an hour later, he'd say, "Where's my cup?"

The guy was really getting on my nerves. And all the more so because he wasn't bringing any business in, and I was busting my ass.

When I was at Pressprich, I'd had a client down in Houston, Texas, named Leonard Coe Scruggs, at a company called American General Life Insurance Company. I'd found out that July and August and the beginning of September were a real bitch in Houston; the heat and humidity were so brutal that most of the salesmen from New York wouldn't go there then. But Coe Scruggs, as he called himself, used to automatically give you $5,000 in commission if you called on him during that hot period.

Coe had passed on, but I found out that his successor at American General still had the same policy. I thought, "Gee, that's kind of a no-brainer." So every Sunday night during those hot-as-hell months, I'd get on a plane to Houston—always after 9:00 p.m., because that's when the ticket prices dropped. I'd sleep at a Super 8 Motel for eight bucks, rent a cheap car, drive from the airport to American General, do business, go back to the airport, and come home. Soon I was going there twice a week. That was ten grand a week in the till, and my partner was giving me shit about it. I said, "Ted, we need asses and elbows on the road right now. What the hell are you doing?"

To save the cost of commutation tickets on the Long Island Rail Road, my partner and I used to drive into the city together every morning from Manhasset. We'd take the Fifty-ninth Street Bridge into Manhattan because it had no toll. One morning as we were crossing the bridge, I turned to him and said, "Look. I can't carry this thing on my shoulders alone; you're gonna have to take a pay cut. You're bringing nothing in."

"Well, what about you?"

"Wait a minute, Ted. I went out and got us $110,000 in fees, and I'm making $35,000. My math puts me at plus $75,000 against all the other costs. You're taking thirty-five grand out, and you're bringing nothing in."

"Well, I don't like the market, and I can't sell stocks if I don't like the market."

"Well, guess what," I said. "You have two children who like to eat three times a day. You haven't got the luxury of not liking the market."

———

But by November of 1974 it had become clear that most of the institutional investors that had pledged annual commissions to us weren't going to come through: the markets were just too shitty. We were literally paying our bills out of our precious capital, not out of revenues.

One day—it was early morning, the Wednesday before Thanksgiving—I was on the phone with one of our institutional clients, Speros "Doc" Drelles, who ran the investment division of the Pittsburgh National Bank trust department. I remember I was talking up Upjohn, the pharmaceutical manufacturer, which had just come out with a new drug. Doc Drelles—I called him "Greek"—was a real piece of work: smart as a whip, and arrogant as hell. He loved to bust my chops by telling me that all brokers were airheads, just empty suits, and that included me. Doc had only one chair in his office—his. Every time I called on him I had to stand there like a kid in the principal's office.

That day he was being relatively sympathetic—after we talked business he asked me how things were going with my new firm.

"Not so great, Greek," I said. "Unlike you, most of my investors aren't coming through on their commitment—you're one of the few who are."

"I've got to go," he said, abruptly.

A little while later, around 11:00 a.m., Jimmy Rau, my head trader, came into my office. "Holy shit," he said. "Pittsburgh National Bank's trading desk just came in with over four hundred orders—a hundred shares of this, ninety shares of that, two hundred thirty shares of something else." In those days we had to write execution tickets for orders, one per transaction, and Jimmy was writing so many tickets for this Pittsburgh National thing that I had to go in and help him. We were writing tickets until 5:30 that afternoon—it added up to around $45,000 in commissions. So effectively, Doc had paid me almost two years' commissions in a single day.

That was a real shot in the arm. But by early 1975 we were still struggling.

I wasn't afraid, but I was anxious, and my anxiety drove me to be almost maniacal about bringing in business. And one day I made a big blunder. I placed a bid on a block of stock that I was positive was headed up and positive I had a buyer for—then, suddenly, it became clear that the guy I'd been so sure of wasn't going to buy. We were left holding the bag—an enormous bag. If the stock went down, we were in huge trouble. Oh my God, I was panicked; I was sitting at my desk with my hands over my head, wondering what the hell I was going to do.

Just then Ted walks in. "What's wrong?" he asks.

"I think I might have blown the firm," I said.

"What are you talking about?"

"Look," I said. "I've made a horrible mistake; I thought I had a buyer, and I don't have a buyer. We could very well go under if this fucking stock goes down."

"Can you find another buyer?"

"I don't know," I said.

He just shook his head and walked away. But after a minute he came back. "You know what?" he said. "I've been thinking; I don't think I've ever made a mistake like that in my life."

"You know what?" I said. "You're right. You haven't done a damn thing in your life; how could you make a mistake?"

My anger gave me the energy to get out of panic mode. I quickly recovered and found a buyer for the stock—at a better price.

My partner didn't stick around much longer after that.

When Ted left the firm—this was May of 1975—he took the capital he'd brought in with him. I'd brought in enough business by then to make up for what he took away, but I was still worried. It was right around then that Allen Mebane, who'd heard about my partner's departure, invited me down to North Carolina to play some golf. We were coming off the fourth tee when Allen turned to me and asked, "How's everything going, Kenny?"

"Allen, I think I'm going to make it," I said. "But I want you to know, it's going to be close."

He looked me in the eye. "I've got you covered," he said.

"Allen, that's very kind, but you really don't have to," I said.

"I won't take no for an answer," Allen said. And he and Charlie Edwards bought one unit of Invemed—6,000 shares of common stock and 750 shares of preferred stock in the firm—for a total of $125,000. That was a comfortable cushion to have, and my little firm weathered the storm.

The best part of the story is that twenty-five years later—it was 2001—when Allen got very sick and retired from Unifi, he called me. He still owned his 6,000 shares of Invemed common stock, which at that point was about 13 percent of the firm. He said, "I'd like to offer you the following deal: I want to sell you my shares of Invemed over a period of twenty years and give the proceeds to my foundation." I agreed, of course. Every year since, I've bought 300 shares of Invemed's stock back, and the Mebane Foundation has given all the money to worthy causes in North Carolina, including helping kids in the public schools in Mocksville, where the Unifi plant is. Allen's gone now, but to date that buyback has put $17 million into those charities. A win all around.

———

In late 1975, Panelrama, the home-improvement company that Gary Erlbaum ran with his brothers Steven and Michael, was struggling. The economy was still down, and their stores were too small; it was just a confluence of problems. One day I went down to Philadelphia to confer with the Erlbaums about what they should do with their company. "Look," I said, "one of the things we have to do is ask ourselves a question, 'Do we have a business?'" The place to start, I told them, was to look around the country and find out who in their business was doing it right.

I knew a little bit about the business. You may remember Evans Products, the railroad-car and building-materials company I'd helped get financing when I was at Pressprich. Evans Products had bought a chain of home-center stores in the mid-Atlantic, Virginia and thereabouts, called Moore's Super Stores. That interested me. And the more I looked into the home-center business, the more I liked it. I liked the demographics; I liked the idea of people doing things in their homes—painting, papering, plumbing. I did it. I hung tile and wallpaper. I painted my house and my in-laws' house. When you get started in life, you can't afford to pay somebody to do that stuff.

The darlings of the industry at that time were a midwestern company called Payless Cashways and another outfit in the Southeast called Lowe's. The home-center industry was feudal in those days; nobody crossed borders. Hechinger shared the mid-Atlantic with Moore's; Rickel and Pergament were in the Northeast. Somerville Lumber was in Boston. I used to go to Rickel and Pergament if I really needed something. They were pretty lousy.

"Who's the best out there, do you think?" I asked the Erlbaums.

"There's a guy in California," Gary said.

"Oh yeah? Who's that?"

"His name is Bernie Marcus, and he runs a company called Handy Dan," Gary said. "He's a nice guy."

Well, I'd heard about Handy Dan, and what I'd heard was that it was in very rough shape. "Gary," I said, "Bernie Marcus may be a very nice guy, but there's only one problem. If my memory serves me right, he and his partners are bankrupt. If Marcus is so damn good, why is he bankrupt?"

"He's not bankrupt," Gary said.

"That's not what I hear," I said.

"He isn't," Gary repeated.

I came back to New York from Philadelphia, went straight up to the office, and looked through my big *Moody's Industrial Manual* for Handy Dan. And standing there, all by myself at 7:30 p.m., I shook my head and said, "Holy shit, Gary's right."

It turned out that Handy Dan was 81 percent owned by a retail conglomerate called Daylin Incorporated. Daylin specialized in pharmacy and health goods and, between bad management and the bad economy, had overextended itself. And Daylin, which was publicly held, was in bankruptcy. But because Handy Dan was a public company—and flourishing!—it couldn't be tarred with that same brush. It was simply an investment on Daylin's books. And a very profitable one. The Moody's manual said Handy Dan was earning a little over $4 million a year, in a sector where earnings were generally spotty.

Moody's also said that Handy Dan was selling for $3.00 a share and earning $1.02 per share. I blinked at that one, it looked like an optical illusion. Most comparable stocks would have been selling for $12.00 to $15.00 a share, or more. If my eyes didn't deceive me, Handy Dan was vastly undervalued.

Right then and there I called Gary up.

"Gary, do me a favor," I said. "I want to talk to this guy, Marcus. Because I'm looking at the manual and it says the stock is selling for three bucks, and earning a buck and a half a share. This has to be some kind of gimmick. Could you see if this guy will take my call?"

"Sure," Gary said. Apparently, Marcus liked what he heard; Gary phoned me right back. "He's in his office," he said. "Call him up."

So I called Bernie Marcus. I was excited, and I didn't hold back. "Mr. Marcus!" I said. "Ken Langone, Gary's banker! Listen, I think you have one of the greatest companies I've ever seen!"

Marcus was cordial but reserved. "Oh, good. Thank you. What can I do for you?"

"Listen, Mr. Marcus," I said. "I'm going through your numbers, and I'm a little puzzled. This $1.82 earnings a share, is it pretax?"

"No, that's after taxes," he said.

"Well, that's extremely impressive," I said. "Now—can you explain to me why your stock is selling for three bucks?"

He sighed. "I know," Bernie Marcus said. "Part of that is people don't understand the difference between Daylin and us. I've got a very nice business here."

"I know you do!" I said. "Mr. Marcus, I'd like to get to know you better. Would you mind if I came out to see you?"

"Sure, sure," Marcus said. "Anytime you feel like coming out."

"How about tomorrow at lunch?" I said.

————

I took the first flight out of New York and landed in L.A. at about 10:00 a.m. local time. We'd arranged to meet at a diner in the City of Commerce, just outside downtown Los Angeles. I took a cab from the airport and got to this damn ugly diner a little after eleven. I sat down in a booth and read the paper for half an hour. About a quarter to twelve, two guys walk in. I didn't know what Bernie Marcus looked like. They immediately come over to me. I'm dressed in a business suit. I start to get up, but I can't get up. What the hell is wrong? Somebody had left a wad of chewing gum on the damn vinyl banquette, and my ass was stuck to the seat!

Was I embarrassed? Sure I was. But I also thought, "This is good luck."

The two guys were Bernie Marcus and his lawyer, Erwin Diller. Bernie was tall, with gray hair and glasses—nice face; I liked him right away—and Diller looked like a lawyer. Serious as a tax audit. I later found out that Marcus had brought his attorney because he, Bernie, was having some stress with the head of Daylin, Sanford Sigoloff (remember that name), and he wanted to make sure he didn't do anything improper when he met with me, such as giving insider information. He also had his lawyer there to size me up. The chewing gum on my ass was a great start!

I laughed it off, they sat down, and we began to talk.

I did most of the talking at first. I had a lot of questions about Handy Dan. "Are there any nonrecurring gains?" I asked. "Are there any onetime charges? Are there any onetime gains?"

Bernie was open with me. He knew that I was trying to help Gary, and he had a good feeling for Gary. He also knew that I was thinking about buying stock and wanted to learn about his company. All his answers were the right answers. It was clear this thing was spotless.

And I was starting to get excited. Hell, I was bouncing in my seat; this company was a major steal! And unbelievably, Bernie Marcus owned no stock in it. He had no options. He was strictly a professional hired gun. He was running that company, and running it very well, for just his salary.

"Mr. Marcus," I said, "I don't know what you do with your money. But I am going to buy every share of stock I can in your company, and—pardon my French—when I get done with this fuckin' thing, it ain't gonna be selling at three bucks a share. I would strongly advise you to get back to your office, mortgage your house, and buy Handy Dan stock. Lots of it. Please—it's not going to be here for long."

The three of us shook hands, and there were smiles all around; well, the lawyer almost smiled. I later found out that after I left, Diller turned to Bernie and said, "Bernie, just my gut—you can trust this guy."

And I got in a cab, sticky seat of my pants and all, and headed back to the airport.

———

When I got back to New York, I began buying every damn share of Handy Dan I could lay my hands on. The total capitalization was about 2.2 million shares, of which about 475,000 shares were in the hands of the public: Daylin owned 81 percent of the company, and the public owned 19 percent, which would turn out to be a very significant number.

Over the next few months, as I bought these shares, naturally the price rose, from $3 to $9 to $12. The stock was doing very well. As a matter of fact, some Fridays, if I wanted to have a good weekend, and the stock was selling for $11, I'd go to the trading desk in my office and say, "Bid $12 a share for two hundred shares of stock," and the damn stock would go to $12, and I wouldn't have had to buy a single share. Understand: I'm a little meshuga. But if the rest of the world is sane, I don't mind being meshuga.

I was able to buy just about all of the publicly held shares, with the exception of one block of fifty thousand, which, it turned out, was owned by the Catholic Congregation of the Most Holy Redeemer in Bay Ridge, Brooklyn, or, as they're also known, the Redemptorist fathers. I knew the guy who'd sold it to them, a broker named Jimmy Keene. Made a nice commission.

I phoned the Redemptorists' financial officer, Father Ray McCarthy. "Father," I said, "would you like to sell your Handy Dan stock?" They'd bought at a little over nine, and now it was at almost fifteen; they'd be making a cool quarter million on the sale.

So the priest says to me, "Langone, Langone—is that an Italian name?"

"Yes, Father." I was smiling to myself; this was feeling right.

"Are you Catholic?"

"Yes, Father, I am."

He said, "Well, under the pain of hell, tell me what I should do. Should I sell you this stock, or should I keep it?"

I said, "Father, I'm not messing with God. You keep your stock."

And that's just what he did. Didn't regret it, either.

6.

CHICKEN SALAD AND LEMONADE

You noticed. I originally named my little start-up Invemed because I was so fascinated by the health-care field, and now here I was, in 1976, up to my ass in the home-improvement business. And happy to be there.

Contradictory? Sure! Life is full of left turns, and I've taken quite a few of them, following my nose, which has very often pointed me in the right direction. The truth is I can't help myself: I am a deal junkie. If the phone rings, I'm like the proverbial firehouse dog—off to the races. Who knows who might be calling? More often than not, it's someone who has a very interesting business proposition. Doesn't matter what kind of business it is.

Handy Dan was an extremely interesting business proposition in 1976. And Bernie Marcus, I soon found out, was very much a kindred spirit. Oddly enough, he had started *his* business career in the health-care field, as a Rutgers-trained pharmacist: this was how he came to Daylin in the first place. Then two friends of his, Amnon Barness and Max Candiotty, knowing that Bernie understood merchandise and markups and service, asked him to go take over this little home-improvement start-up. Which, as we've seen, Bernie turned into a big success, despite the failures of the parent corporation.

After I took my position in Handy Dan, Elaine and I became friends with Bernie and his wife, Billi. Every January, I used to rent a house in Palm Springs to play in the Bob Hope golf tournament, and Bernie and I would golf there together. As we walked the course, we would inevitably talk shop, and Handy Dan continued to fascinate me. I began visiting the stores often, in California and Arizona (where they were called Angels Do-It-Yourself Centers), in Denver and Kansas City and Houston.

I used to love to go to store openings: they always seemed so exciting and hopeful. One Thursday in the fall of 1976—grand openings typically happened on Thursdays, with lots of newspaper and TV ads and hoopla, to get momentum going for the weekend—I joined Bernie at the christening of a new Handy Dan in Houston. And Bernie and I were walking around the store when I saw something in the paint department that knocked my socks off.

It was a big display, depicting two cans of paint, one Handy Dan's house brand and the other a competitor, Sherwin-Williams or Glidden. The display showed the percentage of each can that was pigment and the percentage that was thinner: the more pigment, the better the quality. And here was graphic evidence that not only did the house brand have more pigment than the competition, but the prices were better. Oh boy, I thought that was wonderful.

It was a big display, and the new store was a very big store, thirty-five thousand square feet. Every place I went in it, I saw similar displays and signage, showing how this Handy Dan was going to educate and service the customer. Soon I was literally bouncing up and down; I thought this was the greatest thing I'd

My brother Michael and I,
my first Holy Communion,
Memorial Day, 1943

With Cardinal Dolan at my eightieth birthday party, September 2015

My mother (wearing glasses, second from right) with the ladies who worked with her in the Roslyn Heights Elementary School cafeteria, 1951

Allen Mebane and I, with a Salem Leasing truck leased to Unifi, 1976

Elaine and I the night we renamed
the NYU Medical Center, 2008

With my Bucknell pals Dave Parker
and Art Kinney—looking fit

Dad and I, 1957

With Dick Grasso and Jack Welch at my eightieth

Elaine pinning on Bruce's lieutenant's bars the day he became an officer in the United States Marine Corps, Quantico, summer 1985

My son Bruce with my daughter-in-law Nhung and Rocco

With Bob Grossman and Stan Druckenmiller at my eightieth

Goofing around with Kenny and Stephen on Long Island

Elaine and I with Marjorie and Walter Buckley the night we renamed the NYU Medical Center, 2008

Frank Borman and Ira Harris surprising me on my eightieth birthday

With Gary, Steven, and Michael Erlbaum at my seventieth birthday party, 2005

Tommy Teague and I when we bought Salem Leasing, 1975

With Mom and Dad at my graduation from Bucknell, June 1957—boy, were they proud!

With Marty Lipton
and Frank Blake

Me and The Greek,
Speros "Doc" Drelles

With my assistant,
Pam Goldman, at
my granddaughter's
christening

Dad (lower left) and his union buddies posing in their neckties, 1940s. Look at the size of his hands!

Elaine and I with Dr. John Mountain—my second father

My grandparents. His hands
were worked to the bone.

Speaking to my scholarship students at Bucknell

The beautiful Elaine and I on our wedding day, September 15, 1956

With Ross Perot

Mom and Dad on their fiftieth wedding anniversary

Bob Grossman, Tom Murphy, and I

After 9/11—the memorial set up at NYU Medical Center

BUCKNELL UNIVERSITY
GRATEFULLY ACKNOWLEDGES THE GENEROSITY OF
KENNETH G. LANGONE '57 AND ELAINE LANGONE,
WHOSE BENEVOLENCE HAS MADE POSSIBLE
THIS DISPLAY OF BRONZE BUSTS
AND MEDAL OF HONOR CITATIONS.
THIS DISPLAY WILL SERVE
AS A PERMANENT REMINDER OF THE VALOR
AND DEVOTION TO DUTY
OF
U.S. ARMY FIRST LIEUTENANT
DWITE H. SCHAFFNER '15
AND
U.S. MARINE CORPS SECOND LIEUTENANT
GEORGE H. RAMER '50.

The memorial plaque for two Medal of Honor recipients who went to Bucknell

Being interviewed by CNBC outside the Tribeca Grill just after learning of Eliot Spitzer's extracurricular activities

Frank Borman and Derek Smith at my eightieth birthday party

Bernie, Pat, Arthur, and I—handsome devils!

With Mitch Hart, Tom Marquez, Alan Schwartz, and Tom Teague at my annual golf outing

Gary Erlbaum and Steve Levin—happy to see each other at my eightieth

Elaine's parents,
Marion and Dick Abbe

With Elaine, my son Kenny, my daughter-in-law Jessica, her parents, Marge and Frank Abel,
and my granddaughter Sophia at her christening, November 2015

ever seen. "Holy shit," I said to Bernie. "If all the stores we open are like this, we're going to make a fortune!"

Just then Bernie grabs me by the arm. "Don't get carried away," he says, in a low voice.

"What do you mean, don't get carried away?"

He says, "We're very vulnerable."

"To what?"

"I can't tell you."

"What do you mean, you can't tell me?"

"I can't tell you," he says. "We could be in trouble. Even though this store is great, even though all indications are that it's going to do very well, even though our business is doing very well in general, we could really be in serious trouble."

What I didn't know at that moment was that Bernie had a friend in San Diego by the name of Sol Price. Sol Price had run a retail company called FedMart, whose market was military people; the concept was similar to a commissary on a military base: service members and their families could buy everything from appliances and TV sets to groceries at absurdly low prices. Sol had come up with this brilliant concept of buying in bulk and selling at very low profit margins in big, clearly organized stores. He then sold FedMart to a German company called Hugo Mann for a lot of money and started a new chain called Price Club, which was much like FedMart—only with the new idea, similar to what Costco does today, of charging membership fees to supplement his profits.

One day in the mid-1970s, Price invited Bernie down to take a look at how Price Club operated. As they walked through the aisles, Sol said, "You see this store, Bernie? Someday, somebody is going to do this in home improvement, and whoever does it is going to change the face of the industry dramatically. And if that somebody isn't you, you're going to be in trouble."

Bernie never forgot that.

———

It was hate at first sight with me and Sandy Sigoloff.

Daylin's CEO and I met soon after I'd bought up all the Handy Dan stock I could; Sigoloff understandably wanted to know who was this guy he was suddenly in business with. So Bernie arranged a sit-down, and I flew out to the coast.

Sigoloff was a brilliant man, a former nuclear physicist. He was urbane and articulate, slim and beautifully dressed. I would say he had the morals of a skunk—but that would be unfair to the skunk. He had a reputation for meanness. Bernie later told me that Sandy liked to call himself Ming the Merciless, after the villain in the old *Flash Gordon* serials. When Sigoloff fired people, he didn't just let them go; he enjoyed hurting them, economically and emotionally, so they would think twice before ever turning on him.

Bernie Marcus was still working for Sandy Sigoloff, and not only that, but Bernie, together with his close friend and confidant the CFO Arthur Blank, was making a lot of money for Daylin, which was otherwise in very bad shape. In Sigoloff's twisted view of the universe, Bernie's success made him, Sandy, look bad. And so Sigoloff made it his business to torment and push Bernie around at every opportunity. Once, at a directors' meeting, the two of them nearly got into a fistfight over how Handy Dan was being operated. When they went in another room to try to work it out, Sigoloff's argument was that he was the boss and he controlled Bernie's career. Period. Then he demanded that Bernie repeat those exact words back to him. Bernie acknowledged that Sandy was the boss—period. As for the rest, Bernie said, Sandy could go fuck himself.

Sigoloff was a classic bully, but he wasn't my boss. I wondered if the day might come that he would try to bully me. That would be interesting, I thought.

You'll remember how Daylin retained 81 percent of Handy Dan and put the other 19 percent in public hands (which became mostly my hands: I had 16 percent). This was a common corporate strategy among publicly traded companies in the 1970s. The belief was that the market would place a substantially higher value on a subsidiary if it was trading separately from the parent company, thereby lifting the value of the parent company's shares. Daylin executed that strategy with its subsidiary, Handy Dan. (Tax law required the company to retain 80 percent or greater ownership to be able to consolidate the financial statements of the subsidiary with those of the parent.)

My intense buying of Handy Dan shares raised the price of the shares, and in turn, the public's estimation of the company, but who was to say that what had gone up wouldn't come down again? That's exactly what happened in three similar and very prominent cases, right around the same time: Brunswick Corporation, which had sold 19 percent of Sherwood Medical to the public, suddenly bought all the shares back; Trans Union did the same with its water- and sewage-treatment subsidiary Ecodyne; and National Distillers and Chemical Corporation repurchased all its shares in Almaden wines. In each case, the public issue had been underperforming.

But that wasn't the whole story.

A lawyer I knew named Fritz Brace, a fellow board member of Sealy, represented all three of the companies that did these repurchases. And Fritz told me a fascinating thing: underperformance wasn't the only thing that Brunswick, Trans Union, and National Distillers were worried about. What those big companies were also losing sleep over was their fiduciary responsibility to the minority stockholders. If the company made a move that the majority of the

19 percent didn't like, the stockholders might have a right to sue the company to change direction. In other words, the minority stockholders might really have the whip hand.

It sounded backward, but it made perfect sense.

A beautiful thought suddenly dawned on me. I phoned Sandy Sigoloff and said, "Sandy, I need to come see you."

He didn't sound too eager to see me, but out to L.A. I flew.

I strutted into Sigoloff's office, just as arrogant and cocky as I could be, because I hated the son of a bitch. I sat down, looked him in the eye, and said, "Sandy, I think you and I need to have a talk about how we're going to run Handy Dan going forward."

He looked shocked. "What do you mean, *we*?" he said.

"Look, Sandy," I said. "I'm going to be reasonable, but I control a majority of the 19 percent of Handy Dan that's in public hands, and there is a very solid body of legal thought that says your fiduciary duty to me effectively gives me as much control over the company as you have." I gave him chapter and verse about Brunswick, Trans Union, and National Distillers.

He looked like he was about to shit a brick—which of course made my day.

"I'm a minority shareholder," I said. "But if you do something that hurts my interests, you've got a problem. If you want to make any kind of move that affects the company, the only way you can insulate yourself from big legal problems is to come to me beforehand and say, 'Hey, I'd like to do this,' and then to pledge you're going to vote your shares in direct proportion to the way the 19 percent votes.

"I can tell you this, Sandy," I said. "I'm a very reasonable guy, and the likelihood of my saying no is going to be remote as long as you're doing the right thing. But I just think you and I ought to be in constant contact about our plans for the company."

He was a petty tyrant, and all this "we" and "our" stuff was making him crazier every minute. I've run into guys like this my whole career: they think they're the whole ball game, and they're always wrong. No one succeeds alone. Steam was practically coming out of Sigoloff's ears. "This is the stupidest damn arrangement I ever heard of!" he yelled.

I smiled sweetly. "Okay, Sandy," I said. "I just hope it doesn't get to the point where one day we have to test it."

One day about a month later, Sigoloff phoned me. One of his henchmen, a Daylin senior VP by the name of Jeff Chanin, was going to be in New York; Sandy said Chanin wanted to stop by and see me. It didn't sound like a friendly meet and greet to me. I phoned Joe Flom, the merger-and-acquisitions king at Skadden, Arps—he and his firm were known to be scrappy fighters—and said, "Joe, I don't know if I'm going to need a lawyer. But if I do, I want you to have the meanest, toughest SOB you've got standing by."

"I've got just the guy," Joe said. "Bob Pirie."

On the appointed day, this Jeff Chanin walks into my office, takes off his jacket, and immediately starts making threats. He's a lawyer, it turns out, and a thug. He tells me Sigoloff is taking Handy Dan private again, and my investors and I are going to have to sell out—no ifs, ands, or buts. And if we don't agree, Chanin says, he and Sigoloff are going to squeeze us out with something called a cram down, a legal way of forcing out minority stockholders.

I knew exactly what a cram down was. If minority stockholders owned less than 10 percent of a company, the majority stockholder had the right to get an independent appraisal and force the minority owners to sell at that price. But a cram down required that the crammer control 90 percent or more of the stock in question. Sigoloff was bluffing.

"Jeff, cut the crap," I said. "I control enough stock that you can't do any such thing. If you're here to threaten me, you've got the wrong guy. Excuse me."

And I stepped out of the office and phoned Bob Pirie.

Pirie came over in a few minutes. He was a story in himself— one of the smartest, most combative merger-and-acquisitions lawyers ever to walk the earth. Talk about bringing a gun to a knife fight. Suddenly Sigoloff's thug realizes he's in for it, but he gives it his best shot. At this point, Handy Dan was trading at about $8 a share. "You can't sell your stock; you've got no liquidity," Chanin tells me, all fake magnanimous. Meaning, because between Daylin, the Redemptorists, and me, 100 percent of Handy Dan's stock was off the market, no one was promoting it or doing research on it, therefore there was no one to buy. "You can't sell," Chanin repeated. "But we'll pay you $10 a share."

"Make it twelve and you've got a deal," I tell him.

"Forget it!" Chanin yells.

I go to stretch my legs while Chanin and Pirie hash it out. When I come back to my office, Chanin says, "Okay, I'll pay you $12 a share."

"Jeff, that offer is off the table," I tell him. "I said twelve and you said no."

"What?" he said. "Now I'm saying yes."

"Off the table," I said. "I want fourteen a share."

"Forget it," Chanin said. "I'm not paying $14 a share."

"Okay," I said. "Good-bye."

I went to the bathroom, leaving my guy to rough up Sigoloff's guy a little more. Then, after a couple of minutes, Chanin comes into the men's room. "All right, I'll pay you fourteen bucks," he says.

"You don't get it, do you, Jeff?" I say. "I said fourteen, you said no. I want seventeen a share."

Well, a funny thing happened. There were two doors into the

men's room, an outer door that opened in and an inner door that opened the opposite way. And this thug lawyer, in his fury, tried to bang the inner door open, but it didn't go the way he thought it was going to go and he smashed into it and got a bloody nose. Blood all over him. I'm thinking, "This asshole is going to say I beat the shit out of him." Finally, he stormed out and left the building.

About a week later Sigoloff calls. "Let's not mess around," he says. "We'll pay you seventeen a share."

"Sandy, stop," I tell him. "You had a chance and you blew it. I don't want to sell the stock. It's all over."

You could've heard his phone slam down from three thousand miles away.

In the midst of all this drama I was still calling on all my institutional clients, including Doc Drelles at Pittsburgh National, who'd been so helpful when Invemed was in trouble. Underneath his prickly shell Doc was a generous guy, but that didn't make him one bit less arrogant or cantankerous. Beating up on brokers, including me, was still his blood sport, and he still had only one chair in his office—his.

Then one day in the spring of 1977 I walked in to find another chair next to Doc's, with someone sitting in it.

The someone was a big, goofy-looking kid, maybe 23, 24 years old, with a huge mushroom of hair on top of his head. He looked like a wiseass to me, and a minute later I found out that's exactly what he was. I was only a few words into my pitch for General Motors, the stock I was pitching to Drelles that day, when Doc, in his usual fashion, started busting my chops about it—"Why General Motors? Why not Ford?"—and then this kid who's working for him picks up the chorus, giving me the same kind of crap: "What's wrong with Chrysler?" It was like a tennis match: they had the racquets, and I was the ball! The two of them were working me over, back and forth, and grinning while they were doing it.

I took it for a few minutes, then I said, "Greek, I can take this for just a little while longer, then I'll tell you what I'm going to do—I'm going to come over there and slap the shit out of you, and then I'm going to slap the shit out of this punk kid, then I'm walking out of here."

They started laughing. And that day was the beginning of my one-of-a-kind friendship with that punk kid with the mushroom haircut, who turned out to be a financial wizard named Stanley Druckenmiller.

———

Steve Sato and his team had turned IVAC into a big success, but management, it became more and more apparent, wasn't Steve's strength. He had a lot of very talented people working under him, but for some reason he kept moving them aside. I soon came to feel that he had a deeply suspicious, almost paranoid, streak: he felt his subordinates were out to undercut him. This wasn't doing IVAC any good, and in 1976 I'd decided to turn another page and sell the company. Steve had been a good steward up to a point, but he wasn't the whole package, so we had to do something. Capitalism can be brutal that way.

We ended up selling IVAC to Eli Lilly; Lilly did very well on the deal, and so did I. I was going from a highly speculative little company to a big company that paid dividends on its stock, and I wound up with a ton of Lilly stock, with the value of the Lilly shares substantially greater than that of the IVAC shares. For the first time in my life, I was a millionaire (though I'd owned a lot of shares in all the deals I'd done at Pressprich, partners weren't allowed to sell without the consent of the other partners: my holdings there were illiquid). Invemed, which had been struggling, was on firmer ground.

The closing was November 30, 1977, in San Diego. Elaine was

out there with me, and after the closing we drove up to L.A. That night, Bernie Marcus invited us to have dinner with him and his wife, Billi, at their home in Encino. Billi made us a nice Chinese meal, and while Elaine and Billi were cleaning the kitchen up after dinner, Bernie said, "Come on in the living room; I want to talk to you."

We went into the living room. Bernie lowered his voice. "Do me a favor, will you?" he said. "Get Sigoloff off my back. Sell him the stock."

"Are you out of your damn mind?" I said, though I put it in slightly more picturesque terms. "What the hell do you mean?"

I looked at Bernie for a moment. I could tell he was hurting. He was between a rock and a hard place, with that rat pressuring him on one side and me on the other, supporting him but hating Sigoloff with every fiber of my being.

"You know what's going to happen once I'm out?" I asked my friend. "He's going to fire you. He hates you, Bernie. The only thing he's got of any value in that mess of a company is Handy Dan, and he can't take credit for it, because you're there, and he ain't going to screw with you as long as I'm here."

Bernie looked me in the eye. "Please, Kenny," he said. "Please. I can deal with the guy. Believe me, it's going to be better for me."

"Listen, Bernie," I said. "It's no sweat off my back. I just sold a company; I've got a ton of Lilly stock. I'm in hog heaven. If you want me to sell, I'll sell. But personally, I think you're out of your fuckin' mind."

Elaine and Billi were still in the kitchen talking, so Bernie and I went into his bedroom and he called up Sigoloff's other lawyer, a guy by the name of Ed Kaufman, a partner at Irell & Manella, a big L.A. firm. I'm only hearing Bernie's side of the conversation. "I've got Langone here at my home, and I've got him persuaded to sell you the stock," Bernie says. He listens a moment, then he cups his hand over the phone. "How much do you want?" he asks.

"I'm going to make them an offer," I told him. "If they don't want it, that's the end of it, and let's drop it. If they want it, that's the price."

"What's the price?" Bernie asked.

"Bernie, I want twenty-five fifty a share," I said.

"Why the odd number?"

"Because it has to look like we had some real hard bargaining here."

Bernie told Kaufman the number. The lawyer said he'd call right back.

The phone rang five minutes later. "Have that son of a bitch in my office at ten tomorrow morning so we can get all the papers signed," Kaufman told Bernie.

The next morning, Bernie picks me up at the Century Plaza Hotel and we drive down Avenue of the Stars to Irell & Manella's offices. We park in the garage below the building, we get out of the car, and we're looking at each other over the car roof. "Bernie," I said, "I'm going up there and I'm signing your damn death warrant. You understand that?"

"You're wrong, they need me," Bernie said. "They don't know the business. Trust me, Kenny, this is the best thing for me."

"Bernie, you don't own any stock!"

"I know, I know. But they're going to make it right."

I shrugged. "Okay."

We went upstairs and I signed about a hundred legal papers, making over all my Handy Dan stock to Sandy Sigoloff at $25.50 a share. Not a bad return on investment from three bucks a share!

That was December 1, 1977.

On Saturday, April 15, 1978, I got home from a business trip late in the afternoon, and my middle son, Bruce—he was fifteen at the time—told me that a Mr. Marcus had been calling for me all day. I had two soundalike Marcuses in my life, Bernie Marcus and Tom Marquez, of EDS, the first guy Ross Perot had hired for his new company. "Did he say where he was calling from?" I asked Bruce.

"Yeah, California."

I picked up the phone and called Bernie Marcus. "Let me guess—you've been fired," I said.

"Is it in the papers? Is it in the papers?" Bernie asked.

"No," I told him.

"Then how'd you know?"

"Bernie, you've been calling here all day. What else am I supposed to think?"

Understandably, Bernie was very upset. Not only had Sigoloff fired him, but he'd also shit-canned Arthur Blank and Ron Brill, Handy Dan's director of internal audit. A regular Friday Night Massacre. "And he wants to put me in jail," Bernie said.

"What? What did you do?"

"We had a labor-law violation," Bernie said. He explained. San Jose was (and still is) a big union town, a very liberal city with a big General Motors assembly plant and heavy UAW representation, and there was an effort afoot to unionize the two San Jose Handy Dan stores. One of those stores was going to have a union-representation election, and a group of employees went to Bernie and Arthur Blank and said they wanted to decertify out of the union. And Bernie and Arthur transferred to San Jose a number of employees from Phoenix who they knew would vote against the union. It was ballot-box stuffing, for sure—unfair, maybe; but illegal?

Sigoloff clearly thought he had a lever in his battle to seize total and final control of Handy Dan.

"You don't go to jail for that," I told Bernie.

"I hope so. But Sandy's pressing the U.S. attorney for the Northern District of California to bring charges against me."

Ming the Merciless strikes again.

"How soon can you get to New York?" I asked Bernie. "I want to talk to you. Can you get in here tonight?" It was about 1:00 p.m. L.A. time. I said, "I'll tell you what I'll do. I'll meet you in the Waldorf Astoria tomorrow morning, at Peacock Alley for breakfast at 9:30. I've got to go to Mass out here, and then I'll drive in."

Bernie said he would get on a plane.

"By the way," I said, "do you know a good labor lawyer? I want to get to the bottom of this union *mishegoss*."

"I've got a great labor lawyer. He lives in Jersey."

"Well, call him up and see if he can make it."

We meet the next morning at the Waldorf, Bernie, his labor lawyer—Jerry Glassman is his name—and me. Bernie looks like shit. It's only been forty-eight hours since he was fired. Owned no stock. Got no severance. No health care. Nothing. And Ming the Merciless telling him, "I'm going to put you in jail."

"Okay, I've got a simple question," I say to Glassman. "Is Bernie going to jail?"

"No, of course not," Glassman says. "This is a garden-variety violation of NLRB rules."

"He's not going to jail?" I say.

"He's not going to jail. At worst the union is automatically certified as winner of the election, and all the employees become union members."

"Then, pal," I say to Bernie, "I think you got hit in the ass with a golden horseshoe."

"What do you mean, Kenny? I'm out of work. I'm broke!"

"Bernie, cool it. Cool it. We're going to start a company."

"Are you crazy?" Bernie said.

"No," I said. "Remember Houston? Remember when you told

me that there was something out there that if somebody did it, it's going to wipe out the industry? You were scared that if someone outside Handy Dan did it, you'd be sunk. Now you're the one outside Handy Dan!"

He looked at me, still miserable. "Kenny, I have *no money*."

"Don't worry about it," I said. "I'll come up with the money."

———

For a brilliant nuclear physicist, Sandy Sigoloff was a pretty dumb guy. Because when it came to Handy Dan, his most valuable holding, Sigoloff just had no clue. Bernie Marcus knew, and I knew, that the home-improvement chain Bernie had turned into a major success had huge vulnerabilities under the surface. There were just too many stores, too set in their old ways, to switch over to the Price Club model. Handy Dan's profit margins were okay, but they could have been better. The stores' service levels were generally subpar or nonexistent. And Handy Dan's product selections were minimal at best. Bernie and I knew that customers are much more likely to buy something if they feel they have choices.

And meanwhile, believe it or not, Sigoloff had started to put himself into Handy Dan's advertising, strutting across TV screens and magazine ads like some second coming of Lee Iacocca or Frank Perdue. It was a total vanity exercise, though, as we've seen, Sigoloff's vanity knew no bounds. He just assumed that thanks to his personal fabulousness, people would flock to his home-improvement chain and Handy Dan would keep minting money indefinitely, when in reality it was ripe for the plucking.

I had a plan for Sandy Sigoloff. Was it personal? Sure it was. He had done dirt to my good friend and tried to squeeze me. Yes, I had come out of the business in fine fettle, but Bernie was still hurting badly, and Sigoloff's nonstop victory dance galled me, and not just because it was in bad taste.

After he took back Handy Dan, I started buying up Daylin stock, because I knew where the real value of the company was. And I had a powerful friend in Peter Grace, the chairman of W. R. Grace and Company, which in the late 1970s and early 1980s was buying everything in sight. There was a famous story about Peter Grace: One late night in Southern California, he walked into a diner called Coco's Bakery. A total greasy spoon, but something about it appealed to him. Grace says to the waitress, "I want to see the owner." Some guy comes out with a sailor's cap on, a filthy apron. "I'm the owner," he says. "What do you want?"

Peter goes, "I want to buy your restaurant."

"It's not for sale."

"It is for sale; I'm buying it." And he bought it and opened up a chain of Coco's that eventually included 145 locations. Made a good deal of money.

I was at a black-tie-and-tails Knights of Malta dinner at the Waldorf Astoria in 1979, and I spotted Peter Grace. I went up to him and said, "Mr. Grace, you ought to look at the Daylin Corporation. Daylin itself isn't worth doodley-squat. But it's got Handy Dan, which is worth a lot."

I eventually persuaded Peter Grace to do an unfriendly takeover of Daylin. In the meantime, I bought up a crapload of Daylin stock. Grace had a business-development guy named Bill Reilly, and in early 1980 Reilly paid a call on Sandy Sigoloff. As Reilly is walking into Sigoloff's office, Sigoloff's phone rings. Sigoloff picks it up. Reilly's standing right there. The guy on the phone says to Sigoloff, "W. R. Grace just announced they're doing an unfriendly takeover of your company."

Sigoloff puts his phone down and says, "I know why you're here." Somebody had jumped the gun. He says, "You're going to do an unfriendly deal on me." Reilly said, "That's right." They negotiated the deal, and Sigoloff was gone. So I made money twice on that company.

I said publicly a couple of times, "Every time I get near Sandy, I do nothing but make money. I hope he does something else where I can go after him."

Bernie's revolutionary idea for a new chain of home-improvement stores sounded great—on paper. His vision was of enormous, high-ceilinged warehouse spaces, fifty-five thousand to seventy-five thousand square feet (by comparison, the biggest Handy Dan store was thirty-five thousand square feet), featuring a broad spectrum of steeply discounted products. The discounts would be possible because Bernie and Arthur planned to buy directly from manufacturers—unlike Handy Dan, which purchased its limited selection of merchandise, the bestsellers in every category, from middlemen and warehouses.

In Bernie and Arthur's vision, the new stores' huge size, wide inventory, and low prices would produce $7 million to $9 million in annual sales per store (Handy Dan stores averaged $3 million in sales per annum), at gross profit margins of 29 to 31 percent (the industry standard was 42 to 47 percent). Sheer sales volume would compensate for the lower profit margins.

And not just volume. The salespeople in the new stores wouldn't only be there to operate cash registers. They would be highly trained in home repair and home improvement, ready to answer all questions and guide customers through any project, small or large.

It all sounded great on paper. I believed in it wholeheartedly. All Bernie and Arthur needed, I figured, was a year: a year to study America and figure out where the first stores should be opened and how close to the ideal the stores could come. I calculated that the initial stage would take a couple million dollars in venture capital—to pay Bernie and Arthur's salaries and fringe benefits and enable them to come up with a detailed business plan.

The problem, in May 1978, was that the business climate was lousy. Jimmy Carter was president, and national confidence was sagging. Interest rates were climbing; energy prices and inflation were out of control. Not the best moment to drum up confidence in a daring new venture. I needed a contrarian with a couple million dollars lying around.

Who else but Ross Perot?

I took Bernie down to EDS's Dallas headquarters to meet Ross, and the initial meeting went well. I set the table, telling the story of how Bernie had built Handy Dan into a great company, only to be kicked to the curb by Sandy Sigoloff. Ross sat there behind his big desk, all ears.

Then it was Bernie's turn to talk. And to his credit, as impressed as he was by Ross Perot's success and commanding presence, and as much as he wanted Perot's help, he spoke straight from the shoulder. "Ross," he said, "I'm not interested in doing anything with you unless I know that I'm going to deal directly with you. I don't want to deal through intermediaries, and I will not become part of your existing organization. If I have a problem, I will call you, and you and I will agree on how we proceed. I'm not going to be a captain or a lieutenant; I'm not interested in that nonsense. If we get caught up in corporate crap, I won't be part of it."

But straight from the shoulder was right up Perot's alley. "I like straightforward people," he said. "No, I wouldn't put anybody between us; you have my word."

Everything seemed to be moving along smoothly. We set a second meeting, to explore the start-up in greater depth and to introduce Arthur to Ross.

A fourth guy also showed up at that next meeting, a retired CFO of Texas Instruments named Bryan Smith who was Perot's financial adviser. The second we all shook hands and sat down, Perot piped up: "Okay, what's the deal? What's the deal?"

I said, "Here's the deal. You're going to give us $2 million, and we're going to take the $2 million and use it to study America—to see where we can make our concept work. And if for whatever reason we can't bring it to fruition after a year, you get whatever's left of the two million, and these guys go out and find a job."

That seemed okay with Ross. We laid out the basic ownership arrangement if the new company got up and running: the deal was going to be 70 percent for Perot, 25 percent for Bernie, Arthur, and their team, and 5 percent for Invemed. We agreed that until we went public, if Bernie and Arthur wanted to bring people in to work for the company, their stock would come out of Marcus and Blank's 25 percent. It was—potentially, anyway—a very generous deal for Bernie and Arthur: in typical venture-capital deals, the founders get just 10 percent of the company.

So far, so good. Except for Bryan Smith, who from the jump was the skeptic in the room. He was a very nuts-and-bolts guy who simply didn't believe that—no matter how great the new stores' service and product selection and sales volume—Bernie and Arthur could make a go of it on a 27½ percent gross margin (markup), when the industry standard was 44 percent. No matter how hard I insisted that service and selection and store size were certain to create big sales volumes, Bryan Smith kept shaking his head.

And there was another little detail. As proof of how parsimonious Bernie and Arthur were going to be with Ross's two million, I told Perot that instead of getting new company cars, Marcus and Blank would just move the car leases they'd had with Handy Dan over to the new company.

"Arthur, what kind of car do you have?" Ross asked. I smiled.

Now Perot would get to see what economical guys he was dealing with.

Arthur said he had a 1972 Pontiac. Great. "Bernie?" Perot said.

Bernie said he had a 1973 Cadillac, a five-year-old car with over 100,000 miles on it. But suddenly Perot's eyebrows shot up. "Cadillac? Cadillac?" he said. "My guys drive Chevrolets! They don't drive Cadillacs!"

Bernie turned to me. "Can we talk?" he said.

"Sure." I said. "Ross, can we use your conference room?"

Bernie, Arthur, and I went into the conference room and closed the door. Bernie was whispering anyway. "Kenny," he said. "This guy's going to own 70 percent of our company, and he's busting my chops about an old Cadillac? What the hell else is he going to drive me nuts about? Let's get out of here."

I looked at Bernie. "Are you nuts?" I said. "This guy's about to give you two million bucks!"

But he was dead serious. "I don't think I want to have this guy as my controlling shareholder," Bernie said. "In fact, I'd rather starve to death than have this guy as a partner."

I took a deep breath. Back we went into Ross's office, where I tried to put the most positive spin possible on what had just happened. "Look, Ross," I said. "We're all thinking about where we are. Bryan's clearly got reservations about the deal. Why don't we all think this over for a couple of weeks, and we'll come back and see where we are."

"Okay," Ross said. "If you want to come back, come back."

We knew we wouldn't be coming back. As we waited for the elevator outside Perot's office, Arthur was despondent. "Oh my God, what are we going to do, what are we going to do?" he said. "We haven't got any money!"

"Arthur, here's what we're going to do," I said. "I'm going to go out and raise the two million bucks. You guys are going to get

45 percent instead of 25; the investors are going to get 50, and I'll get 5."

Arthur looked amazed. "Hell, that's a much better deal than we would've had with Perot," he said.

"Yes, Arthur," I said. "In the retail business, when you can't sell something, you guys mark it down. In my business, when you can't sell something, you mark it up."

———————

So I went back to New York and started raising the money. The first people I approached were the individuals who'd held the big block of Handy Dan stock that I'd sold back to Sandy Sigoloff at $25.50 a share. Those people had done very well indeed on their initial investment. I went to them and said, "Look. You had a good experience with Handy Dan; now we're starting a company that's going to be much, much better."

My initial plan was to sell forty units at $50,000 apiece. Each unit would consist of preferred stock and warrants to buy common stock. I also approached my old friend Frank Borman. Frank was now an executive vice president and board member at Eastern Air Lines (he would become CEO the following year): he had a decent salary, but no ownership at all. When I told him I wanted him to put fifty grand in my new start-up, he told me he'd have to borrow the money. I told him to beg, borrow, or steal it right away; that was how strongly I felt about this thing.

Frank was on the board of Southeast Bank, down in Miami, and when he went to them for a loan, the most they would part with was $25,000. I said, "Fine, Frank, I just split the units two for one, and now you've got a $25,000 unit."

That half unit, like the others I worked so hard to sell, eventually became worth many millions of dollars. Mitch Hart, too, was one of our first investors and would sit on our board from the beginning. And I put in $100,000 myself; I'd made a pretty good buck selling my own Handy Dan shares.

I did the whole deal piecemeal like that, and it was ass-busting work. I particularly remember two guys I'd persuaded to put up fifty thousand apiece, Artie Long and John Cornwell, who owned a New York proxy firm called D. F. King & Company. On the day we were going to close, they called me up, separately, and said they could only do twenty-five each.

"Oh shit," I said to myself, because the whole deal was predicated on raising the full two million. So I called two other guys, the real-estate developer Fred DeMatteis and Tom Marquez of EDS. Both were already in for $50,000 apiece. "Look," I said. "Do me a favor. Will you take another twenty-five each?" They said yes, and I had my financing.

———

One day that summer Bernie called me from California and said, "Kenny, you gotta come out here. I've got somebody I want you to meet and something you have to see."

"Give me a hint, Bernie," I said. "What is it, and who is it?"

"Somebody that's doing what we're trying to do," he said. "I mean, *exactly* what we're trying to do."

I flew out. Bernie picked me up at LAX, and we drove down to Lakewood, near the Long Beach Airport. The guy he wanted me to meet was named Pat Farrah, he told me, and what he wanted me to see was Farrah's tremendous (130,000 square feet) store, Homeco. There it was, shimmering in the sunlight, a huge warehouse at the end of a giant parking lot. We parked and went inside.

The first thing I saw when we walked in was a mountain of cans of Coca-Cola, maybe twenty feet high. It was an amazing sight, but a puzzling one. I turned to Bernie and said, "Is this a home center, or is he selling Coca-Cola?"

Bernie smiled. "No, no," he said. "He's selling *brands*."

Well, that was pretty interesting. The first thing somebody sees when they walk into this store is this drop-dead display of one of the most popular brands in the world. It's welcoming, it's appetizing, and it's lifting the image of this store by association with a great brand.

The inside of this gargantuan warehouse was home-improvement heaven. Merchandise stacked to the ceiling. Lumber sold right in the store. Forklifts shuttling pallets of goods around. The sales associates wore tennis shoes, khaki shorts, and brown T-shirts with HOMECO on the back and a silhouette of a house on the front, and they *ran* to greet each and every customer and ask what they were looking for. You could see by the smiles on the customers' faces that it was a sales strategy that was working like gangbusters.

The store was also Farrah's headquarters. Bernie and I went up to the mezzanine level and down a long walkway that led to the executive offices. Lined up along the walkway were blue plastic milk boxes full of papers, into which a young woman carrying a big stack of papers was depositing more papers, one by one, very rapidly. I was struck by how fast she was moving: she wasn't even looking at each piece of paper before she plopped it in this box or that.

"Excuse me," I said. "I'm curious: Could you tell me what you're doing?"

"Oh, these are the invoices from the vendors," she said. "I'm filing them."

"How do you know where to put what?" I asked.

"Oh, I just stick them wherever there's room," she told me.

"Oh boy, this guy's in trouble," I said to Bernie.

"I know," he said.

We walked into the offices and there was Pat Farrah, a force of nature, giving off so much energy that he was practically bouncing off the walls. A big, heavy Irishman with an Afro haircut, blue leisure suit, shirt unbuttoned to the navel, and gold chains hanging all over his chest. He was captivating, he was exciting, he was crazy. Bouncing up and down. Bursting with ideas that bubbled out of his mouth in no particular order.

As his store demonstrated, the guy was a retail genius. As his filing system demonstrated, he was no businessman. He didn't know a profit margin from a paint can. It turned out that Homeco was bringing in piles of cash, but it owed mountains to its vendors, who rarely if ever got paid. Within six months, Pat Farrah filed for business and personal bankruptcy.

And Bernie said to me, "We've got to get this guy; we've got to."

"I agree," I said. It clearly wasn't his financial acumen we wanted him for; it was his marketing and merchandising brilliance.

So Bernie and I romanced Pat, and Pat agreed to come on board and bring his head full of ideas with him. We had a team.

———

In June 1979, we had our first four stores ready to open—all in Atlanta—and we needed more money. Bernie had a buddy at Security Pacific Bank in L.A., the guy who had been the banker for Handy Dan: Rip Fleming was his name. Bernie went to see Rip, and Rip turned him down. But finally, after Bernie showed him a business plan on paper, Fleming said, "I can get you a $3 million line, but I need collateral."

Collateral, collateral . . . One afternoon Bernie and Arthur and I were sitting at the bar in the Century Plaza Hotel, and I was doodling on a cocktail napkin while they told me their troubles. Suddenly I wrote down a couple of figures and said, "Here's what we're going to do."

My idea was to return to the original investors once more and have them go to their respective banks and get letters of credit. If an investor had originally put up $50,000, for example, he would put up a letter of credit for that same amount, which would give him a warrant to buy $50,000 of stock in the company at a later date. If the loan went bad, the investor would have to pay Security Pacific $50,000.

But the loan wouldn't go bad; I knew it, and my complete confidence in our start-up was what convinced the investors to do it.

Now all our start-up needed was a name.

The hunt didn't begin auspiciously. The first idea on the table was "MB's Warehouse," which nobody liked. Then Bernie and Arthur hired a Toronto consultant who came up with a real doozy: "Bad Bernie's Buildall." It wasn't just a name; it was a whole marketing concept: ads for the stores would feature a cartoon Bernie behind bars, in a striped prison uniform, saying, "They locked me up because I sold at such low prices!"

Rip Fleming, the banker, nixed that one. Thank God.

One night Elaine and I were having dinner in New York with our good friends (and original investors) Marjorie and Walter Buckley, and I was complaining to them about the difficulty of coming up with a name for our newborn chain of home-improvement stores. They listened and sympathized. I could tell that Marjorie, who's very gifted verbally and in many other ways, was thinking deeply about the question. The Buckleys live in Bethlehem, Pennsylvania, and they drove back home that night.

The next morning Walter called me up and said, "We were driving back into Bethlehem, and we saw a restaurant built in an old train station; it was called the Main Street Depot. And Marjorie said to me, 'Why don't they call their stores the Home Depot?'

"How about that?" Walter said.

How about that, indeed.

The Home Depot didn't exactly get off to a flying start. At first we had so little cash that we could only afford to open two of the four stores we'd planned to open, and we had nowhere near enough stock to fill those two stores. One of our suppliers, the faucet manufacturer Price Pfister, gave us an open credit line, but the other vendors weren't so generous. Miles of empty shelves were not going to inspire customer confidence. Then Pat Farrah came up with a genius idea: he went to the vendors and asked them for boxes—just boxes, with the product label on the outside and nothing inside—to fill our empty shelves. Customers would walk in and see what appeared to be prosperous stores, packed with merchandise.

And at first Bernie was so worried about attracting customers that he used to shuttle back and forth between the two stores, standing outside the entrances and handing out dollar bills to anyone who'd go in.

After those hiccups in the opening year, 1979, our two Atlanta stores started to do so well that we were able to open the other two locations, which also did very well. With four stores now running in the black, we decided to go public in September 1981. It was time to expand beyond Georgia. We had our eye on Florida. And opening more stores meant that we needed more money.

I went to the typical players, Drexel and Merrill Lynch and Bear Stearns. Drexel turned me down out of hand. I had a relationship with Bear Stearns, but they were hesitant. They wouldn't get off the dime until I told them—it was pretty much true—that Merrill Lynch was interested. (Merrill Lynch would eventually bail.) I finally got Bear Stearns to agree to underwrite a $6 million equity offering. Half of the money would redeem the initial investors' preferred stock; the other half would go into Home Depot's business operations.

But it was a dicey moment. The economy was in a recession; the market was in the crapper. Ronald Reagan had just become president, but Reaganomics hadn't yet worked its magic. Inflation was still through the roof; Paul Volcker and the Fed were pushing interest rates higher. And the week before the deal was set to get done, Bear Stearns told me it only had orders for $3 million of the $6 million. We simply couldn't raise enough money to redeem the preferred shares.

I didn't have a cocktail napkin this time, but I did have another idea. I went back to the original group one more time. "Look," I said. "We've got a simple decision here. If we don't get this underwriting done, we're not going to have the money we need going forward. So either we're going to have to put up more money, or there isn't going to be any more Home Depot."

Now nobody wanted to put up any more cash. I'd expected that. My idea was to, in effect, create cash for the IPO by having the investors convert their preferred shares into common stock in the shares that were going public. Instead of taking cash for their preferred shares, they were putting it back into the company. I don't have to tell you they never regretted their decision.

And Bear Stearns was now able to sell the IPO for the complete $6 million.

If there's anything I would take a bow for throughout this whole process, it would be this: never giving up, and thinking creatively, instead of just reactively, when the chips were down. It's a style I recommend highly. You get to enjoy lemonade instead of the lemons God gives you, and chicken salad instead of the much less tasty alternative.

7.

GUY WALKS INTO MY OFFICE . . .

By 1978, my good friend (and original Invemed investment-banking client) Gary Erlbaum had concluded that his Philadelphia-area home-improvement chain, Panelrama, did not have a bright future. The economy stank at the time; it looked as if there was no way out.

"Gary," I told him, "It's over. What we've got to do is get as much money as we can get for your business and go look for something to invest it in." Gary agreed. I helped him liquidate the company, and we ended up getting about a million and a half bucks for it.

One day not long after that, I got a call from my friend Joe DiMartino, who was one of the highest-ranking executives at the Dreyfus Corporation. A broker he knew at Shearson (then Shearson Hayden Stone) had sent him a client to ask about getting investors for an invention of his, Joe told me, and he didn't know what the hell the guy was talking about. "Will you meet with him?" he asked.

"Sure I'll meet him, Joe," I said. "Send him up."

The guy's name was Gordon Gould. Gould walks into my office, and I can't believe what I'm seeing; he looks like a mad scientist. Wild hair. Disheveled clothing. Wires hanging out of his pockets. Pocket protector with about forty pencils in it. He's invented an important device, he tells me, and though the government has given him a patent on one part of the technology, he can't afford to fight in court for the rest. A guy named Eugene Lang, who started something called the I Have a Dream Foundation, has given him some money and promised to help him, Gould says, but Lang has done nothing for him. Meanwhile, dozens of companies are using Gould's ideas, ripping him off right and left.

"And what did you invent?" I asked.

"I invented the laser," he said.

"No shit," I said. "You've got the same problem I have."

"What are you talking about?" he asked.

"Well, I invented the wheel, and they won't give me a patent either," I said.

"No, no!" Gould said. "There's a patent-law firm in New Jersey that's done all the work; they'll tell you."

It was so bizarre that I had to follow up on it. And the patent lawyers in Jersey told me that indeed this guy had invented the optically pumped and gas-discharged lasers (the former powered by light, the latter by an electric discharge in a gas medium). He'd first applied for the patents in the late 1950s, and he was lucky he didn't get them: there weren't any practical uses for lasers at that point, and the patents would have expired before Gould could have made any money on them. Talk about being ahead of the times.

I made some more calls; then I said to myself, "Son of a bitch, you know what? There may be a business here if we can get the rest of those patents."

I told Gary Erlbaum about it, and he was interested. So we took the proceeds from the Panelrama liquidation and formed a

holding company called Patlex, the name stood for patent litiga-
tion. The plan was to take the assets that were in the business to
fund the exploitation of Gould's patent and the acquisition of additional patents. It was a real pie-in-the-sky scheme, but I thought
it was just crazy enough to work.

I couldn't do the deal myself, because I owned too large a
percentage of the company, and I knew no established investment
bank would go for it. Instead, I found a fellow named J. Morton
Davis who ran a firm called D. H. Blair, which underwrote companies of a highly speculative nature. And Mort Davis went for it; he
was excited about getting me, Ross Perot's banker, involved. Davis
did a financing for us, but the way he sold this deal into the market
was so bad that I had to go back in the next day and buy all the
stock back for my clients.

A few years pass while we litigate the patents; now it's the mid-
1980s. Then, in 1986, we won two important court battles, and by
the end of 1987 we held the patent rights on the vast majority of
lasers manufactured in the United States. Soon we were signing
licensing agreements with the likes of Kodak, Chrysler, Eveready,
and Union Carbide.

We had a two-pronged plan of attack. The first part was to get
a very legitimate guy to be the public face of Patlex. Conveniently,
right around this time Frank Borman was retiring from Eastern
Air Lines. I went to him and said, "Frank, if you'll agree to take
charge of this company, you can headquarter it anywhere you
want in America." And Frank wanted to live in Las Cruces, New
Mexico, so we gave him the company with the patents in it, and
Patlex continued signing annual licensing deals right and left.

The second part of the plan was to do these deals at very low
prices—fifty, sixty thousand bucks a pop, per annum. Because if
you charged these big companies a lot, they might challenge the
patents. They had deep pockets and legal resources; they might be

able to get some court somewhere to say, "We don't give a shit what the Patent Office says; we're disallowing the patent."

But that never happened, because we were so very reasonable. And we went out and got between two and three hundred licensees—bringing in a total of $10 or $11 million a year for Patlex. It was great cash flow. Gordon Gould had a piece; Gene Lang, who had done squat, had a piece. Gary Erlbaum had a piece, and so did I.

That wasn't the end of it.

A couple of years later, I got a call from a guy who'd started an automobile finance company for subprime borrowers—people with bad credit. Was I interested in buying the company? I was interested. We bought the business, changed its name to AutoFinance Group, and folded AutoFinance Group into Patlex.

We brought in a guy from Mercedes-Benz Credit, Al Steinhaus, to run AutoFinance, and he built it into a solid business. We were one of the first subprime finance companies, and we knew how to do it: we were very careful about vetting the borrowers and collecting payments. We took the loans to Wall Street, and Wall Street sold bonds against the loans—another income stream. It was a first-class operation, and we made a lot of money.

Success attracts attention. In 1995, Bob Gillespie, the president and CEO of KeyCorp in Cleveland, got in touch with me and said he was interested in buying AutoFinance. Great. I told him what we wanted for the company, and Gillespie told me what he was offering. We were a buck and a half apart, and neither of us would budge.

So I went to Cleveland to meet with Bob Gillespie. Over dinner he told me that the banking laws wouldn't allow KeyCorp to keep the patent laser business. "Wait a minute," I said. "I've got an idea. You keep the automobile subprime business, but you give us back the patents for the lasers, and I'll give each of our shareholders their proportionate share in it. We'll set up a new company, and we'll put the patents in."

Which is exactly what we did. We sold AutoFinance to Gillespie for $600 million—it was a stock deal; we got paid in KeyCorp shares—and held on to the patent laser business. Now we're right back where we started from before we went into the automobile finance business. So I'm going hunting for something to do with Patlex, because I've got this cash flow from the licenses, but it's not going to last forever: the patents are going to expire in 2003. And suddenly applications for lasers are going through the roof. Every place you look, lasers are being used: laser pointers, CD and DVD players, surgery, industrial cutting, weapons systems.

Remember I talked about left turns? Following my nose?

Bear with me now.

You'll recall Jack Hight, the co-founder of EDS and the guy who introduced me to Ross Perot. Jack came to see me one day and said, "I've got a company in Florida called Database Technologies; they use clusters of PCs to mine motor-vehicle registrations, census data, arrest records, and more. A cop having this technology in his car, if he's chasing a guy who's speeding, can input the guy's license plate number and find out everything about him: whose car it is, where the guy lives, whether he's got a gun license; you name it. He's got all the information before he pulls him over."

Database Technologies had been founded by a guy named Hank Asher. I did some due diligence on Asher and found out he was a pretty dicey character: apparently, he'd been engaged in drug running in the Caribbean in the early 1980s, then joined forces with the DEA to hunt down drug runners. He was suspected of playing both ends against the middle.

I phoned Hight. "Jack," I said, "this guy Asher—I think he's a bad guy."

"I know, I know," Jack said. "But his technology is amazing. Just meet with him."

Gary Erlbaum and I went down to Florida and met with Hank Asher. He was as advertised, and then some—slick, shady, the whole nine yards. But his technology really was amazing. We made a deal to merge Database Technologies with Patlex, under the Database Technologies name, and we listed the company on the New York Stock Exchange. And in 1999 we threw Hank Asher out.

In 2000, I got a call from a fellow named Derek Smith who was running a data-aggregation company called ChoicePoint and was interested in buying Database Technologies. ChoicePoint used to be—ready for it?—none other than Retail Credit Company, the very outfit that fired me in 1957 for making up background reports on people who were applying for insurance or seeking jobs. And forty-three years later, in 2000, we sold Database Technologies to Derek Smith in return for a 30 percent ownership stake in ChoicePoint. Eight years after that, in the fall of 2008, Reed Elsevier would buy ChoicePoint for $4.3 billion, and all the former shareholders of Database Technologies who'd been wise enough to hold on to their ChoicePoint stock would reap a substantial windfall from that deal. Invemed and I together would get $100 million, cash.

In business, sometimes what goes around really does come around.

———

A case in point. Remember the goofy kid with the mushroom haircut who helped Doc Drelles bust my chops back at Pittsburgh National Bank? Stanley Druckenmiller was just a management trainee back in 1977, but he was smart as a whip, and he got even smarter by studying at Doc's feet. He became head of investment research at Pittsburgh National, and soon I was calling on him as well as on Doc. We became close friends: years later he would even ask Elaine and me to be godparents to his youngest daughter, Tess. Stanley started a hedge fund called Priority while he was at the bank, then he left in 1981 to start his own money-management firm, Duquesne Capital, with less than a million dollars in assets. He was successful right away.

In the summer of 1985, Stanley called me and said he wanted to talk. He came to town and we had breakfast at the Waldorf-Astoria. He told me that Howard Stein, the chairman and CEO of the Dreyfus Corporation, had offered him the job of portfolio manager of the Dreyfus Fund, an open-end mutual fund. As part of the deal, Stein was even going to let him continue to manage his private hedge fund—what did I think?

"Shit, there's no downside, Stanley," I said. "Do it."

In the early eighties, Druckenmiller had asked me if I wanted to put some money into his hedge fund. By then, between my Lilly stock and my shares in Home Depot, I was beginning to feel flush, so I gave Stanley a quarter-million dollars.

I won't tell you how much that quarter-million bucks became. In the almost four decades since he started Priority, Stanley Druckenmiller hasn't had a single down year.

A brief side trip to Ross Perot's 1992 presidential campaign, where I almost changed the course of U.S. history. Take note of that "almost."

When Ross decided to run, he called me and he said he'd like my help. There was even a story in *USA Today* at the time that speculated that if Perot won, I might be asked to be secretary of the Treasury. Ross was quoted in the article saying, "Ken would be great in government in any position that he was asked to do." A wonderful compliment.

As you may remember, Perot funded his own campaign. And

one way I helped him was to go on these various TV shows—*Larry King Live, Crossfire* (they were mostly on CNN then; Fox News didn't exist yet)—and be the spin doctor. Another way was to schmooze the reporters in the greenroom after the televised presidential debates.

After the final debate—in East Lansing, Michigan, on October 19, 1992—Ross had to fly back to Dallas, and he asked me if I would give his daughter Suzanne and her husband, Patrick Mc-Gee, a ride back to New York on my plane. I said, "Absolutely. But I've got to go on *Larry King* first." Ross said that was fine.

So I go on *Larry King Live,* and as I get off the set, a reporter comes up to me and says he just saw Jim Baker—James Baker, chief of staff to George Bush, the sitting president—going into Perot's suite. Did I have any idea what it was about?

"I've got no idea at all," I told him.

"Do you think maybe Bush is trying to make a deal with Perot?" the guy asked. Because at this point, at the end of the campaign, Bush's numbers were sagging, and it was clear that Bill Clinton was running a much more effective campaign than people had given him credit for. It looked like the election was going to be a real dogfight.

I told the reporter again, truthfully, that I had no idea.

When we got onto my plane, Suzanne and Patrick and Elaine and I, I asked Perot's daughter about it. "Suzanne," I said, "Jim Baker went into your father's suite; a reporter just asked me about it. Do you have any idea what was going on?"

She shook her head. "I don't know anything about it," she said, and I could tell she really didn't.

The next day I was back in the city, walking to lunch at Christ Cella, the old steak house on East Forty-sixth, when it hit me like a hammer: "Holy shit," I thought. "If we can think of a way for Ross and Bush to join up, we win!"

So I went to the pay phone in the bar at Christ Cella and called up Arlen Specter, the Republican senator from Pennsylvania. Specter was in a dogfight of a race himself; he was campaigning in Pennsylvania with his old pal Bob Dole, senator from Kansas and head of the Republican Party. "Arlen," I said, "I may need a contact in the White House; I've got an idea."

Specter asked me what my idea was.

"Well, Arlen," I said, "I haven't talked to anybody; this is in my head and my head alone. But if we can get Perot to drop out of the race and endorse Bush, I think we might be able to do something."

Specter goes bat-shit. He tells Dole, and they're both excited as all hell to get it done. He calls me back and asks what he can do. "You need to tell me who I can talk to high up in the Bush campaign," I tell him, "because we've got to be damn sure that this thing is airtight." Specter agrees.

Now, I haven't talked to Perot about this at all. Nothing. This is just between Specter, Dole, and me. Next thing, I get a call that I'm to phone Jim Baker in the White House. I contact Baker. Baker says to me, "Have you talked to your principal yet?"

"I've talked to nobody," I said. I'd given some thought to how Perot could be useful to Bush. The main issues of Ross's campaign were the economy and the rise in the national debt; he came back to those subjects again and again. So I wanted to say something meaningful to Baker, but at the same time I knew that a presidential candidate can't offer someone a cabinet position in return for their support. It's against the law. You can wink and blink, but if you say it specifically, you're in trouble.

So I said to Baker, "I think that if the president was willing to consult with Ross on the appointments for Treasury and Commerce and Council of Economic Advisers and Labor, all of the departments that relate to the economy, I might be able to persuade him to do it."

"Okay, why don't you find out," Baker said.

"Look, Secretary Baker," I said. "I have not talked to my principal yet. What I'd like to do is fly down to see him, but I may not have time to do that. I'll get back to you whether I see him or just talk to him on the phone. But I must stress to you the importance of this not leaking."

"I understand," he said.

Now, I eventually found out why Baker had gone into Perot's suite after the debate. The ambassador to Iraq just before the Gulf War was a woman named April Glaspie, and there was a rumor that she had given a wink to the Iraqis—that the United States would accept their invading Kuwait. Perot had said during the debate that night that George Bush ought to come clean with everything Glaspie had told the Iraqis about Kuwait—that whatever it was, the American people had a right to know. So Baker went into the room after the debate to say to Perot, "Ross, there's nothing more to tell you. We've told the world everything; there was no wink." That was the whole purpose of Baker's going into Perot's room.

I phoned Ross, but he was in some interview or other. He finally calls me back and says, "What's up?"

"Ross, please—I don't know if it makes sense, but I've got an idea and I just want you to think about it," I said.

"Okay, what is it?"

"Ross," I said, "it looks to me like Clinton is going to win this election. Now, would you ever consider endorsing Bush? I have a hunch, Ross, that he and his team would be receptive."

"You can't trust these people," Perot said.

"What do you mean?"

"I just got a call a half hour ago from a guy at Goldman Sachs asking me that same question."

"What?"

"Yes, somebody just called me from Goldman Sachs and asked if I was approached by the Bush people, would I be interested."

"Oh shit," I said.

"Ken, you can't trust these people," Perot repeated, and that was the end of the conversation. He felt strongly that if he talked to Bush's team, they would leak that he was willing to drop out of the race, and he would be badly wounded if he stayed in.

It turned out that the guy from Goldman was someone who worked for Baker when he was secretary of the Treasury. Baker didn't know who the hell I was; I guess he didn't realize I had the access to Perot that I had. So he went to his pal and said, "You sound Perot out."

Which meant that, no thanks to Jim Baker, my call to Ross inadvertently killed the whole deal.

Years later, I met Baker at a Bohemian Grove gathering where Frank Borman had invited me as a guest. "Isn't it too bad we couldn't put that deal together?" he said.

I was very polite, because I was a guest there. But I said to myself, "You dope, we couldn't put that deal together, because you had to do what you did and you destroyed any chance of getting it done."

I am convinced I could have persuaded Ross to do that deal if Baker hadn't leaked. And I'm convinced that if Ross Perot had thrown his support to George H. W. Bush, Bush would have beaten Clinton.

Nostalgia doesn't interest me much. I'm a hell of a lot more excited about the deal that's around the corner than the one I did yesterday. This is true across the board in my life. For instance, I have warm feelings about my Bucknell days, but those feelings have less to do with what I did as a young idiot than with the wonderful things my alma mater gave me.

And so I give back. I've always felt a huge debt of gratitude to Bucknell, and I donate freely to it—both my time and my money. It deserves nothing less.

For a long time, I felt differently about NYU Business School. It was only a night program when I went there, and my memories were mostly of running around from building to building for my classes, freezing in cold classrooms in the winter, sweating in hot classrooms in the summer, painstakingly putting together the credits I needed for my MBA. I certainly didn't feel any sense of rah-rah about the place. In fact, after my graduation in 1960 I really lost contact with the school until the early 1980s, when the dean, a fellow by the name of Dick West, got in touch with me and asked for a contribution. Fair enough, I thought. That was when I made the modest gift I mentioned earlier, endowing the Abbe-Bogen Faculty Lounge.

But after West left, a man named George Daly took over his post, and George was a more hands-on leader. One day he came to see me at Invemed, and I told him how grateful I was for the night program but said I was worried about the school's future. NYU Law School, I reminded him, used to have a night program that they ended because they felt it detracted from the school's stature. I worried aloud that a similar mind-set might lead to the end of the business school's night program.

Daly told me that that wasn't going to happen. "We're known for our part-time program," he said.

Then he asked me if I'd be willing to make a major gift to help it along.

At that point, Home Depot was on its feet and expanding aggressively; Invemed was doing well. I was just starting to feel pretty flush. And so I said yes to George Daly. I made the business school a gift of $10 million, and they renamed the night program the Langone MBA for Working Professionals. By the way, naming it after me was the school's idea, not mine.

The school then asked me to join its Board of Overseers—a body with advisory capacity only. Henry Kaufman, a very prominent economist and a partner at Salomon Brothers, and a good friend, was the chairman. I was honored to join the board, and I sat on it through the 1980s and 1990s as—thanks to a $30 million gift from my fellow alumnus Leonard Stern—the business school's full-time program grew to include both undergraduate business majors and MBA candidates.

In 1999, George Daly and Henry Kaufman came to see me, wanting to know if I would be interested in succeeding Henry as chairman of the Board of Overseers of what was now the New York University Stern School of Business. "Look," I said, "I appreciate the honor, but you've got guys who want it; why don't you give it to them? I'm happy where I am." And that was it.

Now, strangely, a few days later, I got a call from Marty Lipton. Marty, a founding partner of Wachtell, Lipton, Rosen & Katz, is a man who has been very important in my life, as a friend, adviser, and lawyer. Anytime I've had a business crisis or challenge, he has always been there. In 1998, Marty had become chair of the NYU Board of Trustees. And now he was calling to ask if he could come see me along with Jay Oliva, the president of the university. Fine, I said.

Marty and Jay came over, sat down in my office, and proceeded to lay out a whole litany of problems the school was having. The school this, the school that. I listened, nodding wisely, then suddenly realized what they were saying didn't sound quite right. "Marty," I said, "are you talking about the business school?"

"No, no," he said. "We're talking about the medical school."

Who knew NYU had a medical school? "Where the hell is the medical school?" I said.

"Downtown, on the East Side," Marty said. "And we've got a real mess on our hands. We just merged our hospital with Mount Sinai, and there are a lot of bad feelings on both sides."

The institution's condition, from a business standpoint, was critical. NYU Medical School had been around for 175 years, but the university as a whole was in tough financial shape, and the medical school was a money pit. That was the rationale for this merger, yet the merger was a nightmare. The NYU doctors felt that if you're going to have a medical school, you've got to have your own hospital, because that's where you teach your kids. But if you don't control your hospital, you really have no control over how you teach. These docs were seriously worried that they were going to be swallowed up by Mount Sinai. And their new boss was the head of Sinai! Morale couldn't have been lower.

"How can I help?" I asked.

"I want you to become chairman," Marty said.

I looked at him. He was serious. I thought about it for a minute. It was early 1999; it wouldn't be long until I turned sixty-four. Home Depot was flying higher than ever; my role in helping to found it had made me more money than I'd ever dreamed of. I knew that in a few years I'd be out of the company, and I wanted to put my good fortune to good use. Being chairman of NYU Medical School would be hard work, but I like hard work, and I had time for it. The only problem was that I knew absolutely nothing about what the job might entail.

"Marty, I'll tell you what I'll do," I said. "I'll spend a lot of time studying it, but I'm not going to give you an answer now."

I went to talk to the chairman at the time, Henry Silverman. Henry, the private-equity investor and the founder of Cendant, had a mess of his own to deal with. He had just merged Cendant, which mostly owned hotel chains, with a direct-marketing firm called CUC, and it turned out that prior to the merger CUC had cooked its books. The founders wound up going to jail. "Look," Henry said, "I'm trying to turn my company around, and the NYU Medical Center has got a real problem. I can't fix both things at the same time."

One thing suddenly occurred to me. "I want to be honest, Henry," I said. "New York is a Jewish town. I don't need the suspicion that I pushed a Jew out of this position."

"I don't think anybody would say that," Henry told me. "But if they did, I'd tell them the real story."

I met next with the NYU Medical School's new dean, Bob Glickman. I was shocked at how depressed he was. Glickman, who'd previously been the chief of medicine at Beth Israel at Harvard, felt he'd been lured to NYU under false pretenses: he'd been promised the medical school was ready to make all kinds of changes, but when he arrived he was told the money simply wasn't there.

I took this news to Marty Lipton. "Marty," I said, "I want to tell you one thing right now. I will do this job. But I will not be part of a group that reneges. I saw the letter to Glickman, and unless we're committed to actually do the things he was promised, I'm out."

"I'm with you," Marty said. Simple as that. It was all I needed. It was then and there that I decided to give $100 million, anonymously, to NYU Medical Center.

I went back to Glickman and told him about the gift. "Bob," I said, "the challenge now is not doing what you were promised but how we do it and how fast we can do it. But we'll do it."

He almost smiled.

We held our first town meeting with the doctors, Bob Glickman and I sitting on the stage in front of a full auditorium. "I'm taking this job," I told them, "and I want to assure you there's one promise I can keep. None of you are going to get everything you want, but all of you are going to have more than you have right now." The docs seemed happy with that, but Bob Glickman was still frowning. I looked at him. "And if I had the capacity to write prescriptions," I said, "the very first thing I would do on taking this job would be to double Dr. Glickman's dosage of Prozac."

Well, that got a laugh—even from Bob.

I began. "Bob, so you don't get nervous, you run the place," I told Glickman. "I don't know a needle from a suture. I should have nothing to do with the quality of care except to know if it's bad. I've got two roles. I've got to walk around this place and make sure everybody's spirits are right, and I've got to raise a lot of money. It's that simple. If I see something I don't like, I'm going to bitch. If you push back, you win. I can tell you what I think, but I won't poke my nose into areas where I have no competence."

I knew a few things about health care, and as I went around and interviewed these NYU docs, I saw that the quality of care at NYU Hospital wasn't just good; it was spectacularly good. These were old-fashioned docs who understood the meaning of quality patient care. They would never rush a patient through a hospital stay just to clear a room: they paid real attention to their patients as people.

I also had a leg up. Dr. John Mountain, the surgeon Elaine had worked for when we were newlyweds, was still active at North Shore Hospital, and he was an incredible source of knowledge for me. Dr. Mountain said to me, "There's a doctor at NYU who is one of the most respected and accomplished cardiovascular surgeons in the world. His name is Frank Spencer." When Dr. Mountain himself needed carotid artery surgery, he went to Spencer. That's the highest tribute one doctor can pay another.

Whenever Mountain got his hands on an outstanding resident who wanted to do cardiovascular surgery, he would call Frank

Spencer and say, "Frank, take this kid as a fellow; this kid is good." He sent a number of residents to Spencer, and when they came back to see him, they would always say, "The medical staff at NYU is first-class."

At the same time, I saw that the facilities were a shambles. I was amazed how well these doctors were doing with what little they had. I knew at once that facilities could easily be upgraded—it was just a question of money—but that you couldn't fix an institutional morale problem with the wave of a wand.

"Marty, look," I said to Marty Lipton. "Always take on the difficult, but never take on the impossible. This merger has got to go. It will be hard to undo, but it's got to go. The poison, the angst, that's been driven through this place is not going to go away as long as we don't control our hospital."

Marty agreed. I put the dissolution in the hands of the lawyers. Now it was time for what I was good at—raising money.

I went to Larry Tisch, Marty's predecessor as chair of the NYU Board of Trustees. "Larry," I said, "I'm going to give $100 million to NYU Medical Center. Will you match it?"

Larry said he wouldn't. Didn't say why; just said no. "Okay," I said. "I'm going to do it anyway."

And I found some good people who said yes. Early in my tenure, Joel Smilow committed $35 million for a new medical research facility. Later, Stanley and Fiona Druckenmiller gave $150 million; Helen Kimmel gave $150 million; Billie Tisch and the Tisch family gave us $100 million; Ike and Laurie Perlmutter gave us $50 million; so did Ron Perelman.

At my next meeting with the NYU docs, I told them, "Look, we've got a lot of work to do, but the hard part is done. If I'd been offered a great facility and a lousy staff, I would've never taken it on. But this is easy. We've got some of the greatest doctors practicing some of the greatest medicine in the world. The only problem with you guys—and frankly, the one thing I'm good at and that you stink at—is I know how to brag and you guys don't."

What I meant was, I'm a salesman. These doctors were in no position to sell themselves or their facility. They were badly beaten down. "Trust me," I told them. "Watch and see what happens."

You'd think it'd be easy to give an institution $100 million. It wasn't easy. One of the first things I found out was that the medical school owed the university $55 million. So I went to the university and said, "I'm going to give the school a hundred million. Why don't you forgive the fifty-five million?"

They said absolutely not.

"Okay," I said. "I'm not foolish enough to think my job is to run that place. I know my main jobs are really cheerleading and raising money. But understand, if I go to my friends for donations, and their motives for donating are me and the medical center, then you get nothing."

In most cases, universities get a percentage—usually around 15 percent—of the philanthropy that their constituent schools raise. If you're an alumnus of Harvard Business School and you give Harvard Business School money, a percentage of that money goes to Harvard University.

What I was telling the people at NYU was that if they didn't forgive the $55 million, we would pay them—and we did pay them, over a period of four years—but that anything I brought in for the medical school belonged to the medical school, free and clear.

They were thrilled. One minute the medical school owes them big-time, and they're afraid it's sucking them into bankruptcy; the next minute, this nut promises to pay them back and become chairman of the medical center.

But not forgiving the debt was very shortsighted on the part of the people at NYU. If they'd let it slide, they'd have earned their 15 percent, not just on my $100 million, but on all the subsequent donations we brought in. Their cut would have added up to substantially more than $55 million. They were penny-wise and pound-foolish.

As I began my tenure, my first role was just to lift morale. It was a big lift. I decided to do some of the same things we did at Home Depot: hold town meetings, walk the halls, talk to the staff. Put my arm around people's shoulders, tell them how much we appreciated them and what we were going to do for them—and deliver. In other words, don't promise pie in the sky unless you've got the recipe to make it.

There was a natural suspicion of me at first, as an outsider and a nonmedical person. A rich guy who maybe just wanted to throw his weight around. I got it. And I'm proud to say that I defused it—by never pretending to be anything I wasn't, by being genuinely interested in everyone I met, but mainly by being *present*.

I immediately saw that we needed all kinds of things, not the least of which was a whole new hospital building. But we also needed a new chief of radiology, and one of our best moves early on was to hire Bob Grossman.

One reason we were able to get Grossman was our acknowledgment that we had to completely redo our imaging technology. One of the biggest manufacturers of medical-imaging equipment was and is GE, and at that time I was on the GE board. I knew Jeff Immelt, the CEO of GE, formerly the head of its Medical Systems division. But Bob Grossman had a very strong bias against GE's imaging technology: he felt the company had fallen behind in the field. He liked Philips much better; he liked Siemens even more than that.

Still, in view of the size of the buy, nothing was clear-cut: if GE (for example) didn't have a certain bell or whistle, they might very possibly say, "Look, we'll give you 30 percent off and guarantee we'll have that enhancement in six months."

One day Grossman and Glickman came to see me, and they were hemming and hawing. Finally, I said, "What's up?"

"I want to be honest," Grossman says. "This is a very big buy we're doing in imaging, and we want it to be a totally open and competitive process. And frankly, I'm worried about your being on the GE board and also being chairman here. Is that something I need to worry about?"

"Let's make it easy," I said. "As of this meeting, I recuse myself. I'm going to appoint two of our trustees, Tom Murphy and Andy Pearson, to oversee the selection process." Murphy had been head of Cap Cities/ABC, and he was and still is one of the most revered and respected businessmen in the world. Andy Pearson had been president of Pepsi and was known to be one of the ten meanest bosses around—a tough guy but a very smart and fair guy.

"All I want," I told Glickman and Grossman, "is to know, once the process is complete, what you did and why you did it."

I called up Jeff Immelt and said, "Jeff, I can't and won't do anything to help your cause. I'm going to be purer than Caesar's wife."

Jeff agreed that was the right way, and the selection process began.

And in the midst of all this, I suddenly found myself locked in battle with a guy who was out to make me look anything but pure.

————

A bit of background.

In my years around the New York Stock Exchange, first as the holder of two seats on the exchange and then as a member of the Specialty Firms Advisory Committee, I'd become friendly with Dick Grasso, who became president of the exchange in 1988. Dick had started as an $82-a-week unionized clerk at the NYSE in 1968 and worked his way up the ranks to a mighty $203-a-week position before being elected to leadership.

In the past, a talented guy like Dick would have bumped his head on the exchange's glass ceiling and been left to find work elsewhere. Also in the past, the leaders of the NYSE had all been big cheeses: guys like Mil Batten, who'd retired as the head of J. C. Penney; Bill Donaldson, who'd co-founded the Donaldson, Lufkin & Jenrette securities firm and been an undersecretary of state in the Nixon administration; and Jim Needham, who'd been an SEC commissioner. But in 1982 the exchange's board of directors, prodded by Stanley Gault, the former CEO of Rubbermaid and Goodyear, decided to change course. "We've got to figure out a way to retain these guys so they don't leave us," Gault said. What resulted was a new system, one where somebody could start at the bottom, like at any other corporation, and one day run the place.

The Compensation Committee established a number of incentives for NYSE employees to stay. They created a supplemental employment retirement package; they set up a savings plan where employees could put money in an account and earn a guaranteed 6 percent rate of interest. And they wrote a rule that gave every employee—retroactively—a pension of 2.5 percent times compensation for every year of service. For example, Bill Donaldson was at the exchange for a total of five years: his pension was 2.5 percent times five—12.5 percent—times the average of his compensation for that period.

And so Dick Grasso, who'd begun as a lowly unionized clerk, had the motivation to stay on and become president of the NYSE and in 1995 be elected chairman and CEO. He was compensated appropriately, and his pension grew proportionately.

He worked his ass off for the money. When he first took over, the exchange had twelve hundred listings (companies listed on the NYSE); by the time he eventually left, in 2003, it would have over twenty-eight hundred listings. Grasso realized that as the market became more computerized, the big, highly liquid stocks—General

Motors, U.S. Steel, Exxon, Mobil, and the like—could be traded more like commodities: in millions of shares a day, with moves of fractions of a penny. This was great for the big companies. But the smaller, less-liquid companies, whose stocks traded far fewer shares (and whose trades were more labor-intensive), needed to be persuaded to spring for the annual fee to join the exchange. And Dick was the guy who had to do the persuading.

He cultivated me early. I talked up the NYSE anywhere I had influence, because I knew Dick, and I believed in him. I encouraged EDS to be listed, and Home Depot, of course. Also Unifi, Database Technologies, Ohio Mattress, and Yum! Brands.

Dick would fly around the United States—always commercial, always coach—persuading CEOs. His schedule was nuts. He'd go to a company in Milwaukee and the next morning visit another company in Midland, Texas. He'd have to fly from Milwaukee to Chicago, change planes, fly to Baton Rouge, and get on a puddle jumper to Midland. For a while, he all but lived in Silicon Valley. We used to beg him to charter a private plane. Dick wouldn't do it. But he did a masterful job, and our numbers grew off the charts. Everybody on the floor of the exchange was making a fortune: volume and revenues were exploding. We were raising Grasso's salary and bonuses accordingly, and it's important to note that because the New York Stock Exchange was a not-for-profit (not a nonprofit: big difference), with no shares or shareholders, all the revenue the exchange earned went straight back into exchange expenses—including Dick's pay. He was directly contributing to his own good fortune.

In 1999, there was a downturn. The NYSE's market share—the number of shares traded on the exchange versus over the counter—fell a couple of percentage points below 90 percent. I went to see Dick. I said, "Dick, I want to tell you something. We're good friends. But if our market share drops below 80 percent, you're out of work."

Dick said he understood completely. Again he went the extra mile—visiting institutional investors, visiting the head of Merrill Lynch—to pitch for order flow and the transparency of buying and selling shares on the floor of the exchange versus over the counter. And the market share held, but that wasn't Grasso's only challenge that year.

In 1999, as we were about to flip the calendar to the new millennium, there was great angst on the exchange about Y2K. What would happen if someplace in our behemoth computer system we forgot to ratchet 1999 over to 2000? We spent a billion dollars on crash-prevention hardware that year; we paid $80 million in sales tax on the hardware we bought! We had backup systems for backup systems for backup systems.

And then, when the clock ticked over to 1/1/2000 . . . nothing happened. All our concerns evaporated. We had entered the new millennium with phenomenal operating numbers: making a shit-pile of money, every penny of which we needed, not just for those crash-prevention systems, but for trading technology and big-time taxes—income taxes, real-estate taxes, payroll taxes. And Dick Grasso bore a lot of responsibility for our success.

In 1999, I had succeeded Bernie Marcus as chairman of the NYSE's Compensation Committee, so when Dick's contract was up in late 2001, I went to negotiate a new one with him. He was in a very strong position. He had been instrumental in getting us back up and running after 9/11—a truly heroic feat. The Treasury Department had requested we wait till the following Monday to reopen, but Grasso could have done it on September 12. And not only had he brought the exchange to a very good place; he had thirty-three years of service.

So I wasn't at all surprised when he said, "Ken, I would like to take some money off the table. My entire net worth is in my job here, and I'd like to get some diversification." He didn't have stock, because there were no shares in the stock exchange; it was made up of members rather than stockholders.

Now understand, that 2.5 percent times Dick's income for all those years of service had really added up: he already had almost $140 million in the bucket simply by virtue of the incentive programs that we'd established in the early 1980s. The Compensation Committee had nothing to do with it; it was there on the books. I agreed he should get what was rightfully coming to him.

But the Enron scandal broke right around the same time, and the issue of executive compensation suddenly became very sensitive. Suddenly it seemed less than ideal, optically speaking, that I was a member of the stock exchange, regulated by the stock exchange, and also chairman of the Comp Committee, which was paying the head of the stock exchange. So we on the NYSE board (which I'd joined in 1998) agreed that if you were not independent— if you were a member of the exchange—you couldn't be on certain committees. You couldn't be on Audit. You couldn't be on Governance. And you couldn't be on Comp.

We agreed that I would come off the Compensation Committee and Carl McCall, who had previously been comptroller of the State of New York, would take over as chairman. I told Carl that Dick and I had agreed to the terms of his new contract, including his request to draw down money, but the contract wasn't finalized, and therefore Carl and the new committee were free to do as they chose.

Then I went to Dick and told him there was a new committee, and they were going to look at his payout with fresh eyes. "If they want to go along with it, they'll go along with it," I said. "If they want to make changes, they'll make changes, and you'll decide if it's agreeable to you or not, but you have no deal yet."

"Fine," Dick said.

The new committee considered Dick's request and approved it. Enter the Sheriff of Wall Street.

Eliot Spitzer had started his career defending white-collar criminals, but once he became New York State attorney general in 1999, he began going after them with a vengeance. In the past, New York State AGs had pursued local fraud and consumer-rights cases, but Spitzer had lofty ambitions: he wanted to be governor and, eventually, the first Jewish president. Taking down some candy-store owner in Manhasset who was overcharging for Baby Ruth bars wouldn't do; Eliot Spitzer wanted headlines, and Wall Street was the place to get them.

When Spitzer first heard Dick Grasso was negotiating a new contract with the exchange, he called him and said, "Dick, I can't tell you how excited I am that you and I are going to be working together in the future"—he as a regulator and Dick as the head of a major institution and also a regulator. Dick thanked him. And they were good friends for a while.

In 2002, Spitzer picked up his lance and began crusading, suing a bunch of investment banks—including Bear Stearns, Deutsche Bank, Goldman Sachs, and J. P. Morgan Chase—for inflating stock prices, among other things. Ten of the firms paid big fines to settle, and the headlines started.

That was also the year the WorldCom accounting scandal was uncovered and the company filed for bankruptcy. Corporate greed was all over the news.

The following year Spitzer went after a group of mutual-fund brokers for privileging bigger investors over smaller ones, letting select clients engage in certain types of trades closed off to the rank and file. More big fines, more headlines.

This investigation led Spitzer to the board of the New York Stock Exchange. When Dick Grasso nominated Sandy Weill, the head of Citigroup, to be the board's representative for public investors, Spitzer (who was also investigating Citigroup for conflicts of interest in its investment bank) told the newspapers that the exchange's board had become an old boys' club, packed with corporate and financial CEOs. Weill withdrew, and Dick found himself square in Spitzer's sights.

Grasso's new contract and $140 million payout were announced in the spring of 2003. And the following month the New York State comptroller, Alan Hevesi, among others, started putting enormous pressure on Dick to resign, charging that in the climate of corporate reform—and also at a down period in the market—his compensation was too high to make him an objective regulator and business leader.

There was a huge public outcry: everybody kept talking about that $140 million, conveniently ignoring the fact that it was legitimately Dick's money, accumulated over three decades of exemplary service. At the same time, Spitzer seemed to be investigating everybody in sight, including several members of the exchange's board.

We held a special meeting, and I spoke up. "Look," I said, "there isn't a guy or a gal in this room who was on the Comp Committee who didn't know every single thing that was done regarding Dick, who didn't have a chance to vote up or down on his pay package, and you all voted up. We all agreed this guy did a hell of a job. And it was only a month ago that we were all praising his talents."

But meanwhile, my fellow board member Hank Paulson, the Goldman Sachs chief—who just the month before had voted to approve Grasso's compensation package—was conniving to get rid of Dick. "We can't take the pressure," Paulson kept saying. "This publicity is killing us." This was a guy who was supposed to have the courage and character of a leader.

Now, mind you, Dick never had a thing to do with what he was paid. Bernie Marcus and Dick never talked about it when Bernie was the head of the Comp Committee; Dick and I never talked about it when I succeeded Bernie. Neither of us ever asked Dick, "What do you want?" We would always go to him with a fait accompli. "Dick," we would say, "here's what the committee thinks you should get." And Dick would always say, "Thank you, I'm blessed." That's all he would ever say.

The pressure kept rising, and one evening in September we had a conference call, with all twenty-four members of the board. I remember it was the night of the opening of the New York Philharmonic—I was on their board too at the time—and I was getting into my black tie in my apartment. Once again, Hank Paulson was pitching that Dick had to go, that it was the only way we could stop the heat that was being put on us.

Suddenly Carol Bartz piped up—Carol was then head of a computer-aided design company called Autodesk. Tough lady. "Wait a minute," Carol said. "This man never asked us for a thing. We always gave it to him. We're a bunch of wussies. If anybody's going to resign, we should all resign. He didn't do it. We did it." And she didn't stop there. There weren't many people on the conference call with testicles, Carol said.

But Paulson wouldn't let up; he desperately wanted to get a unanimous vote asking for Dick's resignation. It didn't happen. We held the vote the same day, and it was 13–7 against Dick. Seven of us—Chris Quick, a floor broker; Bill Summers, of KeyCorp; Carol Bartz; Mel Karmazin of CBS; Bobby Fagenson, a big specialty-firms guy; Jimmy Cayne, the CEO of Bear Stearns; and I—said, "No way, we don't want him to resign." But Dick resigned anyway—forced out, really—on September 17, 2003. He took his $140 million but had to leave another $54 million in back salary on the table because the climate had become so toxic.

The blood was in the water. Rallied by Spitzer, state treasurers and comptrollers around the country vowed to "clean up Wall Street."

Then Spitzer filed a lawsuit against Dick. And me.

He charged Dick with misleading and bullying the board to get his compensation package, which Spitzer claimed was a violation of not-for-profit laws. And he named me as a co-defendant, saying I'd padded Grasso's payment with an extra $18 million that the other members of the NYSE board weren't aware of. Soon there were pieces all over the newspapers—Spitzer had a lot of friends in the press, and he loved leaking to them—calling me a "serial overpayer." The papers couldn't stop talking about the big pay package I'd pushed for General Electric's CEO, Jack Welch, when I was on the Compensation Committee at GE, and the rich contract I'd gotten Bob Nardelli when he became Home Depot's CEO back in 2000. What they never mentioned was the basic equation of capitalism: Welch and Nardelli had earned the money by creating value. I pay people for performance.

And Spitzer conveniently left out the fact that Carl McCall was chairman of the committee that gave Dick the compensation package. I was already out at that point. But I was a rich guy, high profile, outspoken, so I had a nice big target on my chest. And Eliot Spitzer, who badly wanted to be governor of New York, had no desire to alienate Carl McCall, who had major political juice in the state.

The suit was total bullshit. But the Mighty Crusader was all over the newspapers, battling Wall Street greed, and he loved every minute. His path to the governorship was strewn with rose petals.

Every member of the exchange board was told to get his or her own lawyer. It was a field day for lawyers! I naturally called Marty Lipton. But Marty couldn't be my attorney, because Wachtell,

Lipton was representing the exchange. "There's a guy downtown, Gary Naftalis," Marty said.

I hired Gary Naftalis.

A lawyer will always try to feel you out when you first start working together. So when Naftalis asked me about the case, I said, "Gary, I want you to understand something. I thought Grasso earned every nickel we paid him. I voted for that pay package, and I would vote for it again. I think Grasso should still be the head of the stock exchange. I voted not to take his resignation, and I would vote that way again."

People gave me credit for being loyal to Dick. I wasn't being loyal to Dick. I was being loyal to my judgment. I believed this guy earned what he got.

And I said one last thing to Naftalis at that initial meeting: "Gary, no settlement. No fucking settlement."

A few days later, Gary calls and tells me he's been invited to a meeting with Spitzer on a Friday afternoon. He goes to the meeting, and Spitzer says, "Gary, we don't want Langone. We want Grasso to give back the money. He shouldn't have gotten that much money; that's the long and short of it. So let's settle our case with your guy."

Gary comes out of the room and calls me up. "Spitzer wants to settle with you," he says.

"Gary," I say, "I want to tell you something right now. Don't you ever forget this. The next time the word 'settlement' comes out of your mouth in connection with this case, you're fired. You go tell that son of a bitch right now, I'm either going to win or I'm going to lose, but he's not going to decide. The court is going to decide. And if he wants to fight, let's go. I'm ready to sue *him*. There will be no settlement. You understand that, Gary?"

Gary walks back into Spitzer's office and says, "I just spoke to my client. No chance of a settlement."

"Well," Spitzer says, "tell your client that 90 percent of all court cases get settled on the courthouse steps." And Gary's response to him was "What about the other 10 percent?"

———

What's the old saying? When it rains, it pours? Sometimes when it rains you find yourself standing in the middle of a fucking monsoon. In the spring of 2003, as Grasso and I were battling Spitzer, the National Association of Securities Dealers, or NASD, a regulatory agency for the New York Stock Exchange, announced it was bringing a lawsuit against Invemed for, of all things, illegal profit sharing.

Here's what it was: 1999 and 2000 were go-go years on the NYSE and Nasdaq—lots and lots of hot IPOs. And Invemed was in the thick of it, doing what we'd done all along: seeking out new companies to invest in and take public, especially those that were developing innovative medical products and technologies, outfits like Immunex, Cell Genesys, and Pharmacyclics.

The bull market was so hot that when some of these new issues hit the market, their stock price could rise by a factor of twenty within days. Our brokerage customers naturally wanted in, and some of them were quickly selling the shares they were allocated and making big profits. And NASD was accusing us of forcing our customers to kick back some of the profits to us in the form of inflated commissions.

Now, some of the big investment banks, like Credit Suisse First Boston and Merrill Lynch, really were doing this. Credit Suisse, our underwriting partner on several IPOs during that period, actually had a kickback system in place: it based the number of shares of a hot new issue it would allow an institutional customer to buy directly on how much the customer was willing to pay Credit Suisse for the privilege.

But Invemed wasn't doing that. We always let our customers decide how much commission they wanted to pay us, within the bounds of legality: there's a rule that says a broker may not charge more than a 5 percent mark-up on any transaction. When some customers flipped a hot stock and made a big profit, they rewarded us by paying us a generous commission, but never more than the rule allowed. NASD singled out one instance where the price of a hot IPO, VA Linux, went from $15 a share to $300 on the day of issue, and a customer of ours who'd bought it low and flipped it high paid us a commission of $8 a share. That was a lot more than the industry norm, but a lot lower than 5 percent, which would've been $15 a share.

And it was the customer's decision, not ours.

And by the way, the customer was Jim Davin, the chairman of NASD!

That didn't matter to NASD's enforcement division. There I was, a wealthy, conspicuous guy, and just like Spitzer they wanted to make a big fat example of me. And to make matters worse, the big banks they were going after started to fess up—and pay up. Merrill Lynch, Morgan Stanley, Credit Suisse, and Citigroup paid many millions of dollars in fines for the same violation. The momentum was all on NASD's side. One of my lawyers at Wachtell, Lipton, David Gruenstein, came to my office and told me that if I chose to fight the suit in a hearing, my chances of winning were between slim and none. I burst into tears. If this charge stuck, my reputation—and very likely my business itself—was shot to hell.

———

When I went to Marty Lipton and told him about the charges being brought against me, he called in his senior partner, my good friend Ed Herlihy, and said, "Let's put together the strongest possible team to defend Ken."

And they sure did. Besides Marty, Ed, and David Gruenstein, I had George Conway, Maura Grossman, Allan Martin, and Ted Mirvis working with me—the best lawyers in New York's greatest law firm, and every one of them handling my case as if it were his or her reputation at stake, not mine.

My team and I went down to Washington to meet with Mary Schapiro, the NASD's head of enforcement, and her henchmen. Sorry, her associates. Talk about closed minds; they'd already come to their conclusion: "You had a deal with your customers that they had to pay you exorbitant commissions from the profits they made on the hot new issues that you allocated to them."

We argued that none of the commissions violated the 5 percent rule. They were unfazed. "You still had a deal with them," they said. "Those were kickbacks."

Nothing we said would change their minds. On the plane back to New York, Ed looked gloomy. He told me what I already knew: "You're a big name; they want to get you."

"Ed," I said, "we have nothing to do with commissions. We've never put a number on them; we've always let the customer decide."

"Always?"

"Every single time."

"You sure of that?"

"I'm positive," I said.

"Well, there's only one way this is going to go away," Ed said. "We're going to have to show them. Do you think you can get your customers to sign an affidavit?"

I personally called every one of our customers, seventy or eighty of them, and read them the affidavit I wanted them to sign. "Invemed never suggested a commission to us," it said. "We determined their commission completely on our own. Nothing was taken into account except the overall service Invemed provided.

There was no tie-in between the number of shares we were allotted and the size of the commission."

They all signed. Every single one of them. We took all the affidavits back to Washington to show to Schapiro and her thugs . . . sorry, associates.

"Sorry, we're bringing the case anyway," they said.

So my team and I girded ourselves for battle.

———

A couple of days later, one of Schapiro's minions called Herlihy at twenty to ten in the morning and told him he had twenty minutes to start settlement talks or the NASD was going to make an announcement that it was bringing profit-sharing charges against us. Herlihy called me up to tell me.

"Ed," I said, "do me a favor. Tell them not to waste the fuckin' twenty minutes. They should bring their case right now."

———

Typically for him, Spitzer made the battle between us a war in the media, periodically leaking bad things about Grasso and me to his newspaper buddies. Then these reporters would call me, and I would fire back. Much of 2004 and 2005 proceeded this way: I got a lot more famous than I wanted to be. The only thing that disappointed me about that episode in my life was the number of my friends who called me saying, "Why don't you settle with this guy?" I wasn't offended, but I was hurt that they didn't understand how I'm put together. My stand had nothing to do with loyalty to Grasso. It had everything to do with feeling I'd done the right thing. And I would do it again. Anyone who really knew me knew that I'd sooner jump off the Brooklyn Bridge than settle with that weasel.

And little did I know at the time how bad a guy Eliot Spitzer really was.

———

While this thunderstorm was booming all around me, Bob Glickman said in early 2005 he felt he'd done all he could as dean of the NYU Medical School and wanted to go back to being a doctor. We appointed a search committee, headed by Joe Zuckerman, the chief of orthopedics, and we saw right away that one of the strongest candidates, and a complete natural for the job, was Bob Grossman.

Meanwhile, the bidding for our new imaging system was still under way, and Grossman was deep in negotiations with his favorite, Siemens. Bob felt that the German company's technology was far superior to everybody else's.

But he turned out to be a tough bargainer as well as a great radiologist. Bob told Siemens that if they sold us their equipment at a bargain-basement price—the drop-dead price—NYU would allow them to use our facility as a beta site, meaning Siemens would have the right to bring prospective customers here to see our imaging system in operation and talk to our doctors.

And not only that. Bob also wanted Siemens to give us—*give* us—and install (at their cost!) a 7 Tesla magnet, a scanner so powerful that the images of the body it generates look as if the skin has been taken off the bones: they're like photographs of the skeletal structure. At the time there were only five of these devices in the world. Its magnet is so powerful that it has to be encased in a three-foot-thick concrete shield on all sides. Grossman's argument to Siemens was that once this very advanced equipment was installed, NYU staff would become the best possible salesmen for it.

Then, while Siemens was still considering the deal, Grossman walked into a search-committee meeting and announced, "If I can't get everything we want from Siemens, you shouldn't give me this job."

I sat there, my heart in my mouth. After the meeting was over, I grabbed him and said, "Let me tell you something. I'll bet my last dollar you're a Catholic kid who was given to a Jewish orphanage at birth and adopted by a Jewish family, because you can't be that fuckin' stupid and be Jewish. That's just not possible."

"What do you mean?" Bob said.

"Why would you bet your career on a bunch of Germans who might decide to dig in their heels at your outrageous demands?" I asked him. "What if you don't get the deal and then you don't get the deanship either? Are you out of your mind?"

He wasn't dumb or crazy. He was just being Bob. Some people are too honest for their own good. That doesn't mean you should lie—just that you shouldn't undercut your own case.

So I called up John Sexton, who had succeeded Oliva as president of NYU, and asked for another shot for Grossman. And Bob came back to the search committee, without setting any conditions this time, and blew them away.

And by the way, Siemens agreed to everything he asked for— and then some. They also offered to loan us $500 million to build a new hospital. When I told Jeff Immelt about it, he thought Siemens was crazy. "Any competitor of mine that wants to lose that kind of money, it's okay with me," he said.

In the end, we wound up not borrowing the $500 million from Siemens; in the end, we raised the money ourselves. Which allowed us to hit them even harder on the price of the system. We made out like bandits.

A year later—the deal had been completed; the system was installed—I held a dinner at my home in Sands Point for the Siemens team and the NYU team. The head of Siemens at the time was Klaus Kleinfeld—a perfect name for the head of Siemens, right? A very nice guy. I seated Kleinfeld next to me at the dinner. As dessert was being brought out, I leaned over to him and said, "Klaus, tell me something. How much did you lose on our deal?"

"Lose?" he said. "We've made over a billion dollars so far."

I must have looked a little surprised.

"Ken, we're selling installations at *list price*," Kleinfeld said. Every time Siemens brought potential customers to NYU, he told me, our docs would show them the difference between our system and the others they were considering. Our doctors were so passionate about that 7 Tesla magnet and all the other technology that they were Siemens's best salesmen.

Never underestimate the power of a good product. And a smart doc.

There's nothing wrong with a win-win, either.

———

Spitzer's suit against Dick Grasso and me dragged on throughout 2005 and 2006, while Dick and I made our lawyers rich. By the time it was all done, my legal bills were $23 million and Dick's were $30 million. All of it was paid by NYSE Directors and Officers Liability Insurance. Strangely enough, the lead underwriter was AIG, whose former CEO Hank Greenberg was forced out in a 2005 accounting scandal. Spitzer went after Hank too. Between Dick and me and the other board members, the lawyers made out to the tune of $100 million. Speaking for myself, it was worth every penny of AIG's money.

Dick and I argued that his compensation was exactly what he was entitled to and not a cent more, that the board of the exchange had fully reviewed and approved his pay package on several occasions, and that Spitzer's suit against us was pure grandstanding in his campaign for the governorship of New York State. He'd announced his candidacy in late 2004: very early for an election that wasn't to take place until November 2006. But then, he wanted to build up a big head of steam, and his lawsuit against Grasso and me was a key part of his PR initiative.

That's why in 2005, despite being a lifelong Republican, I threw my support behind the gubernatorial campaign of the Nassau County executive, Tom Suozzi, a Democrat. I liked Tom, and I still do, but I'll admit that my main motivation was to stick it to Spitzer.

I wasn't just being vengeful. I thought that this was a genuinely bad guy, determined to run over everyone and everything in his path to power. He ruined several lives in his quest to add scalps to his belt. One night in October 2005—the occasion was the Al Smith Dinner at the Waldorf Astoria, the annual white-tie benefit for Catholic Charities—I was standing and talking with George Pataki, then the governor of New York, and Mike Bloomberg, who was then the mayor of New York City, when I saw Spitzer walking toward us.

What the hell could he want? I wondered. I figured he had to be coming over to say a few words to George or Mike: after all, legal ethics prohibit a lawyer from speaking to an adversary in a suit without talking to the adversary's attorney first.

Instead, though, Spitzer walked straight up to me. "Good evening, Mr. Langone," he said.

"Good evening, Mr. Attorney General," I replied. He grinned at me; maybe he thought I was making nice.

"You know," Spitzer said, "I think in a different life you and I might be good friends."

I looked him right in the eye. "Not likely," I said, and I walked away.

He won his political campaign, but he didn't get to enjoy the fruits of his victory for very long. A little over a year after he took office, he was forced to resign in a prostitution scandal—you remember, he was Client 9 for this $1,000-an-hour hooker—and I can't say I wept for the guy. I did feel terrible for his wife, whom he made stand next to him while he confessed. Why humiliate the woman in public? I wondered. You've already humiliated her enough.

My Wachtell, **Lipton dream team** worked on the NASD profit-sharing case for almost three years, and in February 2006 the NASD convened its hearing panel.

Or should I say kangaroo court?

The hearing officer was a NASD employee. The other two members of the panel worked for firms that belonged to the NASD.

The hearing lasted for more than two weeks, and on March 6 the panel issued a ninety-four-page opinion unanimously exonerating us.

After we won, I insisted on a meeting with the executive board of the NASD, which had now changed its name to FINRA, the Financial Industry Regulatory Authority. Mary Schapiro, God bless her, was obligated to attend. And when we'd all sat down, I said, "Let me tell you guys a story."

In the early 1960s, I told them, the chairman of the New York Stock Exchange was a man by the name of J. Truman Bidwell. The Feds brought a big tax-evasion case against Bidwell, and it was slapped all over the front pages of the newspapers. And when J. Truman Bidwell was exonerated, the article was two column inches, back in the obituary section.

"If you're bringing a case against someone who's ripping people off and will continue unless you do something," I said, "you should make a public statement that you're bringing the case. You want to warn people that they could lose money. But where it's a legitimate contest, you can't make an announcement until the case is fully adjudicated."

And FINRA agreed to that. I call it the Invemed rule.

If I've done something wrong, then shame on me. But if I've done nothing wrong, I'll fight to the death to prove it. There's nothing more important in my life than the name I leave my kids.

———

For years there have been whispers, and some talk louder than whispers, that in my desire to get back at Eliot Spitzer I hired a private detective to shadow him and that it was my detective's sleuthing that ultimately led to Spitzer's downfall. The following is my story, and I'm sticking to it.

On March 10, 2008, I came into the city to attend another dinner, this one at the Tribeca Grill, in honor of Medal of Honor recipients. Dick Grasso was going to be the host. I had arranged to have a drink beforehand at the Four Seasons with my friend Ed Herlihy and Tony Carbonetti, who had been Rudy Giuliani's chief of staff when Rudy was mayor. Ed and Tony and I were sitting in a banquette in the Grill Room, discussing a business deal, when Spitzer's name came up. Rumors about his indiscretions had been swirling, and the news of his scandal had finally broken that afternoon, pushing everything else off the front page. Tony lowered his voice. "I got a call today from a friend of mine who told me a couple of months ago he was waiting in line at the Grand Central Post Office, and who was standing in front of him but the governor of the State of New York, Eliot Spitzer. And when Spitzer's turn came, he bought a $2,800 money order."

Tony gave Ed and me a look. I got it. What was the governor of the State of New York doing standing in line at the post office? He had secretaries, he had security guards, he had all kinds of lackeys. What on earth might the governor of the State of New York have needed a $2,800 money order for? I leave it all up to your imagination.

How the story of the sighting of Spitzer in line at the post office got out, how it turned into a rumor that I hired a detective, and how (or if) the whole thing was related to Spitzer's unmasking, I also leave to your imagination.

Was I thrilled that he got caught? What do you think?

Anyway, I said good-bye to Ed and Tony and went downtown to the Medal of Honor dinner. And I don't know how the press knew I was going to be there, but when I got there, I saw a gaggle of TV trucks and cameras and mike booms. Dick had played it smart and gone in the back door. Stupid me, I went in the front, and the reporters grabbed me. The subject was Spitzer. "What do you know?" they asked.

I told them the truth: that I didn't know anything. But I also said this: "We all have our own private hells, whether it's a sick kid or a bad marriage; we all have something that's on our shoulders. We all have our own private hells; I just hope his is a little hotter than everybody else's."

And on July 1, 2008, Dick Grasso and I got legal vindication when the New York State Court of Appeals dismissed all claims against us, ruling that because the New York Stock Exchange was now a subsidiary of a for-profit, multinational corporation (in 2006, the exchange had merged with the Chicago-based Archipelago Exchange), the State of New York had no oversight over the company's affairs and that the former prosecution was not in the public interest.

Sweet victory.

As for Spitzer, I feel he deserves every bad thing that's happened to him.

Now, the tragedy of all this for me is that a basic tenet of my faith is forgiveness, but I can't find it in my heart to forgive Eliot Spitzer. Dick Grasso and I had the wherewithal to defeat him; many others weren't so lucky. He destroyed lives and careers just because he wanted a headline. What he did to his wife and children was miserable.

And he made me a hero! After he resigned, people would come up to me on the street and shake my hand. "Hey, go get him, thank God for guys like you," they'd say.

Well, I thank God every morning for all I've received and pray to be a better person. And maybe it makes me a worse person not to be able to forgive that schmuck. If that's what I have to live with, I'll live with it.

Let's end the chapter on a more positive note.

When Elaine and I gave $100 million to the NYU Medical Center in 1999, we stipulated that the gift be anonymous. And when we donated another hundred million a few years later, we made the same stipulation—only this time things turned out differently. Bob Grossman and Marty Lipton came to me and said they were certain that if Elaine and I were willing to attach our names to the medical center, others would be more willing to come forward with major gifts. As it turned out, they were right, in spades. The medical center's name today, NYU Langone, brings me a great deal of pride, and at the same time as a Catholic I know pride is a mortal sin. My argument would be that my pride has less to do with vanity than with the knowledge that I've helped others to do a great deal of good.

When Bob Grossman took over as CEO of NYU Medical Center in 2007, our medical school was ranked thirty-fourth nationally and our hospital didn't even make the honor roll. Within a decade both were in the top dozen. We've been number one in quality, patient care, and safety for the last three years. I'd thought that nothing in my business life could top the success of Home Depot. I can't tell you how much more the success of the medical center means to me. And I love Home Depot.

Don't forget, I took the NYU job when I was sixty-five years old. At that age, most guys are looking for some pasture to chew grass in. At that age, I helped bring new life to an institution that in the years since has healed tens of thousands of people. Sixteen years on, helping that institution get to where it is now continues to be the most exhilarating experience I've ever had.

Marty Lipton: thank you, thank you, thank you.

8.

HUMAN NATURE AND OTHER DISASTERS

Everybody talks about the bottom line, but as I've seen time and time again, you ignore the human element of business at your peril. Most of the seven deadly sins can and do come into play, and chemistry between people—good chemistry or bad—always has an effect, sometimes a huge effect: in boardrooms, in executive offices, in sales meetings. I've had quite a few chemistry lessons over the years.

This story starts in the spring of 1999, when I'd recently joined the board of General Electric. I'd been on the board for only two months when Jack Welch said, "I want you on the Comp Committee"—a.k.a. the Management Development and Compensation Committee, or MDCC. Coming from Jack, it sounded less like a request than a direct order.

Now, normally at GE, the chairman appoints committee members in consultation with the Governance and Nominating Committee. But Jack was Jack, and it was his call. "Jack," I said, "you've got guys here who've been here ten or fifteen years. Is that going to sit well?"

God bless Jack. He knew what he wanted, and he didn't hold back. "I don't give a fuck," he said. "I want you on that committee."

"Okay," I said.

Sure enough, as soon as the announcement was made, a guy who'd been on the board for nine years—he was the head of a major bank—went to Jack and said, "I've been here nine years; why didn't you put me on that committee?"

Jack says to him, "I don't want some fuckin' banker telling me what I should pay my people. I want an entrepreneur who understands the importance and value of talent."

That's Jack. And that was that.

Welch was turning sixty-five in November 2000, and—that was GE's mandatory retirement age—he was due to leave the company at the end of the year. There had been speculation for years about his successor, articles in all the business magazines. Lots of names were flying around. But by mid-2000, the list had narrowed to three people: Jeff Immelt, Jim McNerney, and Bob Nardelli. Immelt, as I said earlier, was head of the Medical Systems division. McNerney had been executive VP of GE Capital and CEO of GE Aircraft Engines and GE Lighting. Nardelli was head of GE Power Systems. All three had been protégés of Welch's, and each man, with good reason, saw himself as Jack's logical successor.

Jack had set it up that the two guys who didn't get his job would get a very wet financial kiss from GE, but they would leave the company. It made perfect sense from a psychological standpoint: Welch didn't want two guys still at GE who in the world's eyes (and their own) had been passed over. He was going to give them packages that, when they went someplace else, would have to be met by the company they moved to.

This created the opportunity for Home Depot to hire one of the two.

Let's rewind a moment. In 1999, Bernie Marcus had passed

the reins to Arthur Blank, who had been running Home Depot for about three years. Bernie still sat on the board. One day we were having an Executive Committee meeting, and I said, "Arthur, if you get hit by a train, who is your replacement?"

"We haven't got one."

"We don't have someone in the company who could step up?"

He said, "No, we don't."

"That won't do," I said.

Arthur agreed. So we hired one of the best-known headhunters in the business, Gerry Roche of Heidrick & Struggles. We told Gerry there was no rush. Arthur was going to be chairman and CEO; we were going to bring in a president and COO. A CEO is more strategy and big picture: he's responsible for overseeing the COO, who's in charge of the numbers, the results. The CEO is the interface with the board of directors and their lead director, of course.

We told Gerry there was no rush, but in very short order he said, "Well, what about the two guys who don't get Jack Welch's job?"

It made perfect sense. All three of the candidates for GE's top spot were world-beaters: established leaders in their own right, eminently qualified to run the day-to-day operations of a major corporation like Home Depot. I talked with Bernie and Arthur about it, and they agreed with me.

I went to see Jack Welch.

"Jack," I said, "do me a favor. When you've decided who's going to succeed you, let me know."

Jack knew right away what I was driving at. "Stay the fuck away from my guys!" he yelled. "Don't you dare go near them!" He was worried I was going to approach Immelt, McNerney, and Nardelli before he made his decision, unbalancing his decision-making process. The three candidates had different skills and talents, but Welch swore to me they were neck and neck.

I tried to calm him down. "I'm not going to front run you,

Jack. All I'm saying is, when you've decided who you're picking, I'll take seconds on the other two."

Welch had previously told the GE board that he wanted each of the three candidates to get three million stock options on top of the benefits he already had. It was a very canny move on Jack's part. For the two guys who would not get the top job, this piece of largesse only had immediate value after they left the company: GE stock hadn't yet reached the strike price, so they'd be walking away empty-handed. But any outside company either runner-up went to would be compelled to compensate him for his loss by matching the value of those three million options. "Oh shit," I thought. "This is going to cost us"—Home Depot—"a lot of money."

I spent the last weekend in October in, of all places, the Meadows, an addiction-treatment facility in Arizona. I wasn't the patient; it was one of our senior people, who had a bad enough drinking problem that Bernie and Arthur and I had to order him to go away. And the saddest thing was that it was Family Weekend at the Meadows, and this guy had been divorced a couple of times and had no family to come out to spend Family Weekend with him, so I volunteered. It was quite a scene—basically family members sitting in circles and screaming at each other: "You did this! You did that!" I didn't do any screaming, but I supported my guy the best I could, and on Sunday night I flew to Greenville, South Carolina, where GE was having a board meeting.

I got to the hotel around 11:00 p.m. to find three or four of my fellow directors sitting around having a drink. "What's going on?" I asked.

"Immelt's getting the job," they told me.

Wow. Okay. Naive me: I'd believed Jack when he told me the three guys were neck and neck, but it turned out that it was likely all along he was going to pick Jeff. McNerney was out early, and I think Welch felt Immelt had more gravitas, more CEO presence, than Nardelli. Jeff was a Dartmouth graduate; he had an MBA from Harvard. Nardelli's BA was from Western Illinois; he got his MBA at the University of Louisville.

With the turbulence and decline in value GE suffered after Jeff took over, I wonder whether Jack now regrets his choice.

Maybe Nardelli wasn't polished enough for GE, but he was perfect for Home Depot. I had a dossier on him made up and sent copies to Bernie and Arthur.

At the meeting the next morning, I went up to Welch and said, "Jack, do me a favor. I'm not going to do anything right away, but let me know when I can approach Nardelli."

"Don't you do a fuckin' thing!" Jack said. "I've got this thing all planned."

The Friday after Thanksgiving, he told me, he was going to send a plane to pick up Immelt and his wife and bring them down to his home in Palm Beach so he could tell Jeff he had the job. The plane's manifest would have somebody else's name on it so nobody would be the wiser.

That Sunday night, Jack continued, he would fly to Cincinnati, where McNerney was running GE Aircraft Engines, to tell Jim that he didn't have the job. Then he would fly from Cincinnati to Schenectady, where Nardelli was running GE Power Systems, to tell Bob he didn't have the job. "And then on Monday morning at eight o'clock," Jack said, "we'll make a public announcement."

"Okay," I told Jack. "I'll do nothing until Monday morning at eight o'clock."

The whole thing went as planned: the Friday after Thanksgiving, Immelt found out he had the job. On Sunday, Welch flew to Cincinnati to tell McNerney, who, by the way, went to work as CEO of 3M on Tuesday morning: he'd set it up some time earlier.

Nardelli was hit hard by the news. When Jack flew to

Schenectady and told Bob he wasn't getting the job, Nardelli argued with him. "Why?" Bob said. "Look at my numbers. Look at those guys and look at me. I've delivered."

"Bob, it's my decision," Jack said. "And this is the way it is."

I went to California on Sunday of Thanksgiving weekend. Whenever I went to the West Coast, I stayed on New York time, and that Monday I woke up at 4:00 a.m. and turned on CNBC. Jack had said he would embargo the announcement until 8:00 a.m. New York time, but because GE owned NBC, he gave CNBC a half-hour head start to announce Immelt had the job. At 4:30 a.m. my time, I quickly picked up the phone and called Gerry Roche. "Get to Nardelli right now, and make sure you get to him," I said. "Tell him we want to talk to him."

Roche called me right back. "Got him."

I phoned Nardelli. "Bob, I know you're disappointed," I said. "But I've got a great opportunity for you."

Two days later Bernie flew to Schenectady and had dinner with Nardelli. When the dinner was over, Bernie called me and said, "That's the guy."

Bernie was on board, and so was Arthur. The following weekend we flew Bob and his wife to Atlanta to look at Home Depot's corporate headquarters and Atlanta, and on Sunday, six days after he'd been passed over at GE, we offered Nardelli the position of chief operating officer.

The whole thing was a whirlwind. Bob met with the chairmen of all our board committees. We had the Comp Committee come in and talk with Bob about his pay package: it was understood that we had to match his three million GE stock options with options in Home Depot stock equal to that value. At that point, GE was trading at around $50 per share, and Home Depot at about $35.

That night, coincidentally, there was a Heidrick & Struggles partners' dinner in Atlanta, so Gerry Roche was also in town. And Gerry dropped by to see us—we were having a meeting of the Executive Committee at the Four Seasons Hotel—and said, "Oh, by the way, guys, Nardelli will only take the job if he's made president and CEO."

Having dropped this little bombshell, Roche went off to his dinner, leaving the six of us on the committee—Arthur, Bernie, Mitch Hart, John Clendenin, Bonnie Hill, and myself—sitting there in silence. "Well, here we are," I finally said. "He won't come on as COO—what do we do?"

Arthur suddenly said, "If he wants to be CEO, it's okay with me."

As lead director, I spoke up. "Gee, Arthur, that's really magnanimous," I said. "Why don't you excuse yourself and let us talk, and we'll get back to you." We had a suite in the hotel, and Arthur went up there. And the minute he left the room, all of us breathed a sigh of relief.

Home Depot was having serious morale problems at that point, and Arthur, who was letting personal issues distract him, was part of the problem. Not only that, the rival chain Lowe's was showing great strength and beginning to get at us. "What do we do, guys?" I asked my fellow directors.

Everyone agreed we should take Arthur up on his offer to let Nardelli replace him as CEO.

The only thing we couldn't agree on was who was going to be the one to go upstairs and tell Arthur.

He was our friend and the co-founder of the company, present at the creation. A great guy who had slipped a little bit. Everybody slips from time to time. But who wants to be the one who calls them on it?

Nobody. That's human nature.

We all sat there for almost an hour stewing about it. "Okay, Bernie, why don't you go up and tell him," I said. "He said it's okay with him."

"Oh, no, no," Bernie said. "You've got to go do it."

"Why do I have to do it?" I asked.

"You've got to go do it," Bernie repeated.

"But, Bernie, you're the chairman."

Bernie wouldn't budge. "No, no, you've got to do it."

Finally, I went upstairs and knocked on the door of the suite. Arthur was watching a football game. "Arthur," I said, "the board is really impressed with your position about what's good for the company, and we've decided we'll accept your offer; we're going to make Bob president and CEO."

Well, Arthur went ballistic. "Get out of here!" he yelled. "I don't want to see you!"

"Wait a minute, Arthur," I said. "You mean you were not in good faith when you said, 'It's okay with me'? Why didn't you just say, 'Uh-uh, I want the job,' and let us have to make the decision? Were you just maneuvering to get a vote of confidence? This really disappoints me."

Arthur was really upset. "Get the fuck out of here!" he said. "I want to see Bernie! I want to see Bernie!"

I went back downstairs. "Bernie," I said, "now I understand why you didn't want to go see him."

"What happened?"

"He blew up," I said. "He wants no part of me; he wants to see you."

"You've got to go up there with me," Bernie said.

I said, "I'm not going with you."

Bernie shook his head. He didn't want to face Arthur alone— human nature! "You've got to come with me," he said.

"All right," I finally said. And we went upstairs.

The minute we walked into the room, Arthur pointed at me and said, "You get the fuck out of here."

I got out, and Bernie had to deal with Arthur himself. Arthur calmed down—maybe he understood he had as much reason to be upset with himself as anybody else had—and accepted the position of nonexecutive chairman.

———

We called Nardelli and told him we were going to make him president and CEO and said we were going to have a board meeting that same night to approve his package, which included the very pricey proposition of making him whole on what he'd left at GE.

By now it was getting close to Christmas. And Bob very kindly invited Elaine and me to the GE Power Systems holiday party in Schenectady—the last one he would preside over. Every division of GE had its own Christmas party, and they were lavish affairs: Barry Manilow performed at Nardelli's shindig.

Anyway, Elaine and I went, and from the moment I walked in the door, I knew we'd picked the right guy to lead Home Depot. Bob's people were literally crying about his departure. Weeping! The affection they had for this man was so powerful. The division's union rep stood up at the party and said, "There will never be another Bob Nardelli again for us."

"Holy shit," I said to myself. "Everybody loves him; he's a real people guy. We've got a great operator here."

So Nardelli came to work. And he really was a great operator. For the first four years he was at Home Depot, every single thing he touched turned to gold. It was remarkable. He grew earnings at 20 percent a year for five full years. That's unheard of. Remember what Bob said to Jack Welch when Jack told him he was passing him over for Immelt? "Look at my numbers." Bob was all about the numbers, and his numbers were amazing.

He slashed costs across the whole organization. He consolidated division executives' responsibilities, which allowed him to cut a number of managers loose. He had a computerized inventory system installed at our Atlanta headquarters.

There was a management method at GE called Six Sigma, a set of statistical tools for maximizing output and minimizing variability; to Jack Welch it was gospel, and Nardelli (whom some people used to call Little Jack) was Jack's most passionate disciple. Nardelli brought Six Sigma to Home Depot. He also brought along his own general counsel, Frank Fernandez: I thought that was an unusual move, maybe a little worrying. He also brought in a former HR guy from General Electric, Dennis Donovan, a guy who lived on charts and percentages. Donovan was maniacal about these percentages: he always had a statistic to back up every conclusion.

The only problem was that Home Depot's great strength was (and still is) its culture, and our culture isn't about statistics.

In our culture, you don't measure the intangible value of a sales associate saying to a customer, "Can I help you?" or, "You don't really need that. Come over here and look at this. It doesn't cost as much, but you'll be fine with it."

A story.

One Saturday morning at one of our stores out on Long Island, a customer comes in with the stem from his bathroom faucet and says to a sales associate, "Give me a new one of these."

Now—remember, I'm the son of a plumber—if you look at a faucet, it's got a handle and an escutcheon (that's the shield under the handle). And beneath the escutcheon, inside the sink, you've got the guts. The way it works is the handle turns a stem, or shaft.

At the end of the shaft, there's a washer. The washer fits into what's known as a seat, and when you shut the faucet, the washer presses against the seat, and the water can't come up. Now, if that washer is old and brittle, the water comes through, and you get a drip.

"What's wrong with the faucet?" the kid asks the customer. (This sales associate is about twenty-eight; to me, anybody under eighty is a kid.)

"Well, it drips," the guy says.

"The reason it drips is—look at your washer," the kid says. "Come on with me." He goes over to the plumbing department, and he takes a little thirty-nine-cent glassine bag of assorted washers off the display, opens it, takes the right-sized washer out, unscrews the screw on the guy's faucet assembly that holds the washer in, takes out the old washer, puts the new one in, and screws the screw back in.

"There you go," the kid tells the guy. "Go back home and put it back in; I'm sure it'll be fine."

And lo and behold, the guy went home, put the faucet back in, and it was fine. Drip gone—problem solved. He paid nothing.

About three or four months later, the guy's wife wants a new kitchen, and she wants to go to some foo-foo kitchen showroom place. The husband says, "Oh, no. I want to go see my friend at Home Depot."

They go in the store. The guy goes up to the same kid and says to him, "We're looking for a new kitchen, and we'd like you to help."

"Let me take you over to Roz," the kid says, and takes them to meet the woman who's the kitchen designer. "Will you please take care of them?" the kid says.

Bottom line: the couple bought a brand-new kitchen—appliances, cabinets, flooring. It was close to a $100,000 job.

That's not statistics.

Between 2000 and 2005, Bob Nardelli nearly doubled Home

Depot's sales. During this time, the company's revenue increased from $45 billion to over $81 billion. He grew net earnings after taxes from $2.5 billion to $5.6 billion. But during the same period, Home Depot's stock stayed more or less stagnant while Lowe's stock price doubled.

Back when the company had first started, I'd recommended a policy requiring every director to visit three Home Depot stores every ninety days, casually dressed and as inconspicuous as possible, and report on his or her findings. What the directors were now finding on their store visits was that something was amiss. Wall Street analysts were also reporting the same issues—morale problems in the stores and, company-wide, an inordinate focus on Nardelli's pay package. The market had picked up on our troubles.

Within three months of Nardelli's taking the reins—this was early 2001—it was obvious there was a problem between Arthur and Nardelli. That spring Bob came to us and said, "Look, this isn't working." So we held a special board meeting at the airport in Palm Beach, and we talked around and around the subject for a while, trying to tell Arthur politely that the management structure wasn't working as it was then constituted—until finally Frank Borman, the tough old fighter pilot (Frank had joined the board in 1980) spoke up. "Hey, Arthur, don't you get it?" Frank said. "It's time for you to move on."

Arthur didn't protest: he was stunned. He went home, though he went home a very wealthy man. The next thing we heard, the Atlanta Falcons were up for sale, and Arthur bought the team.

Bernie remained chairman for a little while. But at the beginning of 2002 he stepped down, and Nardelli added chairman to his other titles.

And the company was still hurting. Nardelli had made no friends among the division executives, and his storewide program of trimming back product-knowledgeable sales associates—like that kid who gave away the washer—and replacing them with cheap part-time help was sweetening our bottom line but souring customer relations.

There was also a pet idea of Bob's, the Store Leadership Program, or SLP. Nardelli thought that installing college graduates and ex-military officers as store managers would improve performance and class up our whole operation. It sounded like a good idea—on paper. I remember going into a Home Depot on Long Island and talking to the manager, a West Point graduate who'd come in under SLP. He was clearly a smart guy, but when I asked him about his ambitions for the store, he said, "Oh, I'm just here for the time being; I've got my sights set on Atlanta." Meaning, an executive position at corporate headquarters. Meaning his own store would receive anything but his full attention.

Meanwhile, Lowe's was continuing to gain on us.

There was also the continuing issue of Bob's compensation. As you'll remember, the early years of the twenty-first century—and here we circle back around to the Enron and WorldCom scandals breaking then and the fight I was starting to have with Spitzer over Grasso's pay—were the silly season for CEO compensation stories. Executive pay was the hot-button item, and Nardelli became a poster boy: the business journals were reporting that Bob's options were worth over $200 million. But they didn't have that monetary value at that point—nothing like it. By applying a commonly used financial formula called the Black-Scholes model, you could place a *theoretical* value of about $40 million on Nardelli's options. But Home Depot's stock would have to rise significantly for that value to become real, and there was no guarantee (especially with Lowe's beating us like a drum) when—or if—Home Depot's stock would go that high.

Bob's contract called for him to make between $15 and $16 million a year, including bonuses. In every year between 2000 and

2005, we paid him twice that; that's how good his numbers were. But just like everyone else in the business community, we on the board of Home Depot were reading all those headlines about that supposed $200 million pay package, and even though the stories weren't true, appearances—optics—matter. We held a special meeting of the Executive Committee.

Bonnie Hill was chair of compensation. She suggested, and we all agreed, that for the sake of appearances, we should pay Bob $1 million less than we paid him last year. In 2006, that is, instead of $31 million, he would make $30 million—still almost $15 million over what his contract called for. We called him in.

First we talked about his numbers—music to Bob's ears. We told him what a great job he'd done and how pleased we were. And then we said, "Bob, for cosmetic purposes, we're going to ding you a million bucks this year."

He stood straight up, right there in the boardroom, as if he'd gotten a jolt of electricity. "Why are you doing this to me?" he yelled. "I worked harder this year than last year! You should be paying me more, not less!" He went on and on like that—*look at my numbers!*—and then he stormed out of the room.

We all sat there stunned. My seat was next to his, because I was lead director. I looked around and said, "I'll be back in a minute."

I got up and went to Bob's office. "You get back in that fuckin' room," I told him. "You don't *ever* disrespect that board again like that—ever. You get back in that room and you apologize to those people. We're paying you $14 million more than we owe you. We don't have to give you fourteen million extra dollars. We're giving it to you, Bob. You did a great job. We just think that for your benefit and our benefit it would be better to get below the radar, and that's what we're trying to do. We think a million bucks does it."

He looked hesitant for a moment.

"Just think about what you just did," I said.

He thought about it. And he went back in and apologized. But the damage was done. And the headlines kept coming.

The Executive Committee continued to talk about how to get Nardelli and his $240 million off the front page. Soon after the meeting with Bob—it was around Labor Day 2006—I went to my place in the North Carolina mountains, around a two-and-a-half-hour drive from Atlanta, for a couple of weeks.

I looked out at those beautiful trees and hills, and I thought and thought. Then I suddenly had an idea.

Home Depot's stock was still in the mid-$30s then, so Nardelli's options weren't in the money yet. Now, we could have asked Bob to give back some of his options, just to get down below that inflammatory (and theoretical) number of $240 million. But I knew Bob too well by now to think he'd give anything back.

What about instead of taking something from Nardelli, we were to give something to Home Depot stockholders?

My brainstorm was to ask Bob to agree not to exercise his options until the stock rose to 15 percent above his strike price—and stayed there for a period of time. That way he would get to keep all his options, all the investors would be making money, and the business journals would get to marvel at his generosity.

A win-win-win!

It was a Sunday night. I called Jack Welch up—he was retired and living on Nantucket—and said, "Jack, I have an idea." I told him all about it.

"Brilliant!" Jack said. "That's a brilliant idea. He should absolutely do it."

So I phoned Nardelli and told him I wanted to see him in the morning. And first thing Monday I drove down to Home Depot's headquarters in Atlanta and told Bob about my plan over lunch in his office.

"Bob," I said after I'd explained it, "this solves everything. There's no downside for you." Because they weren't qualified options, I said, he would have to pay income tax on all the shares he bought at the exercise price, even if he didn't turn around and sell them. The stockholders and the business journals would get to see what an upright, selfless guy he was.

He shook his head. "Well, I don't know if I'll be happy if I do it," he said.

"Listen, Bob. You know yourself better than I know you. If you don't think you're going to be happy, then you probably don't really want to do it."

"Well, let me think about it," he said.

"Fine," I said.

In the car on my way back to North Carolina, I phoned Welch. "Jack," I said, "he's going to call you."

I phoned Jack again when I got back to the mountains Monday night. "Yeah, he called me," he said. "He's thinking like a damn immigrant."

"What do you mean?" I asked.

"He's not going to do it," Jack said. "I told him your plan was brilliant. That he wouldn't have to give up anything, that he could hold on to everything. He wasn't buying."

The fact is that Nardelli *was* acting like an immigrant instead of the CEO of a $90 billion company. He was fixated on what was essentially a petty matter—the details of his compensation—instead of Home Depot's overall strategy. He lived in a permanent state of feeling ripped off. Just like a guy who can't get over being dumped by a girl, he had never gotten over Welch's not choosing him for the top spot at GE. Not long after he first came to Home Depot, *Fortune* did an article about Immelt taking the reins. The reporter talked to Bob, and Bob was still talking about his numbers, still arguing about why Welch should have chosen him instead of Jeff. "I told Jack, 'I need an autopsy here,'" Nardelli said to the reporter. "Let's exhume the body." Not the most felicitous choice of words.

At 11:30 a.m. on the day the magazine hit the stands, Jack Welch calls me up. "You fuckin' guineas!" he yells. "You never get over anything! Tell that guy he didn't get my job and to get on with his life!"

But Bob never got over not getting the GE job. And every time he had a chance to stick it to GE, he did. One of the first moves he made at Home Depot was to substitute Philips lightbulbs for GE lightbulbs, at all twenty-three hundred stores around the country. Now, you could argue that it was the right thing for our customers, because the Philips lightbulb cost the same but lasted 30 percent longer. It was scientifically verifiable, so you could advertise it, and the customers went for it. But take a step back for a second. Do you write down the date when you change a lightbulb? Damn right you don't! And neither does anyone else! Nardelli didn't care how long the damn lightbulbs lasted once they were screwed in; all he cared about was screwing GE.

But lightbulbs weren't the only thing Bob changed at all twenty-three hundred stores. He knew the store managers were grumbling about him, because he was leaning on the managers to drive sales and cut costs, to push their people harder and slash overtime. And so in response to the grumbling, he installed a human-resources person at every Home Depot location in the United States, to the tune of around $100,000 per annum per HR representative. Do the math. That's a lot out the window every year for a function that arguably wasn't necessary outside corporate headquarters.

But Nardelli felt it was necessary in the stores, and I don't think it was for the reason he gave out. Morale in the stores continued to be lousy; people were leaving. Home Depot's mission and culture were in question. You could make the case that the

HR representatives in each store were there to ease staff concerns, but you could also make the case that they were there to monitor discontent and report it to Bob Nardelli. The store managers began to feel that these HR people were Nardelli's spies. Morale sank even further, company-wide.

When I went to Bob and told him that I'd been in the stores and morale was not good, he said, "They're a bunch of crybabies."

"Bob, they may be a bunch of crybabies to you, but they're the most precious thing we have," I said. "They're the only thing that separates us from everybody else. They're our secret sauce, our secret weapon. They're what make us what we are as a company."

It was beginning to dawn on me that in his early days at Home Depot Nardelli had acted like the people guy he'd been at GE, but that was when he could rack up good numbers by making changes (like switching the stores' return policy from cash refunds to store credit) that didn't hurt anyone: he was picking low-hanging fruit. Once the low-hanging fruit was gone, Bob got tougher, but counterproductively so. I realized that Bob was really just a people guy on the surface: that he'd made himself loved at GE only in imitation of Jack Welch, who, as tough as he was, truly was a people guy. Bob Nardelli had liked being seen as Little Jack because he wanted to inherit Big Jack's job.

Around this time, early in the summer of 2006, two of Home Depot's directors, Greg Brenneman and Labe Jackson, called me and said they felt Nardelli's leadership was not helping the company. I held back on voicing an opinion.

That fall of 2006—it was five and a half years into Bob's tenure—an activist investment fund out in San Diego called Relational Investors began to take an interest in Home Depot. Activist funds critique companies they're invested in and suggest improvements. In theory, this is all to the good for a company and its stockholders. But it can get coercive, and counterproductive. If the company doesn't follow the fund's suggestions, the fund may mount a proxy fight to gain control, or at the very least get active in a very public way, much as Nelson Peltz had done with GE and Paul Singer with Arconic (formerly Alcoa) before he actually did launch a proxy fight.

I didn't know about Relational Investors at first. I just had the uneasy sense that with our stock flat and company morale down, somebody might be coming after us. So at our November board meeting my fellow directors and I, Bob included, decided to retain my friend Marty Lipton, who's recognized as the number-one guy in the world in corporate governance, and his firm, Wachtell, Lipton, in case anybody out there was considering agitating for changes at Home Depot. If anybody came after us, we agreed, our first call would be to Marty Lipton.

At a meeting like that, the agenda is the agenda, but you always try to read between the lines. And one thing I could instantly see in that boardroom was how poisonous things had become between Nardelli and the directors.

Afterward, I called Bob up. "Bob," I said, "I want to come down to Atlanta with the committee heads and have dinner with you."

He was nervous. Suspicious. "What's going on?" he asked. "What's the agenda?"

"No agenda," I said. "We just want to clear the air."

So the four of us went down to Atlanta: Mitch Hart, who was the head of the Technology Committee; Bonnie Hill, the head of Comp; John Clendenin, who was the head of Audit; and myself.

We sat down to dinner, and John Clendenin said, "Bob, before we start, I want to say something. I don't know who you are, Bob. I thought I knew you. But I don't know who you are, and that scares me."

"What do you mean?" Nardelli asked.

"What you're doing here," Clendenin said. "Your behavior.

We're doing all we can for you, Bob, and we're trying to help you. We're paying you more than we owe you, and we're happy with that, but for whatever reason it always feels like it's you versus us or us versus you. We've got to fix this."

Well, Bob listened. He said he was trying to right the ship. There was a lot of work to be done to make that happen, he said, but he emphasized that he was all in, and then some. Nobody had ever criticized his work ethic. His tone was conciliatory, and the tension around the table eased. It wound up being a nice dinner.

A week later—it was early December—I got a call from Andy Taussig, our banker at Lehman Brothers. "Ken, I don't know what's going on," he said, "but Nardelli is bringing a group of his senior people up to New York on Monday to meet with us and two other bankers. They've also got three PR firms lined up to interview, and they want us to line up three law firms."

"For what?" I asked.

"Apparently, they've been approached by one of these activist groups, and they want to get ready," Taussig said. "But you can't let Bob know I told you."

This pissed me off. The board had already agreed what to do if an activist group moved on us. The entire board was to be notified immediately, along with Marty Lipton. Nardelli was acting like a law unto himself.

Friday afternoon around three o'clock, Nardelli called me up. He told me he'd received a fax from Relational Investors listing several issues at Home Depot they considered critical and strongly hinting they were about to mount a proxy fight for control of the company.

"When did you get this fax?" I asked.

"It came in on Wednesday," Nardelli said.

"And you're only calling me on Friday to tell me?"

Bob said impatiently that the fax had come in on a machine

in the investor relations department that nobody ever looked at and had sat unnoticed for two days. And thanks to what Andy Taussig had told me, I didn't believe a word he said.

"What are your thoughts?" I asked him. I knew he had moved ahead without telling me, but I couldn't tell him I knew.

"My senior staff and I are coming to New York Monday morning," he said. "We're going to interview three banking firms, three law firms, and three PR firms."

"You'll do no such thing," I said. "Bob, the board has made it clear that anything like this comes directly to the entire board, not just you. Cancel those meetings. We're going to have a board call."

On Friday night at ten, all twelve members of the Home Depot board, including Bob and Marty Lipton, got on a conference call to discuss how we would respond to Relational Investors. We all agreed that Nardelli should cancel the meetings he'd set up. We confirmed that Wachtell, Lipton would represent us legally, but we decided that we didn't want a PR firm or an investment-banking firm yet. We were a wounded company: publicity in a battle with an activist fund would be a delicate matter. And as for which banker we should choose, as Marty Lipton later told me, "Look, you should pick somebody you really trust, because many bankers, when they find out this is going on, will run ahead of you and try to encourage another firm to come after you." To try to take us over, in other words.

Business can be brutal, as I've said time and again. Just how brutal, I would find out very soon.

On the Sunday morning after the conference call, the board had another call. And John Clendenin, who is a very quiet, honorable, decent man, was still fuming about Nardelli. "We're the board!" he yelled. "This wasn't his decision to make!"

Throughout December, it became increasingly clear that the Home Depot's board was losing confidence in Bob. Then, on the day after Christmas, several directors phoned me and told me that Nardelli was seeking their votes to throw me off the board.

"You're kidding me!" I said, though I put it in somewhat stronger terms.

"That's what he said."

I told them I would think about what to do next. That was Tuesday, December 26, 2006—the same day Gerald Ford died. The next day Greg Brenneman and Labe Jackson called me again and said they felt Bob had to go.

I agreed. "But, fellas," I said, "we're going to do this in an orderly way. We're going to decide as a board, not as individuals."

On Friday, December 29, I got on the phone with the members of the Executive Committee, and we all agreed that it was time for Nardelli to step down. We decided to have a special board meeting in Dallas on January 2; we were going to be closed for business on New Year's Day, and Tuesday the second had been declared a national day of mourning for President Ford. I said I would tell Bob to be there.

As for who would replace Bob, the five of us were all agreed: the clear choice was our vice-chairman, Frank Blake.

Nardelli had brought Blake over from GE, where he'd been the general counsel of the Power Systems division and senior VP for business development. Frank had a stellar résumé: he'd graduated from Harvard and Columbia Law, had clerked for the Supreme Court justice John Paul Stevens, and had been deputy counsel to the first president Bush. And he was as quiet and thoughtful as Nardelli was hard charging. Despite his achievements, there was a certain humility to Frank Blake—a quality that, in some people's eyes, might not have made him the first choice to lead a big company like Home Depot. But I believed in him strongly.

We were still on the conference call. I was at my home in Florida; Mitch Hart and Greg Brenneman were skiing in Vail, Colorado. Bonnie Hill was in California. Only Clendenin was in Atlanta, where he lived; I knew that Blake was also there. "John, go talk to Frank," I said. "Tell him it's highly confidential, but ask him if the job were offered to him, would he take it." If Frank was willing, we would then have to get the whole board's approval.

I then got Marty Lipton on the phone, and we called Nardelli to tell him we were going to have a special board meeting on Tuesday the second.

Bob immediately sensed what it was all about. "You can't do that," he said.

Marty Lipton spoke up. "No, I'm sorry, Bob," he said. "Any director can call a board meeting; all he has to do is give you forty-eight hours' notice, and this is more than forty-eight hours."

There was nothing Nardelli could say.

John Clendenin called me back at noon. "I spoke to Frank," he said. "He wants to think about it."

"Tell him he's got three hours," I said.

John called Frank back at three o'clock, and Frank said, "If it's offered, I'll take it." John phoned me with the news.

"Don't say anything to anybody," I told him. "Bob doesn't know about this."

Nardelli phoned me the next morning, Saturday. "Ken, I admire you and love you and respect you," he said. "You're my coach, my mentor, my idol. This is a father and a son having a family spat."

"Bob, when you've got 300,000 people"—the total number of Home Depot's employees—"depending on you to make the right decision, that's not a family," I told him. "That's 300,000 lives. This is beyond family." I said, "Bob, let me make it clear. I'm only one vote, but as far as I'm concerned, it's time for you to go."

"Can I come down and see you?" he asked. "Talk about all this?"

"I don't want to see you, Bob. I've made my mind up. It's time."

A deep silence on the other end of the line.

"Bob," I said, "on Tuesday you're going to have a chance to present your case, and the board is going to have to make a decision. Does it want to continue on, or does it want to make a change?

"I have no authority to speak for any other director, so what I'm saying to you right now is strictly me," I told him. "What the rest of the board does, they'll do. They're all very independent, strong-willed people."

The directors were scattered around the country, so I reserved a couple of conference rooms at Dalfort, the general-aviation terminal at Love Field, Dallas, the most central spot for the meeting. We gathered there on Tuesday afternoon, January 2. Marty Lipton was present, to tell us what our obligations were and what the process should be—to make sure every *t* was crossed and every *i* was dotted. Frank Blake was waiting in another room.

Bob had the floor first, and what he talked about—no surprise—was his numbers: "This is what it was when I took over; this is what it is now; this is what happened in between." Sales. Revenue. Net earnings. All up; all unimpeachable. He never mentioned morale. He never mentioned his twenty-three hundred HR people.

I sat there, fascinated. My first impression of Bob Nardelli—"he's a real people guy; we've got a great operator here"—had been exactly 50 percent right. The guy really was a great operator. But I came to realize—too damn slowly—that the whole people equation of Home Depot, the essence of our culture, had completely eluded him. To me, the whole issue with Bob was the damage to the culture. There's nothing like these people in our stores. They're special. Now, how do you get all these special people? Well, you start by treating them special. You let them know they matter. You let them know you appreciate their opinion. You let them know that if they think there's a better way of doing things than the way they're doing them, they have an obligation to tell us, and we have an obligation to listen. You also let them know that anybody can build a big store space and put all kinds of inventory in it; the glue that holds Home Depot together are these values. We don't just say them. We believe them, and we practice them consistently.

Now, Bob had developed the mind-set that these people, who started at well over minimum wage and got a raise every year if their performance reviews were good, were a cost. And they were a cost! They were a significant part of the company's overall costs. And therefore Bob spent a lot of time trying to figure out how he could take that cost down. In my mind, it was like the reverse of the straw and the camel's back. Nardelli kept taking one straw off, and it reached a point where something very valuable was being lost.

He finally finished his pitch, and we asked him to leave the room so the board could discuss what was going to happen next. Since I was chairing the meeting, I spoke first. "Okay," I said. "First of all, nobody has the luxury of not having an opinion. We're all going to have to take a stand one way or the other."

Bob had brought two people onto the board during his tenure. There was Tom Ridge, the former governor of Pennsylvania and onetime head of Homeland Security, and Helen Johnson-Leipold, of the S. C. Johnson family, who'd just come on a few months earlier. Helen asked to abstain, because she felt she hadn't been around the company long enough to develop an informed opinion. Ridge took the position that Bob should not be fired. All eleven of the other directors felt that Nardelli should leave.

A brief discussion about Frank Blake followed. Some of the directors wanted to name him acting CEO rather than give him the position outright. For one thing, Frank had never led a company; maybe his quiet personality was also giving some people pause.

"Wait a minute," I said. "Let's cut his legs off; he'll have a better chance of succeeding. We've just proven we have the courage to fire a CEO. Let's have the guts to pass power without reservations." And so we voted Frank in immediately.

Marty Lipton and I went into the room where Bob was sitting with his lawyer. "Bob," I said, "the board has made its decision. We wish you good luck. I'm going to hang around to negotiate your severance contract, and there's nothing more to say. We appreciate your service. We think you did a lot of good things. But we think at this juncture it's time for you to go one way and us to go another way."

Marty and I then went to the room where Frank Blake had been waiting and told him the good news. The three of us returned to the conference room. "Ladies and gentlemen," I said, "meet your new CEO." Everyone applauded warmly.

The first thing Frank did was fascinating. When I asked him, "Frank, is there anything I can do for you right now?" he said, "Yes, I'd like to talk to Bernie Marcus."

Bernie had retired at age seventy-three in 2002, but as the company's co-founder he was passionately tuned in to Home Depot's every move, and he hated almost everything Bob Nardelli had done as CEO. He wasn't shy about expressing his opinions to Bob, either, and the blood between them eventually got so bad that the two of them stopped speaking.

I placed the call to Bernie. And when I told him we'd just given the job to Frank Blake, his reaction was short and not so sweet. "Another GE guy," he said.

"Yeah, another GE guy, Bernie, but this is a very different guy. You're gonna see."

"Hmm," he said, sounding anything but convinced. I tried to tell him that Frank was his own man, a totally different person from Nardelli. But Bernie still wasn't having any. I hoped he might eventually come around.

"Bernie," I said, "I've got someone here who wants to talk to you." And I handed the phone to Frank.

"Bernie, Frank Blake," Frank said. "Listen, Bernie, I want to tell you that I'm looking forward to my responsibilities leading this great company that you and Arthur and Ken founded. I think it's a great opportunity, and I'm excited about the future. But I'm going to need your help and your insight."

I could tell from looking at Frank's face that it was a hard sell. But at the end of the call, Bernie, Frank, and I agreed we would meet for breakfast in Palm Beach the following Sunday morning to discuss the path forward.

After Frank left for Atlanta, Marty and I sat down with Bob and his lawyer to finalize his severance.

The board had agreed we'd give Nardelli $18 million. (By the way, he had ninety days to exercise those of his stock options that were in the money, and most of them were not in the money. His option package wound up being essentially worthless: the furthest thing from that reported $200 million.)

If Bob was agreeable to his settlement, we said, we would offer him the choice of spreading his severance over four years to allow for tax planning, or taking it all at once. But the minute we began talking, Bob's lawyer started nickel-and-diming me on some bullshit insurance policy!

"I'm going to tell you something," I said to his lawyer. "My plane is right downstairs. If this contract isn't signed in five minutes, I'm getting on my plane, and I'm flying to Palm Beach, and you're going to be wired $18 million tomorrow morning, and we're all done. If he wants to fuck around, we'll fuck around, and he'll be the loser."

Bob signed the agreement like that, and left. I've rarely seen him since. We're cordial with each other, but distant.

The next morning, bright and early, I ran into Larry Bossidy in the North Palm Beach community where we both live. Larry was a former chairman and CEO of Honeywell; before that he was vice-chairman at GE—a very, very talented guy, and a very close friend. Nardelli's firing was all over the newspapers; his supposed pay package was *the* issue of the time.

"Well, you really screwed this one up," Larry said.

"What are you talking about?"

"Frank Blake worked for me at GE, and he's no CEO."

"Well, we disagree," I said.

Poker is my favorite game, and I'm pretty good at it—don't ever play me in poker! But the truth is that at that moment I didn't know exactly what kind of a hand I was holding with Frank Blake. What I did know is that he was a very smart man and a very good man. I knew he and his wife, Liz, were devoutly religious. I knew he carried himself humbly and wasn't afraid to ask questions. But putting aside how good Blake was or wasn't, I'd pushed for him because I had a gun at my head; I knew we had to leave that room with a leader. Did I know that Frank would be as strong a leader as he turned out to be? Of course not. But I was in poker mode, and I liked Frank Blake's chances.

"Well, Larry, you're wrong," I said. "In fact, I feel so certain, how much you want to bet?"

"I'll bet you ten grand," Larry said.

"Okay," I said. "The loser pays ten thousand to the charity of the winner's choice. Now, how do we decide whether I win or I lose?"

"I say he won't be there in six months."

"I'll tell you how good I feel about Frank," I said. "He's got to make it a year. If it was just six months, we might say, 'Ah, give him a little bit more time.' If he doesn't make it a year, you tell me the name of your charity."

―――――

Frank wasn't a slam dunk by any means. That first breakfast with Bernie set the tone: Bernie was downright chilly with our new CEO. Maybe even a little cooler than chilly. And Frank inherited a company that had been set back on its heels: the stock was flat, morale hadn't improved, and the stores, thanks in part to Nardelli's HR implants, were still riddled with suspicion.

Frank phased out the HR people, but he did a lot more than that. He visited store after store and made it clear at every Home Depot he walked into that he was there to listen and learn. He acknowledged and celebrated the company culture that Bob Nardelli had found so irrelevant. He made a fan of every sales associate he met.

It's easy for a commanding general to impress a foot soldier; Nardelli certainly had an air of command. But Frank Blake had a different way of impressing people. He didn't throw his weight around; he didn't yell. He had a way of making everyone he talked to feel as important as he was. He dressed like a plumber, and he looked like a nerd. It was clear that he was a brilliant man, and like most brilliant people he was endlessly curious. He truly cared about what was happening in those stores, down to the smallest detail. At one location we visited together, in Columbus, Ohio, I noticed he was carrying a piece of paper with some figures on it.

"What have you got?" I asked him.

"I want to go see something," he said, and I followed him down an aisle to a display of augers and auger bits. It turned out that Frank wanted to check the pricing on augers, because someone had told him the tools had been mispriced in our stores. Well, they hadn't been, but Frank had to see for himself.

Proving that the big picture depends on a lot of smaller pictures.

Frank Blake became a rock star to the employees, and he gradually won Bernie's acceptance, and then his deep affection, simply by picking up the phone and calling him whenever he had a question he felt Bernie could answer best. None of it happened right away—Frank's first year was tough—but when it did happen, the company was in a better place than it had ever been in before.

Every now and then, to this day, Bernie still likes to give me a hard time about the ditch Nardelli drove Home Depot into. And what I say back to him is this: "Go ask Frank Blake if he would've come here if Nardelli hadn't been here first!"

———

A year to the day after Frank Blake became CEO of Home Depot—right to the very day—I called Larry Bossidy, first thing in the morning. "Larry," I said. "You got a check around and a pen?"

"What do you mean?"

"Well, I'd like you to make a check out for $10,000 to the Boys' Club of New York."

"Why?" Larry said.

"You forgot? I just spoke to Frank at six thirty this morning, and he was still there."

———

I would like to mention a couple of other small details about Frank Blake, because he would never tell you about them himself. He not only has a superb intellect; he's the best listener I've ever met, hands down. If he's talking with a group of people and someone says something interesting, Frank will stop speaking immediately and give the floor to that person. He has the greatest quantity of humility I've ever seen in a man. I don't need to tell you how rare that is in a chief executive. When we first negotiated his salary, he had three stipulations: Number one, he didn't want his compensation to be such that it would be on the front page of the *Wall Street Journal.* Number two, he didn't want it to be an embarrassment to Home Depot sales associates—the kind of thing customers might bring up in a critical way. And number three, he wanted 90 percent of his pay to be in stock. "When the shareholders win, I win," he said. Talk about having skin in the game.

And on more than one occasion, Frank donated his annual bonus, a sum in the millions, to the company's Homer Fund, which provides emergency money to associates in need and gives scholarships to their children.

I would also like to say a final word about my faulty judgment in hiring Bob Nardelli. As with Steve Sato at IVAC, Bob was a great leader until he wasn't. Was I too slow in both cases to see the writing on the wall? Definitely. Both guys were racking up great numbers but ignoring the human equation, and in business good numbers can be like sunlight: blindingly bright.

But did my insecurity, my need to be liked, get in the way of letting these guys go before more damage was done? Definitely not.

It's no fun to fire somebody. Still, in business you don't have the luxury of not holding people accountable to the highest possible standards: you owe it to the company to do the right thing. And when it comes to making those tough decisions, I have no problem at all.

I also have no problem admitting my mistakes: I'm loaded with them. But I never bought a pencil without an eraser on it, and God invented erasers on pencils for people like me.

9.

NET WORTH

When I was ten years old, I was an altar boy at St. Mary's Church in Roslyn, just across the harbor from the sand pits. The priest, Father Francis Ryan—Father Frank—came from Ireland, spoke with a brogue, and had a boxer's nose: he really had been a boxer. Does it sound like a Spencer Tracy movie yet?

I've always been spiritual, and I loved being an altar boy. The hours were challenging, though. When it was my turn to serve the 6:30 Mass for the week, I had to get up at six every morning from Monday until Saturday and walk about a mile to a spot underneath the railroad bridge at Roslyn Road, where Mr. Harnett, the church sexton, would pick me up in his little Ford Model A and drive me the remaining two miles to St. Mary's. I remember the smell of the pipe Mr. Harnett smoked and the fragrance of the inside of the church, a combination of incense and the wood of the pews and the bindings of the hymnals.

Weekdays I'd serve Mass, then walk back up the hill and go to school. But on Saturdays I had to walk all the way home—three miles. Once I took a ride from my uncle Pat, my father's oldest brother, and his wife, my aunt Agnes. My aunt scolded me the whole way about why my mother and father didn't go to church. I never took a ride from them again.

I've always felt that some of the worst people in the world go to Mass regularly, while some of the best people in the world never set foot in church. I attend Mass every Sunday, and try to make daily Mass as often as I can. I have a routine every morning: I get up and brush my teeth and, still in my pajamas, go off in a quiet corner of the house for twenty minutes with my Bible and a Bible study guide and pray.

I don't know if there's a God or if there's a heaven; I can't prove it, but that's what I believe. There's one part of me that thinks, when you're dead, you're dead. You had your shot; move on. But if there isn't a God, what have I lost by praying? Nothing. It's a no-downside bet.

The first part of my prayer is that when I'm presented for my judgment, our Creator will have concluded that for the most part I've lived my life according to His teachings, and Scripture. I then ask that in the hereafter I'll be reunited with all those people I loved and admired who left before me. I then pray for those who have lost loved ones or have problems: people I can help. I say, "God, let me always do it for your praise, honor, and glory—not mine."

I know spirituality isn't for everybody, but for me it's been an incredibly motivating factor. God is the most important part of everything I do.

Yet I'm very conscious of the fact that *I* get praise, honor, and glory on a daily basis. I'm human: I like it. Do you think it doesn't give me a little glow every time I see "NYU Langone" here, there, and everywhere? Can you imagine, these incredibly brilliant doctors and research people walking around with my name on their chests? Does that make me proud? You're damn right it does! And

I'd be totally dishonest if I didn't admit it. Maybe there's somebody out there who wouldn't feel the same way . . . maybe.

I played golf a few months ago with a guy who was doing some business with the medical center. I took him to my club. As we walked out to the first tee, I saw that his golf cap read NYU-LANGONE. I thought, "Hey, that's my name!"

Now, I'm well aware that pride is one of the seven deadly sins. I'm insecure enough to want people to like me and smart enough to recognize when they only like me because I have money or influence. It's awfully easy when people are kissing your behind to let it go straight to your head. But, boy, if that kind of stuff goes to my head, I've lost myself. That's why it's very important for me to work on not thinking I'm better than I am—or than anyone else. I need to be reminded.

My driver, Alvaro, was taking me down to Mass at St. Pat's the other morning. Alvaro has been working for me for twenty-six years, and he's done very well. Dresses like a banker. People compliment me about him all the time. "What an amazing driver you have," they say. I say, "Guess what? Alvaro is on the team, and he knows it."

Alvaro has bought and sold two apartments in Florida and made enough that he now owns an apartment on the sixteenth floor of a high-rise on Singer Island. I always say I would love to be a fly on the wall when he's on the elevator and some retired banker from New York gets in and says, "What do you do?" and Alvaro says, "I'm Mr. Langone's driver." He couldn't wait to show Elaine and me his new place; he's got a view of the ocean on three sides. To me, that's what capitalism should be all about.

As we were heading downtown, I said, "You know, Alvaro, I'm really lucky to have had you with me all these years."

"Well, I'm lucky to work for you," he said. And then: "There's nobody like you, Mr. Langone."

"Well, there's nobody like *you*, Alvaro," I said. And I meant every word.

———

At the end of each day, Elaine always says a wife's prayer, "Dear God, if you'll make him successful, I'll keep him humble." God delivered; Elaine didn't do very well.

In 1986, I said something to my wife that would have alarmed a less levelheaded woman.

"Elaine, I'm buying a plane," I told her. "If I don't use it, I'll get rid of it," I quickly added.

"Fine," she said. Elaine has always been in my corner: she assumes that I wouldn't do something if I couldn't afford it, and it's a good assumption.

Well, I could afford it, but I'll admit I took a big gulp of air when I signed that check. The plane, my first, was a used Learjet 35, and it set me back $1.7 million—a lot of money. Not only that, but Home Depot had just gone public five years before and wasn't yet hitting on all cylinders, so a million seven was really steep for me then.

But hot damn, I was excited about that plane. Part of the reason I bought it was to feel close to my pal Frank Borman: his father drove a laundry truck, and Frank wound up flying around the moon. My father the plumber drove that old tea company truck, and look where I'd ended up. I was thrilled with my good fortune.

I called my mom. "Mother, I just got a plane," I said.

"That's very nice, Kenneth," she said. "Why don't you tell Dad about it?"

"No, no, I want to surprise him," I said. "Just tell him I'm going on a business trip to North Carolina, and I want to take him with me."

I was going down to see Allen Mebane, the chairman of Unifi, and Tommy Teague, my partner in Salem Leasing, our truck-leasing business. Speaking of fathers, Tommy's dad had been a sharecropper, a tenant farmer, and my dad loved Tommy; both my parents loved the way southern people talk.

"Pack Dad's little bag, and tell him I'll pick him up at five thirty," I said. "Give him some dinner first."

So Mom put Dad's toiletries, clean underwear, pajamas, and a clean shirt into his bag and fed him dinner, and I picked him up. We headed up their street to Northern Boulevard, where you turn right to go to the city—only I turned left, because I was going out to Republic Airport in Farmingdale, where the plane was.

"You're going the wrong way," my father said.

"No, Dad, I know where I'm going," I said. "It's going to be all right."

So we drive out to the airport, and here's this little jet sitting by the hangar; it looks like a fighter jet. We get in, and this plane seems even smaller on the inside than it does on the outside. You can't stand up in there: you basically have to crawl to your seat. And my dad was eighty-one years old—almost as old as I am now—and he wasn't that agile. Short. A little stocky. He crawls in, I crawl in, the pilot starts her up, we taxi to the runway, and then we take off like a damn rocket.

A couple of hours later we landed in Winston-Salem. Tommy was going to pick us up. And as we were getting off the plane, I looked eagerly at my father's face. "Dad, what do you think?" I asked.

"I like the big planes better," my father said.

————

About ten years later, thanks to the success of Home Depot, I found myself a very wealthy man. And though I'd been very aware of making my first million back in 1977, I felt superstitious about where I was now. When I play poker, I have no trouble counting my winnings after the game is over, but I've always found that when I counted my money while the game was in progress, I lost. So even though some people around me seemed excited about how rich I was, I thought, "I ain't counting."

I'm still not. I'm not counting until I leave the table, and I'm not leaving the table until I have to.

Still, my success has given me all kinds of freedom I didn't have before. Today I own a plane that cost me over twenty times what that little Learjet cost. It has a cabin you can walk around in; it sleeps four. I can fly to Europe whenever I want, and I do, regularly. I have a beautiful house on Long Island and several other beautiful homes around the country—in Manhattan, in Palm Beach, on top of a mountain in North Carolina. I belong to some of the greatest clubs in America. I don't even think about what it costs to go to a great restaurant if I want to take my family or friends out every night.

At the same time, I'm always thinking that there's got to be a greater meaning to my life than all this money I've made. The Bible says there's a better chance of a camel getting through the eye of a needle than of a rich man making it to heaven. The Bible says that if I want to be *really* rich, I'll give everything away. Warren Buffett's a little less strict than Scripture: he says that wealthy people should give away at least half their wealth to philanthropic causes. I signed Warren's Giving Pledge years ago, but in my case it was academic: I'd already given away more than half my net worth.

Should I follow the Bible? I'll be honest: I'm not giving everything away. Why? Because I love this life! I love having nice houses and good people to help me. I love getting on my airplane instead of having to take my shoes off and wait in line to take a commercial flight. You want to accuse me of living well? I plead guilty.

I envy people who aren't as motivated by material things as I am, and I know that envy is another one of the seven deadlies. I don't know if I would have done what I did or sacrificed the time I've sacrificed if I didn't see something in it for me. If that's greed, let the chips fall where they may. As I said, I've been rich and I've been poor, and rich is better.

Yet too many people measure success the wrong way. Money should be at the bottom of the list, not the top. I woke up soon enough to realize that if the only way you can define my life is by the size of my bank account, then I've failed. Fifteen or twenty years ago, a guy asked me how much I was worth, and I answered without thinking, "My net worth is what good I do with what I have."

I know I can make money; I have the talent. I know that when I get in a tight spot, I can figure a way out. But if I forget how important it is to apply my talent to somebody else's benefit, then I've really missed a big bet. And so Elaine and I give. A lot. My firm belief about donating money—I learned this from my old man—is that if you're not sacrificing something, you're not being truly philanthropic. Add up everything I own—the plane, the houses, the cars—and even including all the yearly maintenance, the sum comes to about one-third of the total amount of money that we've given away. To the Animal Medical Center. To the Boys' Club of New York. To Bucknell. To Harlem Children's Zone and its Promise Academy, my charter school. To NYU Medical Center. To the restoration of St. Patrick's Cathedral.

But as much as we give, it keeps coming back: we've made back all the money we've given away, and more. What Elaine and I can't make more of for ourselves is time. We spend it, but we can't get it back.

We will make sure we've given most of our money away by the time we die, with the exception of what we leave to our kids. We want to pass along enough for them to live reasonably well, but not so much that they can do anything foolish with it. We want them to have a roof over their heads, but we also want them to have the meaning in their lives that comes from having to make their own way.

———

In 2008, as I mentioned earlier, I made a big deal to sell Choice-Point, the data-aggregation company that had merged with my Database Technologies in 2000, to the information-technology publisher Reed Elsevier. You'll recall that ChoicePoint used to be Retail Credit, which gave me my first job out of college. By now, of course, the company was all electronic: no more guys going around in cars, knocking on doors. The company had huge data-bases, and Reed Elsevier wanted them. To the tune of $4.3 billion in cash.

Together with his team, Ed Herlihy at Wachtell, Lipton wrote up a contract that you couldn't get a wisp of air through; it was that airtight. Then, on September 15, Lehman Brothers declared bank-ruptcy, and the financial crisis began. Everybody thought the world was coming to an end. And Reed Elsevier tried to declare force majeure to halt the ChoicePoint deal.

"Hey, guys," Herlihy told them, "you've got no leg to stand on; we're closing."

And so we closed. That Friday night, September 19, 2008, in the thick of the biggest financial crisis since the Great Depression, Reed Elsevier had to wire in $4.3 billion. We at Invemed got $200 million for our ChoicePoint shares. It was a nice time to have a lot of cash.

Now the story gets more interesting.

A few weeks later, a close friend of mine, a big deal maker who will remain anonymous, called me up and said, "Bernie Madoff knows all about you, and he would love to talk to you."

I'd never met Bernie Madoff. All I knew about him was that he was a weird, reclusive guy with the reputation of being the biggest option player on Wall Street. He had some kind of fund that nobody knew anything about; it was very successful, but nobody understood how it worked. A black box. But as a courtesy to my friend, I said, "Okay, I'll see him, for you."

Now, I don't know beans about options: puts and calls and strips and straddles and all this other crap. All I do is pick stocks, and I never buy anything I don't understand. But I have an investment partner, Steve Holzman, who loves to screw around with options, and he's done very well with it. So I phoned him and said, "Steve, do me a favor. Bernie Madoff wants to meet with me. I don't know what the hell he does; would you come along so there's somebody knowledgeable in the room?"

Steve sounded less than interested. Madoff's fund wasn't his cup of tea, he said, and it probably wasn't mine either.

"Please, Steve, do me a favor," I said. "I'm doing this as a courtesy for a guy who's a very dear friend of mine."

So Steve agreed, and we went to the meeting. Four thirty on a Monday afternoon. I had a dinner date with friends at 6:30 at an Upper East Side restaurant: I remember thinking I should be able to make it easily. Madoff's offices were in the Lipstick Building, that ugly-ass oval-shaped pink skyscraper at Third Avenue and Fifty-third. Steve and I go up there and shake the guy's hand, and the first thing he does is start showing us his art collection. He had contemporary art all over the walls: Warhol, Jasper Johns, Frank Stella, Roy Lichtenstein. Prints, mostly. One piece was four different parts of a bull in four separate frames; I don't know what the damn point was, other than to make work for the framer.

Bernie Madoff was smooth. Urbane. He really wanted us to know how much he knew about art. And while he's showing us all these pictures, all I can think about is the fact that I have a dinner date uptown at 6:30. Finally, I said, "Bernie, I've got to go to a dinner; can we sit down and talk?"

"Sure," he says. Cool as a cucumber. As if he just remembered why he asked us up there.

We sit at a conference table, Madoff and I on one side, Steve on the other, and Bernie goes into his pitch, very low-key, soft-voiced: his computer geniuses, he said, had developed a new wrinkle that he thought could add approximately two percentage points to his already solid long-term record. Something about a split-strike conversion strategy . . . I glazed over. All the jargon sounded right, but I didn't know what the hell he was talking about. I was glad I'd brought Steve along.

Then something occurred to me.

"Hey, Bernie," I said. "Why are you coming to us? Why aren't you making this offer to all your happy clients? I know a lot of them down in Palm Beach."

In HBO's movie about Madoff, when the actor playing me asks this question of Madoff (excellently played by Robert De Niro), Madoff gets flustered and starts stammering, whereupon the movie Langone gets up and stomps out of the office. In real life, it wasn't like that at all. In real life, Madoff answered my challenge with complete coolness.

"Oh," he said, "that'd be a real rigmarole. Getting people to come out of existing products into something new like this—" He shook his head. "No," he said, "it's easier to find new money."

What kind of new money?

He was only looking for 500 million, he told us.

"Bye-bye," I thought. "These people, these clients, have been with you thirty to forty years, and you're going to a guy you've never done business with before? If this thing is so damn great, all you're doing is screwing them. And what's to keep you from screwing me next?"

I looked across the table at Steve and rolled my eyes. I could tell he agreed.

Madoff finally wrapped up and handed each of us his business card. When we left the office, I looked at Steve and said, "What the fuck is this guy's problem?"

A story comes to mind: Salomon Brothers used to have an event every year at the 21 Club. They'd put rows of seats, like a theater, in the big dining room upstairs, and they would bring in a prominent economist to give a talk. One year somebody got the idea to bring in a fraud, an actor pretending to be an economist. Now, here are all these powerful heads of insurance companies and banks sitting there and having cocktails, and this guy is up there talking about this Y-curve and that X-curve and this graph, and the intersection of this and that. None of these powerful people have any idea what the hell he's talking about. And when the guy gets done, he says, "Well, fellas, are there any questions about what I just said?" And then, "Let me tell you something. I hope you understand what I said, because I don't—because I'm not an economist."

And everybody laughs; they've been had.

The next year, they have a legitimate economist come in. The guy who was the head of New York Life, Donald Ross, had a few drinks before the presentation. So he's sitting there, and now the guy starts presenting. This is a real economist, a serious guy, talking about X-curves and Y-curves. But Donald Ross says, "I ain't listening to this bullshit this year," and he gets up and walks out.

The moral? Smart people can have the wool pulled over their eyes as easily as dumb people, if not more so.

I'm not saying Steve and I are smarter than anyone else: we just happened not to like the flavor of what Bernie Madoff was selling. Steve later told me the complete lack of volatility in Madoff's fund put him off: Steve is a firm believer that volatility is part of the equation in high-end investment, that wealthy investors ought to tolerate more uncertainty in return for higher numbers.

Two weeks after the meeting, on December 11, 2008, my office phone rang, and my assistant Pam told me Steve Holzman was on the line. I picked up. "Holy shit, did you hear the news?" Steve said. He'd just seen on his Bloomberg terminal that Bernie Madoff had been arrested for securities fraud.

"I feel like the guy who flirted with Lorena Bobbitt at a bar," Steve said.

Of course, after Madoff was arrested, it hit me exactly what he'd been doing: as the crisis unfolded and his clients stampeded out the door, he needed money to pay them off and keep the game going. For me the scary part about the guy was how he could act as if life couldn't have been better for him at the same time the roof was blowing off him. I told you I was good at poker, but I wouldn't want to play with that SOB; he'd clean my knickers.

Steve Holzman had a little gizmo made for his house in Florida: Madoff's business card is mounted inside a Lucite box, and when you walk by, a motion detector triggers a recording of my voice saying, "What the fuck is that guy's problem?"

What indeed. Did you hear the story about Madoff and Swiss Miss?

There's a canteen in his prison, a place where the prisoners can go to buy snacks and toiletries, little things like that. And apparently one thing the prisoners really like is Swiss Miss hot chocolate mix, the powder that comes in little envelopes. And apparently Madoff cornered the market on Swiss Miss—bought up the prison's entire supply—and was gouging his fellow prisoners if they wanted it, because he had it all.

The guy can't stop!

———————

Capitalism gets a bad rap these days. Madoff didn't help; the financial crisis didn't help. When Bernie Sanders campaigned for the presidency in 2016, I'm afraid he got a lot of college kids to believe that capitalism is bad and that America is headed, or should be headed, toward something that, in my mind, resembles socialism: Guaranteed income. Free college tuition. Single-payer health care.

I disagree. Strongly.

Guaranteed income: Where's the incentive to do more, or to do better, if the money you get is detached from the work you do and the effort you put into it?

Free tuition: Sounds great, but where's that money going to come from?

Single-payer health care: How are you going to feel about going to a hospital with a serious condition when you have no choice about where to go?

I disagree with socialism not (as you might believe) because I'm a rich guy trying to hold on to my money. I disagree because socialism is based on the false notion that we should all be exactly equal in every single way. Take CCNY: City College of New York. In 1970, during the years of campus protests, City changed its selective admission system to open admissions for anyone who had graduated from a New York City high school. The result? The great school that had been known as "the poor man's Harvard" went to hell in a handbasket, its academic reputation completely shot—until open admissions ended in 1999.

We all have different talents. We are not all equal. Millions of people suffer from inflammatory diseases like psoriasis, rheumatoid arthritis, colitis, and irritable bowel syndrome, and many of those sufferers benefit greatly from a drug called Remicade. We've got a noted scientist on the board of the NYU Medical Center by the name of Jan Vilcek who discovered the molecule from which Remicade came. Now, imagine the quality of life of those people who benefit by Jan's genius, and consider the fact that royalties from the sales of Remicade made Jan a very wealthy man. Socialism would say that Jan (who, along with his wife, Marica, is also enormously charitable) shouldn't have been rewarded for all the lives he made better.

Socialism would say that Bernie Marcus and Arthur Blank and I shouldn't have been lavishly rewarded for the fact that people can go into a Home Depot and get better deals and make more affordable repairs to their homes because of what we did. Well, maybe socialism is right about us! But we know capitalism brings better lives than socialism does. I'll take you to any socialistic country—to Russia, to Romania, to Hungary—and you can see for yourself. Like it or not, we aren't all equal, and I don't feel guilty about having this strange talent that I have. God gave me this wonderful ability to measure risk, along with a good nose for people and which businesses I want to back. If nothing more comes of it than my having created jobs and gotten rich, nobody has lost.

––––––

Wall Street got a very bad reputation after the financial crisis, yet 40 percent of college graduates today are going into finance. I tell kids that that's a big mistake. I tell them they should learn the nuts and bolts of a business before going out and trading that business's stock. I didn't realize how stupid I was back when I was a salesman at Pressprich! I would look in the most superficial way at the companies whose stocks and bonds I was selling: I never truly understood how those businesses worked. It wasn't until I got wealthy enough to buy pieces of companies that I developed a much deeper understanding of them. And by the way, that was when it became easier for me to make even more money, because I could now look at a business and understand it that much better: I could say, "Hey, wait a minute, this over here can be fixed; that over there can be eliminated."

It wasn't just wealth itself that put me in that position; a lot of it was sheer stubborn curiosity. Whenever I served on a corporate board, I was notorious for asking more questions than any other director on that board. I didn't give a shit if my question showed how stupid I was. A lot of people are scared to ask questions because they don't want people to know how dumb they are. I've never had that problem.

A lot of people are also afraid of falling down and hurting themselves along the way. Capitalism works, but you've got to make the effort, and you've got to be able to take the lumps. You have to have the kind of stamina that, when you get knocked down, allows you to pick yourself up and brush yourself off and move on just as if you'd never been knocked down. When I almost went broke in 1970, when I fell almost overnight from the highest mountain to the lowest valley, when I'd go home every day at 4:00 p.m. and weed the garden and cry, I managed to go on afterward.

Capitalism is brutal. It's survival of the fittest. What's a successful business? More money coming in than going out. If it's the other way around, you're out of business—simple as that. If Bernie and Arthur and I had had a bad idea when we started Home Depot, we'd have gone broke. If we'd had a good idea but executed it poorly, we'd also have gone broke. Look at all the automobile companies that have folded: Packard, Studebaker, Hudson; I can go right down the list. What happened? Mostly good ideas poorly executed. They couldn't compete.

Capitalism is brutal, but it's rarely a zero-sum game. Both sides of any transaction should get something out of the deal. Valeant, the pharmaceutical company, had a whole roster of important medications, but when it got caught charging obscene prices for them, its stock went down 90 percent. The market spoke, and Valeant had to listen.

I can't think of one deal I've ever done where I couldn't have gotten more out of it than I did. As I've made clear, I like making money. I'm not some Buddhist monk who wants to eat beans the rest of his life. But it's amazing what you can accomplish when you look beyond sheer profit to getting buy in by other people. I'd rather own 10 percent of a billion-dollar company than 100 percent of a $100 million company. The numbers are exactly the same, but by owning a piece of the billion-dollar company I get the benefit of everybody else pulling with me, and that's a huge benefit.

Back in 1986, Tommy Teague and I decided to take our truck-leasing business private to get the benefit of Reagan's new tax laws. I was putting up the money to buy out the public stockholders: all the company's shares were going to be reallocated to Tommy and me. "Ken," Tommy said, "if there's some way I could get more stock, I'd sure appreciate it." He owned around 8 or 9 percent of the company at that time.

"Tommy, leave it to me," I said.

At the closing, Tommy and his lawyer were on one side of the table, my lawyer and I were on the other. Suddenly I saw Tommy whispering to his lawyer and getting agitated. Finally, he blurts out to the lawyer, "Fuck you, I'm telling him."

Tommy gets up and tells me, "I've got to talk to you outside, Ken."

We go outside. "Did you read the contracts?" he asked.

"Uh-uh, I didn't read them," I said.

"Well, your lawyer fucked up," Tommy said.

"My lawyer didn't fuck up, Tommy," I told him. "Those contracts are exactly as I told him they're to be."

"Well, goddamn it, he fucked it up," he said. "The way it's written, I'm gonna own two-thirds of the company and you're only gonna own one-third!"

"Tommy," I said, "my one-third is going to be worth a hell of a lot more than if I owned two-thirds and you owned one-third."

Now, if I had given Tommy 20 percent of the company, he would've been happier than a pig in shit. But I knew that with *two-thirds* of the company in his hands, Tommy was going to work his ass off to make Salem Leasing succeed. And I was right. Tommy Teague is seventy-six years old today, and he still works seven days a week. We took the company private for a value of about $15 million; today my one-third is worth $150 million.

One of the most important lessons in my life is this: leave more on the table for the other guy than he thinks he should get. And one of the most important rules in capitalism is incentive.

I didn't get rich by accident. I've always been very conscious of terms and conditions and trading, and I bargain back and forth. But I never wanted to reach a point on a deal where the other guy feels he was had. I'd rather have him feel he got me than I got him. I can live with that. I'm not a ten-year-old who needs to go behind the garage and see who's got the biggest dick. If the other guy does better than I do, there's a good chance he'll want to come back to me and make a number of deals. On the other hand, he has to be straight with me.

A guy came into my office one day, he bargained hard, and we made a deal. Then he came back to me the next day and said, "You know, I think you bested me."

"What do you mean?" I asked.

"Well, I think what I agreed to is not right for me."

"Do you think you should have a different deal?"

"Yes," he said.

"Okay, I'll tell you what," I said. "Tell me the deal you think you should have had, and that's the deal we're going to do."

"Really?"

"Really," I said. And he told me.

"Fine," I said. "Now do we have a deal?"

"We sure do," he said.

"Memorialize it," I said. "Get your lawyers; I'll get my lawyers. You got your deal. You can't go out and say I took advantage of you. But let me just tell you something: I never want to do business with you again as long as I live."

What had he done that was so wrong? We made a deal. I thought it was fair. He thought it was fair. But whether he sensed that there was some give in the terms or thought I felt some compunction, he came back for more. In my mind, he reneged.

But the opposite of greed can be foolishness. I belong to a bipartisan Washington think tank called CSIS—Center for Strategic and International Studies. One day a few years ago, I was there for a meeting, and my fellow board member the late Zbigniew Brzezinski said to me, "Do you realize if you guys didn't make profits at Home Depot, how much lower the prices could be in your stores?"

"Yeah, you're right, Zbig," I said. "But who would buy stock in my company to give me the capital to build the business if they didn't get a return on their investment? If there aren't any profits, then there can't be any return."

Why do people buy stocks in one company and not another? Why do people buy stock in Home Depot and not Sears, Roebuck? They're taking a hard look at Sears and saying, "God, that company is a mess; I don't want to invest in it." So Sears stock goes down; our stock goes up. That's capital allocation. And it's brutal. Because there's no place for losers. But there shouldn't be.

There's no pride for the winners, either. You want bragging rights? You're going to go broke. Walk into any Lowe's store, look around, and—except for the blue color scheme instead of orange—you'd say, "This is a Home Depot." They copied us! It's fine. If you have a better idea than mine, I'm using your idea.

No pride, and no complacency. God help you if you rest on your laurels. Back in the 1960s and early 1970s, there was a group of large-cap stocks called the Nifty Fifty. Anheuser-Busch. Black & Decker. Bristol-Myers. The Coca-Cola Company. Dow Chemical. Eastman Kodak. Eli Lilly. General Electric. IBM. Johnson & Johnson. 3M. Xerox. When the state pension funds and the insurance companies started buying equities, they bought these companies blind. The mentality back then was this: buy any one of these companies, set it on automatic pilot, it's just going to keep growing. It'll never stop.

Kodak was a money machine: they made so damn much on those little yellow film boxes. Then one day an engineer walks into their R&D department and says, "Hey, look what I can do. I can take a picture digitally."

"What happens?" the R&D guy asks.

"Well, it goes through the electronics, and it comes up on a screen," the engineer says.

"Where do you put the film?" the guy asks.

"We don't use film," the engineer says.

"What do you mean, you don't use film?"

"No, you don't use film. If you want to print it out on a piece of paper, you can, but this is just digital—nothing but pixels."

You know what happened next. Kodak was reluctant to give up the cash cow it had in film, the kids out in Silicon Valley figured digital photography out for themselves, and Kodak was gone.

Xerox. In 1959, Xerox's stock used to literally double every six months. They had what they called the 914 machine, the original dry print. Then the patents ran out, and all of a sudden Minolta and all the rest of them show up with the same technology. Xerox is a shadow of its former self today.

What a tech company needs to do during the precious period when it has product exclusivity is spend a lot of money to obsolete itself. That's what IBM used to be the best at, but it lost its way through sheer arrogance. IBM stopped obsoleting itself, and other people obsoleted it. IBM thought it could keep producing hardware when the rest of the world—Cisco, Qualcomm, Intel, Microsoft—went to software. Especially Microsoft. IBM gave Bill Gates that business! They didn't want to be bothered with it.

Arrogance ran right through the IBM company culture. They focused on uniformity: you had to wear a dark suit, white shirt, conservative necktie, lace shoes. I say, if a guy has good ideas, let him come to work bare ass!

The most successful software company for medical records is a firm called Epic Systems, in Madison, Wisconsin. We put their software into NYU Medical Center, at a cost of $300 million, and it's phenomenal: people can't believe what we're able to do with it. Epic was founded by a woman named Judy Faulkner. I got her to come to New York to speak to some investors, and at the end of her talk I asked her, "Judy, do you have any kind of dress policy?"

"Well," she said, "we like our people to have clothes on when guests are on campus."

The Nifty Fifty dwindled down to Not So Nifty through arrogance, rigidity, myopia. Companies lose their way the same way people do—and with people at the top who lack vision. IBM focused on the wrong things. Avon is gone. Procter & Gamble has leaned itself way down: they've shed product lines right and left. Now they're looking for inspiration to GE, which Jeff Immelt, before he retired, began trying to recast as the industrial software company of the future. Good luck on that one. That's like trying to get an ocean liner to do a 180.

The one company on that list that's morphed really successfully is Minnesota Mining and Manufacturing—3M. They've made significant investments in new technologies, in new products. They have an abiding belief that they must bring out so many new products every single year. Just think of how much money they made on Post-it notes alone! 3M has been magnificent in innovation.

Another magnificent example is Walmart.

At the end of World War II, Sam Walton bought a northwest Arkansas branch of the national Ben Franklin five-and-dime chain and operated it very successfully by taking low profit margins and passing the savings along to the consumer. Walton was a licensee: he owned the branch but paid a lease to Ben Franklin until his lease expired and he was unable to negotiate a new one that could keep him as profitable as he wanted to be. So he divorced from Ben Franklin and renamed his store Walton's 5&10, and he did all right, but he had greater ambitions.

Then he heard about a guy named Harry Cunningham, up in Garden City, Michigan.

Cunningham—his nickname was Pete—had taken over a failing chain of five-and-dime stores called S. S. Kresge and turned it into Kmart, a chain of super-successful, super-discount stores. Cunningham's original inspiration was a big-box Rhode Island retailer called Ann & Hope, which pioneered some practices that were revolutionary for a department store in the early 1960s: limited sales staff on the floor, shopping carts, giant parking lot. With its low overhead and high sales volume, Ann & Hope was able to offer its customers deep discounts. Pete Cunningham copied Ann & Hope for Kmart, and Sam Walton took notice.

Years later Pete retired to Florida, and I got to know him in

Palm Beach. He told me that every time he went into his original Kmart in Garden City, Sam Walton was there, looking around. Walton was absolutely convinced that Kmart was onto something, and he decided he was going to do it too. So he took a little chain of five-and-dimes in northwest Arkansas and turned them into Walmart, which became the largest corporation in the world, while Kmart proceeded to go bankrupt and merge with Sears.

Pete Cunningham lived right down the street from me in Palm Beach, and one day I invited him to visit a Home Depot that had just opened nearby. We went down, and I was walking the store with some of the kids who worked there when I noticed that Pete was lagging behind us, ten feet back or so, and he kept shaking his head.

After a while we got in the car to drive home, and I said, "Pete, I couldn't help but notice you were shaking your head while you were walking through the store. Did you see something in there that you didn't agree with?"

"Oh, no," Pete said. "No, no." He sighed. "I was thinking this is the way Kmart used to be, and look what happened to it."

What happened to Kmart? After Pete retired, the company had a succession of CEOs who didn't give a damn about the business, who didn't give a damn about the customers, who were only interested in the perks of being a CEO. That'll get you every time.

And what happened to Walmart? Sam Walton kept an eagle eye on every detail of his growing chain: the locations of stores and warehouses, shipping costs (he started his own trucking company), overhead. The more Walmart grew, the greater the volume it was able to buy in and the lower it could make its prices. And once the old man died, control of the company stayed in the family, and the Waltons are smart. They've adapted to the times, with ideas like sustainable packaging and energy reduction in the stores and online sales, and they've stayed focused on their original mission: keeping prices low and optimizing the shopping experience. And they reaped the rewards.

We've tried to do much the same with Home Depot. Complacency is the enemy. If we don't stay focused on our mission every single day, every minute we're awake, Home Depot will go to sleep.

And arrogance is the enemy. For many years, Bernie Marcus and I never, ever went into a Home Depot store—never once—unless we were pushing carts in from the parking lot. I used to pray I would see a piece of trash on the floor so I could pick it up. Why? Those are entry-level tasks for the kid who works in that store. When he sees the top guys doing them, he can say to himself, "If it's not too small for them, it's not too small for me." The minute you take away all the artificial barriers between you and your people, you're on the way to phenomenal success. But it takes a little bit of humility.

To this day, if I walk into a Home Depot and see a customer who looks lost and confused, I walk up to him and say, "I have something to do with this company; can I help you?" If he has a question that's beyond me, I'll go grab a kid and say, "Can you help this customer?"

And it isn't just the customers I have interesting interactions with. One night I went into a new store that was about to open, out in Elmont, Long Island, and a young sales associate saw me and recognized me. "Can I ask you a question?" this kid said. (I call anyone who's younger than I am a kid.)

"Sure," I said.

"Were you guys born stupid, or did you just gradually get that way?"

This was interesting! "What's on your mind?" I asked.

"Some of the shit you guys do in this store doesn't make sense."

"Take me and show me," I said.

He took me to the toilet plungers. They were out of sight, in a box underneath the sales displays. "Shit," the kid said, "half the people who *work* here don't know the plungers are on the lower level in a big box, and when you reach in you get dirt all over you. You don't wake up on a Saturday morning and say, 'Honey, let's go buy a plunger.' Most people, it's three o'clock in the morning, the toilet's stopped up, and the first thing they do is wake up at sunrise and run to the store to buy a plunger. If they don't see them right away, they're not going to be happy. And if the plungers were out where regular shoppers could actually see them, they might buy one just in case."

I said, "How would you fix it?"

"I'd put pipe hooks up and down the wall rack," he said, "and hang the plungers in them like a gun rack. Right at eye level."

This was a Wednesday night before the grand opening on Thursday. Saturday morning I went into the store and made a beeline for the plunger display. I saw the pipe hooks but no plungers. "Where are they?" I asked the kid.

"They're all gone," he said, with a big grin. They were sold out.

Now, this kid can call me a moron, a jerk; he can call me anything he wants. I don't give a damn! The point is that he was right. He was thinking about what the experience for the customer should be, how to make that experience ideal. And for that he deserves praise, not to mention a little sweetener at the end of the year.

We had another kid; Don was his name. Don had made a study of end caps, those special displays you see on the end of a store aisle—in a supermarket it might be Thomas' English muffins or Pepperidge Farm cookies or Heinz ketchup and mustard. Suppliers pay extra for end caps, because customers naturally stop and look at them, and then they buy. Don came up with the idea of a display that would show customers everything they needed to install a toilet. "How will you do it?" we asked him.

"I'm going to put it on an end cap in the front of the plumbing department," he said, "and I'm going to feature all the products, from the copper or PVC supply line and waste line, to the handle assembly and flapper, to the toilet seat. Everything." That store's sales for plumbing went up 30 percent. A huge number. And the end caps in our stores got a new nickname: Depot Dons. We gave Don a significant bonus.

And that's capitalism. Should the Plunger Kid and Don not have gotten bonuses because the other kids in their stores didn't come up with a brilliant idea?

Should Dick Grasso not have been paid $140 million for adding tremendous value to the New York Stock Exchange?

There's a parable in the Bible about a farmer who needs workers. He hires a guy at eight o'clock in the morning, the guy works until 6:00 p.m., and the farmer pays him for the whole day. But at five o'clock in the afternoon, he hires another guy who works one hour, and the farmer also pays him for the whole day. The first guy bitches. The farmer says, "Hey, I didn't take anything away from you. It's my money." That's the essence of capitalism. It's investing, and people are always your best investment.

———

A few months back, my assistant Pam got a call from a Home Depot district manager on Long Island; this guy said he needed to come in and see me. Sure, I said. So Pam made the appointment, and the guy came in and sat down across from me in my office. I'll call him Phil Morelli.

Phil told me he started with us about nineteen years ago as an hourly associate, at a couple of bucks an hour more than minimum wage. He was a lot boy—helping people load their carts and pushing the carts back in from the parking lot. Today he's a district manager, in charge of eight stores; he makes about $250,000 a year. "But I'll tell you why I had to come see you today," he said. He looked at me. "I want you to know, last spring, I paid off my parents' mortgage. In December, I paid mine off. And yesterday afternoon I got a call from my Merrill Lynch broker telling me that my account is now worth over a million dollars, so I'm a millionaire."

This is a kid who couldn't afford to go to college. Maybe he wasn't college material. Doesn't matter—today he's a millionaire. And he's not alone. We've got three thousand people at Home Depot who started out as hourly employees and are multimillionaires today. When capitalism works the way it should, it works for everybody. It's like the tide: all boats get lifted.

Do I expect credit? I don't need credit; I've done very well. But beyond that, I got a huge sense of satisfaction. Here I am, a guy who flew around the country getting doors slammed in my face to raise two million bucks for two Jews who were facing serious legal charges and an Irishman who'd just filed for business and personal bankruptcy, and when I finally put the money together, I went to them and said, "Let's start a company." We started a company, and bang, here's Home Depot. Which, by my calculation, has impacted at least a million and a half lives.

How do I figure that? Home Depot has 400,000 employees across twenty-three hundred stores. The majority of those employees have wives, husbands, kids to feed. Then think of the number of jobs we've created at the companies that make the goods that Home Depot sells. Black & Decker. The Stanley Works. Masco, the faucet manufacturer.

Now, you could make the argument that of those 400,000 employees, 200,000 of them were working in hardware stores that we wiped out, so that's not really a net gain. And there is some merit to that argument. But those 200,000 weren't being paid like we pay them, and they weren't being taken care of like we take care of them, and they weren't getting benefits like those we give them.

For example, we've never paid anybody minimum wage at Home Depot. We had a simple belief: minimum wage, minimum talent. We always wanted to have good kids who wanted careers and not feel they had to compromise their pay. We paid them two or three bucks an hour more than minimum. We reviewed them every six months. And from the beginning we were growing like a weed, so we created enormous upside mobility.

Income inequality is a terrible problem in this country, and I don't have a magic solution. I don't know about mandating a higher minimum wage. I do know that nobody can live on $20,000 a year. But I worry that mandating a higher minimum might hurt the people you want to try to help: the more you increase the costs of any factor of production, the more incentive you give owners to figure out a way to change that factor of production. So, for instance, a kid behind the counter at Wendy's may only be able to perform at that level. If you raised the cost of that function, Wendy's management might have to think about automating it, and then the kid's out of a job.

On the other hand, if a hike in minimum wage over the short term brought wages up across the board, I'd be for it.

There are a lot of people in business who just don't think farsightedly enough. Unifi, the North Carolina textile company whose board I also sit on, has a plant in El Salvador that texturizes acrylic yarn to give it the feel of cotton. It's an enormously profitable facility—180 employees, earning us a consistent $8 to $9 million a year.

A couple years ago, we were having a board meeting, and the company's chairman and CEO were both there. "By the way," I asked them, "what do we pay these people down there?"

Eighty dollars a week, they told me.

"I don't know anything about Salvador," I said, "but how the hell can you live on $80 a week anyplace in the world?"

"Well, that's the going wage," these guys said.

"Let's do some math," I said. "Say these workers make $4,000 a year. If we raise their wages 30 percent, they're going to make $5,200. That $1,200 difference times 180 employees adds up to under a quarter-million bucks a year—out of nine million bucks in earnings. I think we can afford that!" I looked at these two guys. "So what happens if we raise those wages?"

"Well," they said, "you're going to have a lot of other American companies down there pissed off at us."

"Is that right?" I said. "I don't know if this is policy under the purview of the board, but I'm going to make a motion that we raise pay immediately down there by twelve hundred bucks a year." The board passed it like that.

This meeting was on a Wednesday. The chairman and the CEO were going to fly back down on Monday and make the announcement. "I want you guys to call me and tell me the reaction," I told them.

Monday came, they made the announcement, and they called me up. They said they got all kinds of calls from competitors of ours, bitching about the bad example we'd set. But they also said that when they announced it to the people at the plant, the factory workers were crying and hugging each other: they couldn't believe it. Right after that, a number of people who were working at other places wound up in our employment office to put applications in.

Today, that factory still pays more than any other plant in the region—and is more profitable than ever.

The tide rose.

You want my whole philosophy in a nutshell? I want everybody to do well. The world is a lot more fun if we're all rich instead of just some of us.

––––––––

Some guys who get to be wealthy like to brag about being self-made men. I can't imagine they're not leaving somebody out of that equation. The thing I can't say and never will say is that I'm self-made. To make that claim would be to commit a grave sin against all the many, many people who helped me get to where I am; you could fill Yankee Stadium with them, and then some. My parents. Elaine. Her parents. My brother, who taught me my prayers. Russell Headley. Jack Cullen. Bindy Banker. All the young guys we brought into Unit 15 at Pressprich. Ross Perot. The Erlbaum brothers. Bernie Marcus. Marty Lipton. Ed Herlihy. Stan Druckenmiller. Bob Grossman. And let's not forget 400,000 associates at Home Depot.

That's how I got rich. Not by myself: I'm just one guy. I like to think I have a skill for assembling outstanding people, but the fact is also that I'm a collage of many people's efforts.

My mind goes back to the twelve-year-old in blue jeans in 1947 selling Lenny Altman's cardboard liquor boxes for scrap; that was a clever kid. That was initiative. But Lenny saving up all the dollars he no longer had to pay me every week and giving them to me when it was time to go to college, that was even cleverer. That taught me a lesson I never forgot.

So many other people along the way have taught me important lessons. And if there's one lesson I could pass along to kids today, it's this: the opportunities in America today are the very best they've ever been. You might have to look harder for them than in my day, but they're there. Boy, do I wish I were twenty-one again and just starting out.

On the other hand, I have to admit that when I was twenty-one, I was looking at the world one-eyed. Like so many college kids today, I wanted to go to Wall Street and get rich. That's a good way to make a lot of money; it's also a way to fail big. Not to mention burn out fast.

I learned early how essential it was to love the work I was doing. Sometimes I look back and wonder, how did all this happen? Then the answer comes. Shit, I know how it happened: I was at a place where I was having the time of my life! I still remember what Hudson Whitenight said to me sixty years ago: "If you really love your work as much as I think you're going to, you're going to be a big success." So I'm saying to a kid, I learned that ex post facto; you should learn it in front!

Yes, I've been lucky, incredibly lucky, and you can't learn good luck. My old man used to say to me, "You could fall in a bucket of shit and come up with a gold watch and chain." But we all fall in that bucket from time to time. What distinguishes the winners from the losers is the ability to turn adversity around: resilience and creativity.

I still love my work today, all of it. At eighty-two, I'm still excited to get out of bed in the morning, still charged up about what the next deal might bring. And though the money my enthusiasms have brought me has enabled me to live well and help others, I can honestly say that if it came down to it, I would pay to go to work every day.

How many people can say that?

INDEX

profit sharing, illegal, 192–95, 200
Promise Academy (Harlem), 243

Quick, Chris, 189

R. J. Reynolds, 25–26
railroads, 33, 36–39, 54, 81–83, 90, 117, 129
Raleigh, North Carolina, 50
Rau, Jimmy, 127
Reagan, Ronald, 161, 252
recession, 68, 161
Redemptorists, 134, 142
Reed Elsevier, 168, 244
Reilly, Bill, 150–51
Relational Investors, 222–25
Republican Party, 169–73, 199
research analysts, 56–57, 67, 71–75, 81–82
Retail Credit Company, 29–32, 168, 244
Rhode Island, 257
Richardson, Hamilton, 90–91
Rickel home center, 130
Ridge, Tom, 229
Riebow, Ruth, 84–85
risk taking, 85, 94, 122, 250
Roche, Gerry, 207, 210–11
Roslyn Heights, Long Island, 1–2, 4–5, 8, 19, 46, 61
Roslyn, Long Island, 7–8, 22, 237–38
Ross, Donald, 247
Rowan, Eddie, 54
Rudin, Lew, 115–17
Rudin, Rachel, 116–17
Ryan, Francis, 237

St. Mary's Church (Roslyn), 237–38
St. Patrick's Cathedral (New York City), 239, 243
Salem Leasing, 241, 252–53

salesmen, 54–64, 75–79, 105, 111, 125, 180, 250–51
Salomon Brothers, 90, 92, 112, 175, 247
Samuelson, Paul, 13
San Diego, California, 117–19, 121, 137, 144–45, 222
San Jose, California, 147–48
Sanders, Bernie, 249
Sands Point, Long Island, 117, 197
Sato, Steve, 121, 144, 235
Schapiro, Mary, 194–95, 200
Schenectady, New York, 209–10, 213
Schwartz, Alan, 114–15
Scott, Blaine, 98–99
Scruggs, Leonard Coe, 125
Sealy, 124, 139
Sears, 64, 254, 258
Seaver, Harry, 73
securities, 33, 41, 45, 50, 55, 57, 81, 117, 183, 192, 248
Securities and Exchange Commission (SEC), 59, 102–7, 119–21, 183
Security Pacific Bank (Los Angeles), 158–59
September 11, 2001, 185
Sexton, John, 197
Shearson, 163
Shearson, Hammill, 26–27, 69
Showalter, Paul, 17
Shroyer, Bruce, 78
Siemens, 181, 196–98
Sigma Chi fraternity, 13, 15–17, 24–25
Sigoloff, Sanford "Sandy," 132, 138, 140–43, 145–52, 155
Silverman, Henry, 176–77
Singer, Paul, 223
Six Sigma management, 214
Skadden, Arps, 141
Sleeper, Matt, 24–26
Smilow, Joel, 179